The FINAL COUNT
THE LIFE OF DAN KIELY

The Final Count

Published 2023 by Dan Kiely
Copyright © Dan Kiely
Casebound Edition
ISBN: 978-1-916544-20-8

All rights reserved. No part of this publication may be reproduced or transmitted in any form or by any means, electronic or mechanical, including photography, recording, or any information storage or retrieval system without permission in writing from Dan Kiely. The book is sold subject to the condition that it shall not, by way of trade or otherwise, be lent, copied, altered, resold or otherwise circulated without Dan Kiely's prior consent in any form of binding or cover other than that in which is published and without similar a condition, including this condition, being imposed on any subsequent publisher.

Publishing Information
Design & publishing services
provided by JM Agency

www.jm.agency
Kerry, Ireland

The FINAL COUNT
THE LIFE OF DAN KIELY

DAN KIELY

with Jeremy Murphy

Contents

The Basics	07
Brass and Reel	11
The Black Stuff	14
Sweeping Up Before the Baby	17
My Father's Waterproof Clothes	19
The Back of the Hill	22
An Industrious Family	25
Pig Shambles	28
Nearly Killing Professor Coolahan	30
My First Bike	35
Young Kiely the Soldier	38
Emigration	44
Young Kiely the Boxing Champ	50
Back to Kiskeam	55
Uncle Paddy's Home	63
Bound for Idlewild	67
Goldman What?	75
Breaking Ball in New York	82
Taking to the Field	86
A Car for Dad and a Trip for Cathy	92
The Girl with the Marilyn Monroe Hat	99
The Bishop with the Big Red Hat	106

Leasing the Red Mill	114
Far From Run of the Mill	122
From the Mill to the Hibernian	128
The Day That Was in It	132
Breaking Ball in Ireland	137
So Near, Yet So Far	143
Dublin Bound	153
Running with the Hounds	162
The Best of Times & the Worst of Times	167
Gay Old Times	174
Putting My Hat in the Ring	181
In the Wilderness	193
More Ups and Downs	205
The Boss – Working with Charlie Haughey	225
Albert & Bertie	240
One Last Hoorah!	250
One Last Battle	258
Epilogue	287
About the Authors	291

The Basics

I had better start with the basics, who I am and where I was born. I was born in the early hours of May 10th, 1942. Back then babies were usually born at home and I was no different. I was born in our little house attached to the Garda barracks in Tarbert, County Kerry. My father, who was a member of An Garda Síochána, would have cycled all the way to Moyvane to fetch the midwife, Benty Kearney.

Mrs Kearney was a 'mighty woman' as they would have said, and she delivered most of the children in the North Kerry and West Limerick parishes. As soon as my father arrived, she would have rushed out of the door with him. She wasn't a woman to dawdle. She would have hopped in her car, seated him in the passenger seat, his bike in the boot, and set off for Tarbert.

I was one of seventeen children. The rate of children dying in birth or early infancy was high then, and our family was no different. Two of my siblings died during childbirth and another was stillborn, the youngest of the family. The birth of the little stillborn lad was the first time my mother was admitted to hospital for a child, while the rest of us were born in the family home.

My mother hailed from Dunmanway, West Cork. She came from a large family of nine, five brothers and three sisters. Her father had a job with the railway in Dunmanway, and her mother ran a small restaurant, also in Dunmanway. It was in that small restaurant that she met my father, around 1935. He was already in the police at that stage, the 'guards' as we call them in Ireland (short for An Garda Síochána).

He, along with his brother Paddy, had been appointed to the Garda's Auxiliary Special Branch by Éamon de Valera, a special division of the police comprising mainly former anti-Treaty veterans. They were often known by their nickname the 'Broy Harriers,' named in honour of their founder, Eamon Broy.

I will tell you about my Uncle Paddy, who I was very close to, a little later. For now, I would like to tell you about my father. My father came from a small village in North Cork, known as Kiskeam. There were eight in his family, although all five of his sisters immigrated to America during the War of Independence and Civil War. My father, along with his brother Denis, fought in both of those conflicts, first as captain in Sean Moylan's flying column, and later as an anti-Treaty republican in the Civil War.

My father was on the losing side of the Irish Civil War however, the pro-Treaty side, led by Michael Collins, prevailed in the end. After the war, there was no work for those that took the republican side. Rather than remain idle in Kiskeam, something that would have been against his nature, my father immigrated to the United States in 1923, where he worked for a transport company, driving a bus around the busy streets of Manhattan.

He returned in 1932, when Fianna Fáil and Éamon de Valera had secured power, and the political situation had changed as a result.

I can't pass on an opportunity to mention my father's immediate family, particularly his sisters in America, and how good they were to us. During the Second World War, they sent parcels to us by post. We relied on the generosity of these women because of the widespread shortages and rationing during the War, known as the 'Emergency' in Ireland.

I remember one Christmas parcel including a strange item known as coffee, that had a very distinctive smell and taste. Coffee was unusual in Ireland at the time and we were taken by it. When I arrived

An early photo of Dan Kiely's family, including Dan Kiely Sr., pictured in Garda uniform, and Dan Kiely's mother, Mrs Hannah Kiely (née O'Regan). Dan is a baby in this photo, pictured seated on his mother's lap.

in America as an immigrant myself, many years later, I would catch the familiar smell in the air.

Throughout this book, you will read a lot about both of my parents, because I have the utmost respect for them. They were 'salt-of-the-earth' people. My mother would live until she was ninety-six years of age, and that was after an extremely hard life. She laboured all her life, feeding, washing and clothing all of her children.

I will also have much to tell you about times back then, which were so different to today.

We had no running water. All our water was sourced from a public fountain, which was situated in the square in Tarbert. I remember making several journeys to and from that well as a young boy, hauling pails of water back to my mother, who would do all the washing and cooking with it. We also had no electricity, another thing that was wholly foreign to us. When I came home from school, I would take out my exercise book and do my lessons by candlelight. When I see my grandchildren today, doing their homework on shiny state-of-the-art tablets and laptops, I can't help thinking of my little tattered exercise book, lit by the flame of the candle.

Our house, attached to the Garda barracks where my father was stationed, wasn't much. We had to make do with three bedrooms, and electricity and running water didn't arrive until the sixties. But it was home, and by God did we make the best of it.

Brass and Reel

Growing up in Tarbert, our sole source of entertainment was a small, battery-operated radio. Every week, my brothers and I would walk down to the local garage to get our radio charged. It wasn't like the ones you get today that are powered by small disposable batteries. The battery that operated this radio was bigger and more cumbersome, and it needed to be regularly charged.

That small little radio was our connection to the outside world. To me, it was a magic box that provided us with news and a little music to help pass the days. There was very little music on the Irish radio stations at the time, so my brother and I would hack into foreign stations like Radio Luxembourg to get some music. There was always a little bit of music on the foreign radio stations.

However, don't forget, if you are resourceful and imaginative enough you can make your own fun in life. The Kielys were always a very musical family, and in many ways, we didn't need the radio; we could make our own music.

We benefited very much in this respect from the fact that my father was very musical. My grandfather, Tim Kiely, had a brass and reel band in Kiskeam, and they were quite the local celebrities. They played at rallies all across North Cork. I am proud of them, as they entertained people through many difficult years, through the war years and during the War of Independence and later the Civil War; they took people's minds off the bad times.

My mother was also musical. She was an accomplished violin player. Both our parents encouraged me and my siblings to play instruments, and it worked.

We had quite the brass and reel band going in our little house in Tarbert: My brother Tim played the accordion; my brother Pete, the trumpet; I played the cornet; my father played the baritone; and I remember my younger brothers who, when they were too small to play anything, would bang the tambourines. So, who needs the radio when you have your own home orchestra?

My mother would joke that we would 'wake the dead' with our clamouring and racket, but she did appreciate the fact that music gave us a source of entertainment and distraction in what were hard times.

We would play at local events. If the local football team were victorious, they would be paraded through the streets with the sound of Kiely trumpets and accordions.

The musical Kiely family with their various instruments: (l-r) Dan Kiely Jr., Tim Kiely (holding the accordion), Dan Kiely Sr., Denis Kiely and Pat Kiely (both holding bodhráns), and Pete Kiely (holding a trumpet).

You could say it was easy for us, as my grandfather's reel and brass band would always play at local events in Cork and further afield. Whenever they played in places like Brosna or Knocknagoshel, at fairs, race meetings and other occasions, my father and a gang of us would join them. I remember joining my father on stage at the races once and blowing out a few octaves on the cornet.

It was wonderful to create such joy and atmosphere; to watch people lose themselves and have a ball. I was often paid a small fee, ten shillings or something like that – but it was something, and I didn't say no.

Once, if I can remember correctly, a reporter from the *Irish Independent* newspaper came down to interview us and take photographs. Photos of the band appeared in their Sunday edition which was widely read at the time.

Music has stayed in the Kiely family right up to the present day. My brother Pete progressed from the humble trumpet and eventually became a master of the button accordion. Right up to this day, Pete is very proficient at the accordion. Pete's children have also inherited his love of music.

I eventually took to playing the piano accordion and I will never forget the day I got my first one. It arrived from America, a gift from my Uncle Paddy. This was when I was about thirteen or fourteen, and I started playing it straight away. I continued playing it throughout my young adult life. I even played it when I was in America, after emigrating there when I was nineteen.

In America, I would often sit down after a hard day's work, pull it out of its old box and start playing. Someone told me once that my accordion sounded a little sadder in the Bronx than it did in Tarbert. Maybe there was a part of me that longed to be back in Kerry, playing in that brass and reel band, with my father by my side, along with my brothers Tim and Pete. I knew I was always destined for America, but the sound of the accordion was always there to remind me of home.

The Black Stuff

One striking feature of my upbringing, was the amount of time spent doing work; often hard, backbreaking labour.

My mother, particularly, worked so, so hard; every time I saw her, she was working. Whether it was keeping the house clean, washing our clothes, feeding us, or helping load in the turf for the winter.

In the modern age of electricity and modern appliances, it is hard for us to appreciate the amount of physical labour expended on simple, essential tasks. There were sixteen in our household and my mother would have to hand-wash all the clothes. Hand-washing clothes for sixteen people was no mean feat.

Saturday night was bath night in the Kiely household, and my mother would spend hours bathing us in a big, galvanized bathtub. I have memories of my mother hauling up buckets of warm water to fill the bath, and then bending down to scrub us clean; she was a mighty woman!

Fuel is important for any household and any society, and ours was no different. In the Kiely home, it was turf. Turf was our fuel, our means of keeping warm and cooking food. Turf was gold.

Going to the bog in the summer to cut the turf was essential, and something we were all expected to pitch in with. The bog was located a few miles outside Tarbert, so we hired a lorry from the Kelly family – the only family in the village with a lorry – to transport the turf from the bog to our house.

Some people may imagine that the work was in the cutting and the digging of the turf, but that was only the beginning. Cutting turf was hard labour – you are, after all, extracting something from the bowels of the earth. After the turf was cut, my brothers and I would stack it into mounds. We would then leave the mounds for several weeks to dry, before returning to turn them and leave them to dry again for another couple of weeks. When this process was complete and the turf was sufficiently dried, we would load the turf onto a donkey and cart and transport it to the roadway. The turf would remain here until the arrival of the Kelly's lorry, at which time we would load it onto the back.

One of the main difficulties was the constant rain; it was essential that the turf was kept dry, as wet, damp turf was useless.

Directing the donkey safely across the bog, without spilling his load of turf, was also arduous. The surface of bogs are rough, rugged and creviced, and not ideal terrain for a donkey. The animal would often slip, hesitate nervously or get his or her hooves caught in the holes or crevices.

After a fall of rain, the surface was even more arduous. Whenever the donkey arrived at the lorry, we would quickly hurl the turf into the trailer before bringing the donkey back for another load. Eventually, the lorry would be filled, but our work didn't end there. Back in Tarbert, the turf would have to be transported from the lorry into the small shed in our garden, which was part of the Garda barracks complex.

A young Dan Kiely pictured during a day at the bog. Also pictured is his father, Dan Kiely Sr. (who is second from the right, looking at the camera).

We were fortunate in many respects. There was always a strong community in Tarbert and my father was liked by the local people. He had friends that we could rely on when we needed. When it came to cutting turf, we could always rely on a local family called the Mackasseys to lend a helping hand.

The Mackasseys were great people, who did so much for the local community. Later, they would get so many local people working on construction sites in England, through the Murphy construction company. During the turf cutting season, when they were finished cutting their own turf (usually around six in the evening) they would come and help us cut ours. While my brothers and I gave everything we could to our father, we were young and small at the time. The Mackasseys on the other hand, were big, strapping men, so their input helped massively.

They would stay for about two hours with us, from about six until eight, cutting the turf. They nearly did more in those two hours than we had done in the whole day up to that point. To this day, I am grateful to them for their generosity, and I think their kindness illustrated the depth of community bonds that existed in small villages in Ireland at that time.

God bless the work. A group of men working hard in the bog, including a young Dan Kiely (he is second from the left).

Sweeping Up Before the Baby

I have one memory involving my mother and turf, which has stayed with me my whole life. I will never forget it.

It happened one summer's day, just after the arrival of a fresh lorry-load of turf. My mother, despite being heavily pregnant, was pitching in. She helped us stack the sods up before they were hauled into the small garden shed. She then helped us sweep up the turf dust; on the day turf was delivered, the whole yard would be blackened with dust.

My mother was adamant that our house, particularly the yard and garden, which was officially part of the Garda barracks, must be kept spotless. I reckon she was eager to make a good impression, and didn't want to do anything to endanger my father's job.

On this particular day, my mother was out in the yard sweeping up with us, going around with her broom, ensuring every last speck of turf dust was collected. Then, all of a sudden, she stopped. I looked up at her and could see she was in some kind of pain. She was holding her hips and grimacing.

'Mam, are you alright?' I asked her. She told me she was fine. She then called me over and gave me a series of firm instructions. My mother was the kind of woman who when she told you something, you listened. She told me to gather up the remaining turf dust and dispose of it in the garden.

'Yes Mam, that's no problem,' I chirped, and off I went.

The author Dan Kiely, pictured with his late mother, Mrs. Hannah Kiely.

This was after a long, hard day in the bog at this stage, so being in the garden was a joy. Our garden may have been small, but it was lovely in the summer. The flowers were in bloom and the birds, who would nest in the crevices of the old barracks, would be in full song.

That particular evening, I deposited the turf dust as my mam had instructed, and walked back in a relaxed, carefree mood. I must have dawdled longer than I intended because when I got back things had moved at a quick pace. When I got back, I could hear screams coming from the house.

My father had jumped on his bike and was cycling for the midwife, but she wasn't needed on this occasion. My younger brother had already been born. He was in my mother's arms when I arrived in the room.

I'm not sure what I was thinking then, but I can tell you what I'm thinking now: My mother was an extraordinary woman. One minute, she was down on her knees, using every last ounce of her strength to clean the yard for my father, the next, she was giving birth to my younger brother. My mother lived until she was ninety-six and worked every day of her life. She was a remarkable woman, and I am so proud to call her my mother.

My Father's Waterproof Clothes

My father was also a remarkable man. He was the sole breadwinner for a family of sixteen, which was tough going in those days. Other than some small savings he had from his days in America, he provided for us with his Garda wages, which were modest.

My father would go everywhere and do everything on his bicycle. Ordinary, middle-ranking guards like my dad weren't afforded the luxury of a motorcar. Very few people had cars back then. When I was growing up in Tarbert, only three people had a motorcar: the priest, the doctor and the hackney man. Dad had to make do with his bike.

It was a black High Nelly, with a little bell he would jingle every time he was in sight of the house, to let my mother know he was home.

The bike served him well, allowing him to fulfil his duties

A photo of Dan's father, Dan Kiely Sr., on the beat in Stack's Mountain, which is located between Listowel and Tralee, Kerry.

as a Garda, but he was also massively disadvantaged on account of not having a car.

Sometimes, he would return home in the evening soaking wet, having been out all day in the rain. Whenever this happened, my mother would rush over to him and sit him down beside the fire. She would quickly remove his drenched clothes; his waterproof leggings and breeches, his police uniform underneath (which would also be soaked) and his wet socks and boots. Having removed all his clothes, and placed them on the range, my mother would begin drying his bare skin with a towel.

On these nights, he would often sit by the fire for an hour or so, shivering, as my mother towelled him down; his teeth chattering as he sipped hot tea. Seeing my father like this made me angry. I felt he deserved better. He had put down a hard shift for the local community and the country, the least the state could do was ensure he was adequately clothed.

The waterproof leggings and breeches were made of cheap material, and they would often tear. My mother tried her best, mending tears and sewing on patches, but it was never enough.

I remember, one evening after he had returned home drenched wet, saying something that caught everyone's attention.

'Dad,' I said to my father, as I tried to get his attention by prodding his bare, wet leg. (I can't recall what exact age I was, but I must have been young, as my head was level with his leg.)

'Dad, Dad …'

Dan Kiely Sr. pictured in his bus driver's uniform, from his time driving buses in Manhattan.

'What is it young Dan?'

'Dan, don't be bothering your father now, he is after a hard day.'

'Dad,' I persisted, ignoring my mam on that occasion. 'Dad, when I grow up, I'm going to go to America, and when I make it big, I will buy you a motorcar.'

'Well by God, are you now? Here is a young fella who is aiming big.'

The whole house had a good laugh at my expense. My sister, who was making the tea, thought it was gas. As did my mother, who, as you will learn, never wanted me to emigrate, tried her best, the poor woman, to put such notions out of my head.

However, my father had a little glint in his eye. I think, despite himself, he really appreciated what I had said. I remember he pulled me close to him and patted me on the head. I think he appreciated the fact that one of his own was looking out for him and was eager to work hard and make his way in the world. I also reckon my father knew that one day, it might even come true.

The Back of the Hill

Like any other boy growing up, I looked forward to the summers. We were still expected to work hard, mind you, harder really, despite being off school for a few months. During the summer, the turf had to be cut and the local farmers had to be assisted with baling the hay, cleaning the yards and weeding the gardens; and all this would be done during warm summer days and evenings, when you could feel your muscles ache in the heat and the sweat drip down your back. It was hard labour, but still, I loved summers growing up in Kerry.

During the summer months, my parents would often take the whole family for a picnic. We would walk a mile or two outside the village where there was a small little hill.

To get over the hill, we would climb over a small gate. My younger brothers and sisters would be lifted by my father over the gate and caught by my mother on the other side. Then we would walk up the hill and down the other side, to our favourite picnic spot, a small glen by the bank of the River Shannon.

Tarbert is situated on the Shannon Estuary, where the River Shannon, the longest river in Ireland, meets the Atlantic Ocean.

This picnic spot was so secluded, it felt like there wasn't a person in sight for miles. We were alone there as a family, with only the birds and the wild rabbits for company.

We would find a little spot on the ground, a walking distance from the river's shore, and lay out a rug. My father would take a group of us swimming, while my mother made the sandwiches and tea.

It was during those summer picnics, that I learned to swim, and I am forever indebted to my father for that privilege. My father would take us in, one by one, and, while holding us by the waist with our bellies against the water, he would instruct us to begin stroking with our arms and kicking with our feet.

When he was confident that we had the hang of it, he would slowly let us go. After a few attempts, we would stay afloat, kicking and flapping by the shallows of the river. Eventually – after several attempts and kind encouragement from our father – we mastered a basic breaststroke and were able to do a few yards in the shallows.

Aside from the learning experience, it was great craic. Playing in the water with my brothers and sisters, diving off each other's shoulders, feeling the warm sun on our backs; it was lovely.

After the water, we would run back to our mother who would have sandwiches ready for us.

Growing up in the Kiely household, we had this special expression: 'Let's go to the back of the hill.' It was in reference to those summer picnics.

If I said that to some of my siblings today, they would probably know exactly what I meant. Times were tough growing up, but credit to my parents for ensuring we had some light and happiness. No matter how difficult things got, we always had the summers to look forward to, our picnics behind the hill.

Dan Kiely (first on the left) pictured with his mother, Hannah Kiely, (second left), and his father Dan Kiely Sr. in Garda uniform.

An old photo of the Kiely family in their favourite place, the 'back of the hill'. Dan Kiely Sr. is holding a sweet gallon, which would be used to brew the sweetest tasting tea.

It was there we took our first steps into the great River Shannon. It was there we first learned to swim, while being held up by our father as he whispered wise words of encouragement into our ears. They were happy days.

An Industrious Family

They say 'a woman's work is never finished', and boy was that true of my mother. In the evenings, when all her housework was done, when everything was swept, polished and cleaned, and all of us were fed and bathed, you would expect her to have taken a break, but not my mother.

She would sit down and, in the glare of the small lamp, she would knit. She would mend all my father's old clothes and knit the whole family lovely cardigans and jumpers, that would keep us warm during the winter.

Then there were the flour bags. My word! I do wonder what kids today would think of what my mother did with flour bags.

In those days, when you went to the shop for flour, it was sold to you in big, white sacks. I would go to the grocer's and watch as the grocer heaped the white, powdery flour into those big sacks. In our household, the sacks were never disposed of. When we were finished with the flour, my mother would take the sacks, wash away the starch and dirt and knit them together to form bedclothes.

The flour sacks didn't make the most comfortable linen in the world, but they were insulating, they took the edges off the mattress and kept you warm during the winter.

Then there were the sweet cans. The local shopkeeper sold sweets in these big, capacious tins. They were commonly referred to as gallon tins. I don't know whether they literally were gallon sized, but they were certainly very big and, unsurprisingly, my good mother found a use for them.

For our picnics behind the hill, the sweet gallon was used to store water for the tea. While we were swimming with Dad, Mam would insert tea leaves into the sweet tin, balance it over a small log fire, and wait for it to brew. I will never forget the smell of freshly brewed tea, which, for some reason, always tasted sweeter when brewed in those gallon tins. I wonder was it the lingering residue of sweets?

People may dismiss such practices as primitive, but sitting down in the sun, after a fresh swim, with nicely brewed tea and homemade bread was not such a bad life.

While I was growing up, my mother trusted me with some very important errands. Particularly errands that required bargaining, haggling or negotiation of any kind. I wondered later if she saw potential in me. I don't think she was surprised when I went into business later in life. Whenever my mother had sixpence to spare, she would send me up to Tarbert Creamery to purchase some cream. I would always try my best to get a little extra cream off the creamery man.

Handing him our worn sweet tin, I would tell him how big our family was, how some of us had emigrated, and how hard it was to get by. All of which was true of course, but you had to say it. If I didn't say it, I wouldn't get more.

On most occasions, the man would take pity on me and give me a little more cream. I grew to love the sound of cream plopping into a sweet tin, and I loved the smile on my mother's face when she saw me return with a good portion of cream.

I remember my mother asking me once to clean out an old tea chest. It was yet another chore and I was probably a little resentful to be given it, but I did it.

In those days, loose tea came in big, wooden chests. They had wooden legs and were locked with metal bolts. I had no idea why she had asked me to clean out the tea chest, but I did it.

Then, lo and behold, a day or two after cleaning it out, I arrive in the kitchen and find the tea chest, looking sparkling and new, in the corner, but there was something different about it. I walked over and looked inside. Who was inside, but my little brother. He was snuggled up in bed clothes made from flour bags, and nestled in a cot converted from a tea chest.

I remember feeling very proud of my family. We may not have had much, but with industry, resourcefulness and creativity, it is remarkable what can be achieved.

Pig Shambles

'We're going off to help kill the pig.'

Now, that was an expression I heard many times growing up. As I got older, I would join my brothers in that essential communal activity.

In the Ireland of my boyhood, pig killing wasn't a solitary process, done in isolation, it was a communal activity, and all the local families were encouraged to play their part, and we did our bit.

When the day came, my brother and I would walk to a special place in the village, a small old outhouse, where the slaughter took place.

I remember getting a little fright when I first visited it, as the animal's cage was directly inside the door. The pig would gradually become more excited and nervous as more people arrived. Some pigs became very distressed. They barged into the sides of the pin and squealed loudly. It was as if they knew their fate.

I was given numerous jobs and tasks over the years. In the early years, I was tasked with helping to hold the pig down and pin it to the ground while its hair was removed.

This was dangerous work, as a kick from a pig could be fatal. The grownups would hold his feet and head, while us kids would press his belly.

In industrialised abattoirs, the pig's hair is burned off after slaughter, but in Tarbert, everything was done manually. Being held down and shaved like this distressed the animal, and it would struggle and squeal, so it was an important and difficult task.

In today's world, some people have ethical objections to practices such as this, but I think they often forget how hard times were back then. There wasn't an awful lot of food to spare, and the pig was a source of some delicious and nutritious meat.

When the slaughter was complete, our reward was some food to take home to our family. If we were lucky, we would receive some pork steak. I have fond memories of sitting down to dinner with my brothers and sisters, as our mother served us pork steak; all thanks to our labours in the pig shambles.

In their Sunday best. Pictured (l-r) are Dan Kiely, Johnny Coolahan, Cormac Hurley and Dan Cowman.

Pork steak was cut from the prized part of the animal, but even the offal was tasty and received with gratitude. If I got a pig's head, I would bring it home and it would be eaten with satisfaction.

Everything we got, we made last. If we got a slab of bacon, my father would salt it and hang it from a hook in our kitchen. Over the course of a few months, it would cure.

Every so often, he would take it down and cut off some rashers with a knife. The rashers would be eaten on a lean day when we didn't have meat, and they were delicious. The smell of frying bacon still makes my mouth water, and the rashers tasted so much better with a hungry belly after a hard day's work.

Nearly Killing Professor Coolahan

Now, let me tell you the story of how I nearly killed the future great Professor John Coolahan while playing hurling.

There was a group of us growing up in Tarbert who loved playing hurling together. It was me, Cormac Hurley, the sergeant's son (who would go on to become a Garda in Limerick, and who remains a very good friend of mine) and Johnny Coolahan.

We were all in secondary school at the time. Cormac and I attended James Dore's secondary school in Glin, while Johnny went to Mrs McKenna's in Tarbert. I remember being very eager to form a school hurling team, which would have been something of a blasphemy in North Kerry, a football-mad county.

All three of us saved like mad to buy three hurleys. Hurleys, the long sticks hurling is played with, were traditionally made from the wood of the ash, and didn't come cheap.

To raise some money, all three of us went off on rabbit hunting expeditions. Cormac, Johnny and I spent weeks, if not months, traipsing around the glens and hills outside Tarbert, looking for wild rabbits and hares. With the rain pelting down, and with the assistance of my trusty terrier and a borrowed hound, we eventually caught enough rabbits to buy three second-hand hurleys. All three of us were ecstatic with our latest possessions. For a sliotar, the small hurling ball, we manufactured something out of old string and twine.

Armed with our hurleys and homemade sliotar, we spent evenings and weekends playing and training in the fields around Tarbert, or at the local sports field if we were lucky enough for it to be unoccupied by the local football team.

One of my teachers took an interest in us three aspiring hurlers and often joined us in the sports field. He helped train us in the rules and intricacies of hurling.

We learned a lot under his tutelage. After a few months, my soloing – the art of balancing the sliotar on the top of the hurley as you sprinted with pace – had improved considerably.

However, one day, he told us he was unhappy with our tackling. Hurling, especially in those days, was a tough, physical sport, and injuries were frequent. However, we were fouling persistently and needed to hone the art of the good hurling tackle.

The old gang. Pictured (l-r) are Dan Kiely, Cormac Hurley, Tom Buckley, Johnny Coolahan, and Dan Kiely's brother Michael Kiely.

To improve our skills, we practised 'throw-ins'. In a throw-in, the referee throws the sliotar up into the air, and the two hurlers, standing side by side, compete for it.

When my turn came I went up against Johnny, and our *bainisteoir* asked us to take our position a few feet from him, shoulder to shoulder.

'Alright lads, I'll throw up this sliotar and when I blow this whistle, all you think about is get the sliotar, get the sliotar.'

In hindsight, I think my passion and enthusiasm got the better of me. The ref threw the sliotar up into the air, and when I heard the whistle blow, all I could think about was 'get the sliotar, get the sliotar'.

I was small and slight for my age, so I had to push myself harder to compete with my bigger, more corpulent peers. The ref threw the ball in the air, blew his whistle, and an almighty scramble for the sliotar ensued. Both Johnny and I missed the ball, but, luckily for me, it coincidentally fumbled to my side.

Johnny, who was bigger and heftier than me, tackled me from behind and, as I stumbled, I swung his hurley at the sliotar, making contact, inadvertently pushing it into his path.

Not to be defeated, I made one last scamper for the ball. I managed to reach the ball first, but rather than gathering it off the ground – Johnny was breathing down my neck and tackling heavily – I swung the hurley behind my shoulder and blasted the sliotar with venom.

The next thing I knew, Johnny was on the ground and bleeding badly. I had hit him with the hurley, and it was bad. There was blood everywhere.

Luckily for us, our teacher and bainisteoir, to his credit, was a fast thinker, and wrapped one of our hurling jerseys around Johnny's head, to stem the blood. There were no mobile phones back then, so Cormac and I ran to the nearest farm, and the farmer contacted the doctor.

The doctor arrived and examined my good friend. He had a very bad gash and the doctor reckoned he had suffered some form of concussion.

I felt very bad about what I had done to Johnny. I felt I had played too aggressively, and felt responsible for Johnny's injuries. Johnny however was remarkably forgiving and understanding. Later that evening, he returned all stitched up and feeling good. I remember him telling my parents not to punish me, that it was an accident and everything was forgiven.

We were young then, and we didn't know that accidents were very common in sports, particularly in physical-contact sports like hurling.

The injury certainly didn't affect Johnny's career. My friend Johnny Coolahan went on to become Professor John Coolahan, Professor Emeritus of Education at Maynooth University. He was also President of the Education Board of Ireland for many years, where he made a massive contribution to policy making in the area of education.

On his death in 2018, the obituary writer for the *Irish Times* newspaper described John as the 'father of Irish education'. I remember feeling very proud when I read that. It was high praise for my good friend, and it was very much merited. John was an intellectual giant in the world of education policy, philosophy and theory.

Some years before he died, Causeway Comprehensive School honoured John Coolahan. I was chairperson of the school board at the time and was asked to deliver the keynote address.

I told those gathered how John and I had grown up together on the streets of Tarbert village. How I didn't just admire Johnny as a professor and policymaker, I admired him as a friend. I told of how we would play hurling together, and how, on that fateful day, I had almost killed Johnny Coolahan with a hurley.

I remember joking that, by making a gash in his head, I helped open up his considerable brain, and Ireland had been reaping the rewards ever since. I remember looking over at John while I made the joke, and I was happy to see him get a great kick out of it.

I also really understand and appreciate John's belief in the power of education. While I never loved school, I do think the education I received stood to me.

As it happens, my poor father deserves enormous credit for the fact I got any schooling at all.

Secondary school fees were expensive back then. This was long before the Education Act of 1968, passed when Sean Leamas was Taoiseach, which eliminated secondary school tuition fees, and made school accessible to people who would otherwise have been unable to afford it.

My father and mother were desperate for all fourteen of us to receive a decent education. They were eager for us to move up in the world.

To make the tuition fees more manageable, my father split us up, sending half of us to Tarbert school, and the other half to Glin school, which was four miles away. The tuition fees to Tarbert and Glin were payable on different dates, so, by sending us to different schools, my father could spread out the payments, and relieve the financial pressures on the family. Paying one big, lump sum to one school would have been very difficult for us

I think Ireland owes a lot to people like Seán Leamass, Donagh O'Malley, Minister for Education at the time of the Act, and my friend Professor John Coolahan for its educational standards. John came alive in the classroom, teaching and imparting wisdom. I think those classrooms, presided over by teachers like Johnny, helped prepare us for life. Although, we owe a little to the hurling field as well. Playing hurling in those fields made men of us.

My First Bike

Kids these days probably get their first bike on Christmas Day, as a present from Santa Claus. My story is somewhat different. My first bike was less a gift and more an essential means of survival.

My secondary school was situated in the village of Glin, which is about four miles north of where I lived in Tarbert. In those days, schools didn't provide public transport as they do now. You walked to school or cycled.

When I started school, my brother Pete gave me a gift of an old, High Nelly bicycle he had received from a friend of his in Tarbert. Pete had oiled it and spruced it up a bit, so it was ready for me on my first day in school.

My first day of school came, and the bike was there waiting for me in the courtyard. I made two or three attempts to mount the saddle of the bike, but without much success. It was a man's bike, so, after placing my foot on the pedal, I struggled to lift my leg over the saddle.

Eventually, by placing the bike against the wall, I managed to mount it, but then, as the bike rolled away from the wall, I found my feet couldn't reach the pedals, and I lost my balance. My bike crashed to the ground and I fell on my side. My schoolbag, and the little lunch my mother had made for me, landed in the mud.

I made another few attempts to somehow operate the bike, but to no avail. On one occasion, I cycled a few yards, by seating myself

Dan Kiely pictured with his classmates in an old school photo. Dan is seated second from the left on the front row.

under the bar, and somehow succeeding in operating the pedals. However, I lost my balance again after a few yards and toppled over. I couldn't reach the handlebars and therefore couldn't steer properly.

I needed to obtain a smaller bike, and, not for the first nor the last time in my young life, I needed money. I resorted to what was a reliable source of money for me growing up: hunting rabbits. Eventually, I saved enough money to buy a smaller bike and that served me well in my daily commute to and from Glin.

My bike troubles didn't end there, unfortunately. The bike was second-hand and, owing to the length of my daily journeys, it needed constant maintenance. Also, don't forget, the journey was four miles there and four miles back on what were very poor roads. The roads were paved with coarse gravel, so punctures were frequent. And if you got a puncture, there was really no option but to stop on the side of the road and mend your tyre, or replace it with a spare one, which could delay you for up to half an hour.

My mother also found a job for me – as she often did, God bless her. Every Friday, I was to cycle to Mrs Rowan's in Ballylongford to collect the family's weekly supply of eggs. Mrs Rowan lived on the road a mile outside Ballylongford, on the opposite side to Tarbert and Glin, so it added two hours to my daily cycle.

Cycling on that road every Friday, especially in the bad weather, with the rain pelting down and the winds ferocious, was hard.

But there were days I was glad to do it. I was happy to have some time to myself, away from farm work and school work.

I loved cycling up there on spring and summer evenings, with the sun beating down, or a breeze in my face, and the air rich with the smell of flowers and freshly cut hay. Cycling on that road, and hearing the chickens cluck in Mrs Rowan's coops, would give me a rush. When I cycled back the way I came, I would often close my eyes, and feel the wind and sun in my face. I felt like a king.

Young Kiely the Soldier

'With me gone, Dan, you will have to step up to the plate. You will be the oldest now.' This was one of the last things my brother Pete told me before he emigrated to the United States.

After Pete emigrated, I was the eldest of those left behind. As my brother Tim had also emigrated. This meant I had more responsibilities. One of those responsibilities was taking Pete's place in An Fórsa Cosanta Áitiúil (FCÁ) which I embraced enthusiastically.

During the Second World War, or 'The Emergency' as it was called in Ireland, the then Taoiseach, Éamonn de Valera, established the Local Defence Force, the LDF, which was a brigade of army reservists, made up of people from the local community. It was a precaution in case the country was invaded. After the war, the force was renamed An Fórsa Cosanta Áitiúil.

There was a tradition in our house to join and help out. It may have had something to do with my father's military and republican past – he had fought in the War of Independence.

I was very eager to join. The local branch of the FCÁ would often parade through Tarbert village. My brothers Tim and Pete would often lead the procession, holding the tricolour aloft, while the other recruits marched behind. I loved watching them march on St Patrick's Day, particularly on days when the sun shone and everyone in the village came out to greet them and cheer them on.

Dan pictured with his friend and comrade Anto Heaphy, both in Army Reserve (FCA) uniform. Anto Heaphy would go on to successfully run The Listowel Arms Hotel for many years.

I was, of course, very proud of my brothers, but I was also a little jealous. I desperately wanted to join myself.

However, I was disappointed to discover I was too young. I was fourteen at the time Pete left, and the rule was you had to be over seventeen.

My problems didn't end there. I was also small for my age. Although I was fourteen, I was about the height of the average ten year old. Worse again, I looked anaemic. For whatever reason, as a child, I always looked as pale as a ghost.

I remember my father bringing me to speak with the captain of the local FCÁ unit and pleading my case. Neither of us knew what to expect. On the day in question, the captain was standing at the gate near the entrance to the field where the local recruits were completing their drills. As we walked up to him, my heart raced. Watching the soldiers complete the various military manoeuvres filled me with anticipation. Although it was flogging rain, and everyone was covered in muck, I just wanted to be out there, getting involved.

When the captain saw me, he patted me on the head affectionately. He told my father he couldn't believe I was fourteen, but he said he knew my father to be a man of his word, so he took him at it. After a brief discussion with my dad, he agreed to relax the rules and let me take part; he said I could pitch in, help out and do some of the more menial jobs until I developed sufficiently to become a full recruit.

He also noticed my paleness and commented on it to my father. I remember them whispering something to each other, out of my earshot, and laughing to themselves. I noticed both of them looking at me and smiling, as if they were plotting something. At the time, I was so excited to have been accepted, I didn't take much notice. Alas, I would soon find out.

Some days later, I was standing in the FCÁ barracks in Listowel waiting for my new uniform. A boy of about seventeen or so came in and handed me my gear. He smiled as he handed me the uniform, but I was so excited I didn't notice.

Only after I had changed, did I realise! I almost tripped on the ends of my pants leg, it being so floppy and big. I remember catching my belt strap and pulling it outwards, and thinking I could nearly have fit another Dan Kiely in here if I so wished.

This was significant to me, as the prospect of wearing a lovely, shiny new uniform and boots was a big incentive for joining in the first place. Clothes were very simple back then. Most of the clothes I had growing up were homemade, except for the clothes sent to us from my father's sisters. My mother would take strips and pieces from my father's old suits and knit jackets and pants out of them for me.

Don't misunderstand, I am not complaining, these did us, growing up. If it wasn't for my mother's work ethic and industriousness, we would have gone without clothes.

I loved the idea of wearing an FCÁ uniform. In my childish dreams, I imagined myself marching through Tarbert on St Patrick's Day, with a shiny new beret on my head.

I would be lying if I said I wasn't disappointed to be handed that oversized apparel. Luckily, I didn't allow the uniform's imperfections to destroy the pleasure I took in finally being a member of the FCÁ. Luckily for me, my mother was adept at sewing and she adjusted the uniforms for me.

When the captain said menial tasks, he really meant what he said. I wasn't allowed to participate in the military training or drills, or, much to my chagrin, the shooting practice. I did have one important job in those early days; polishing the recruits' boots and buttons.

This was important work, as participating in parades and processions was an indispensable part of what the FCÁ did. When marching on St Patrick's Day, it was important for all the reservists to look their best, with shiny boots and buttons, and I was proud to play my part in that.

My mam and dad were delighted I was accepted. It meant that when I was accepted as a full recruit there would be some extra money coming into the house. Remarkably, back then, an FCÁ recruit's annual annuity would be the equivalent of two weeks of my dad's Garda wages.

Even though I was new to the FCÁ, I did get an opportunity to do some target practice at the shooting range. I got my hands on an old Lee-Enfield rifle, with 303 cartridges, and I discovered I was a dab hand at it.

The FCÁ did their target practice in a field outside Tarbert, and I have fond memories of sneaking up there. I got friendly with an older recruit, who shared my enthusiasm for learning more about firearms and becoming more skilled in using them. One day, he arrived with an old, rusty contraption and a sack. He looked flustered and excited. I asked him what the contraption was. He smiled and said to me, 'I found this in the back of the barracks. It's old, but still good.'

I had no idea what to expect as he began to assemble it. It was a launch pad for grenades, and the sack had a few unused grenades.

I remember him carefully placing a grenade on the bolt, while I released the latch. Once released, we threw ourselves to the ground with our fingers in our ears. It made a small, but loud explosion several yards away. Looking up, I could see thick, black smoke forming around our bomb site.

It was a small explosion, but I think it taught me something about life. To this day, while I consider guns a necessary evil, I'm always at pains to emphasise that they should be treated with respect. I discovered I had a good shot, and a little later I got the opportunity to shoot for the Irish Defence Forces.

I eventually discovered what my dad and the captain found so amusing. Next Sunday, my dad pulled me aside and, with a smile on his face, he said to me, 'Dan, on your way back to school after lunch tomorrow, call into the Ivy House public house and ask Mr O'Shaughnessy for "a cure". I told him to expect you. Do it every day until you are put right. Do you hear me, Dan?' I nodded obediently. 'That's a good lad, Dan,' he said to me.

The next day, on my way back to school after lunch, I called into the Ivy House. Mr O'Shaughnessy was standing behind the counter and he smiled when he saw me.

'How can I help this young man?' he asked.

'My name's Dan Kiely and I've come for the cure.'

'By God, you have,' Mr O'Shaughnessy said, as he smiled at three men sitting at the bar counter.

Mr O'Shaughnessy fetched a small glass and, placing it under a keg, waited until the black liquid came out. As I mentioned, I was unusually small for my age, so one of Mr O'Shaughnessy's patrons had to lift me onto the counter so I could take the glass.

'Now, young Kiely, you drink one of these every day until we see a bit of colour on your face.'

I remember being a little frightened by the black liquid and the creamy, frothy top, but I did what I was told and, slowly, took a few exploratory sips. Satisfied it didn't taste too bad, I slugged the small glass back. At that stage, Mr O'Shaughnessy and his three locals had begun cheering me on, finding great sport in the young fella having his first glass of 'the black stuff'.

I'm not sure if it restored some colour to my cheeks, but if drinking a small 'pony' of Guinness everyday was the price I had to pay to join the FCÁ, then it was one I was prepared to pay.

Emigration

Growing up, I watched as so many of my brothers and sisters emigrated.

My sister Eileen was the first to leave home. I was so young when Eileen left that I hardly remember her leaving. Eileen went on to become someone we were all very proud of.

Her first destination was Dublin, the nation's capital, or the 'Big Smoke' as we called it growing up. Like legions of Irish women from rural towns and villages, Eileen trained to be a nurse, a profession she excelled at, owing to her work ethic and compassionate nature.

Eventually, like so many Irish women of the time, she joined the nuns, the Columban missionary nuns to be exact. Her work with the Columbans took her to the Philippines, where she did Trojan work and service, helping some of the desperately poor.

Later in life, she was put in charge of managing the Columbans' international assets, work that would take her across the globe, to far-flung places, meeting dignitaries and philanthropists.

It is remarkable to think that a small girl from Tarbert, County Kerry, who grew up in the house attached to the Garda barracks, would go on to achieve and do so much. But that was Ireland for you; we didn't have much, but we achieved a lot.

The first of the Kielys to leave the country was my sister Cathy. She set off to America at the age of fourteen. I remember her leaving, but I reckon it was hard on my parents, seeing such a young girl, at such a tender age, make such a plunge.

When she arrived in the Big Apple, she juggled education and work commitments, getting a job in a telephone company while working at night. We were all very proud of Cathy; how she survived New York, worked hard, and was eventually in a position to help her brothers and sisters when they joined her in America.

My brother Tim was the next to venture out to new pastures. He, like Cathy before him, stayed with my Aunt Margaret at first, until both he and Cathy managed to get an apartment of their own.

Initially, Tim got a job at the flight kitchen in Shannon Airport, helping prepare the meals for the transatlantic flights. Every day, Timmy would help prepare dinners for passengers travelling to places like New York, Boston and Chicago. Fate would have it that one day, thanks to Cathy's assistance and his own determination, Tim himself would make that journey. The boy who had spent years watching those planes bound for America take off from Shannon Airport, one day stepped onto one himself; made the journey that many Kielys made before him, and many would make after him.

After Tim joined Cathy in New York, my brother Pete followed soon after. Before we knew it, three Kielys were living together in an apartment in the Bronx at 1272 Nelson Avenue, to be precise. Those of us living in Ireland were always reminded of this by the parcels sent back. Tim, Pete and Cathy were all very generous to my mother and father, sending what they could afford for Christmas, birthdays and special occasions.

Naturally, from a young age, I was eager to join my siblings in that strange and wonderful new land.

I made it known to my parents that my heart was set on emigrating. I longed to see the Statue of Liberty and America's shores. I wanted to make a man of myself in New York City, follow in the footsteps of my brothers Pete and Timmy and my sister Cathy.

I think my parents knew I had the emigrant's fire in my belly. I knew it ever since I told my father that I would buy him a car when I go to America when I'm older. I think they recognised that fire and drive in me, and respected it as well as feared it. I think my parents, my mother especially, had mixed views on emigration. On one hand, she hated it, as it meant parting ways with her children and having her family scattered around the world. On the other hand, she accepted it as an economic necessity; unlike today, Ireland was poor and underdeveloped, and it was necessary to emigrate for more opportunities.

However, she didn't want me to emigrate. I think she probably thought that since so many of her children had emigrated, she was entitled to have one or two of them at home. I do remember, with some regret, having many arguments with her. I was stubborn when I wanted to be, and I had that insatiable drive to go to America, discover the world and better myself.

I was so eager to go to America that I continuously wrote to Cathy asking her to help me with the fare. I also convinced her to assist me with the paperwork. In those days, emigrants needed to have work and accommodation arranged prior to travelling. When this was complete, I convinced my mother to take me to Dublin for my compulsory X-ray; a necessity in those days if you wanted to emigrate to the United States.

Arriving back in Kerry after my X-ray, I was as determined as ever. I remember it all coming to a head one day in school. French wasn't my favourite subject in school. I guess I couldn't see the merit in learning a language whose practical value didn't seem obvious to me, but my teacher, to her credit, refused to give up on me.

During one lesson, I struggled with the pronunciation of 'Je m'appelle Dan et j'habite à Tarbert.' After making a pure hames of it, I expected her to move to the next pupil, but she insisted I keep repeating the sentence until I pronounced it correctly.

Eventually, I lost my temper and explained to her that it was pointless for me to learn French as I wasn't going to sit my Leaving

Cert. I was planning to emigrate to America and all of those 'je suis' and 'je m'appelles' wouldn't do me any good on the mean streets of Brooklyn and the Bronx.

I remember the poor lady being very disturbed by what I said. She even kept me back after class to try and persuade me to finish my Leaving Cert. She kept telling me that the Leaving Cert was a good, solid qualification and a good educational basis for life that would serve me well in whatever I did.

Looking back, I think she did have my best interests at heart and there was sense in what she was saying, but when you have a young, headstrong fella with a dream his heart was set on, there is no talking to him.

I remember the last summer before I left for America, I avoided my mother, avoided discussing the topic with her.

I did, however, make one vow. The idea struck me after walking down Main Street in Glin and passing Costello's shop.

I remember something inside the window catching my eye. I pressed my nose against the glass and looked in. I had never seen a gas cooker before then. I remember running in and asking Mr Costello, the shop owner, about it, and he explained what it was.

New modern appliances like cookers and washing machines were revolutionising domestic life for millions of families, relieving them of the burden of physical work. They were having a transformative effect on the lives of women, especially women like my mother, who never stopped working and labouring.

From the minute I saw the magical machine in Costello's shop, I knew I wanted to purchase it for my mother. I asked Mr Costello how much it cost. I remember he paused and rolled his eyes. 'It ain't cheap young Kiely!' 'Go on, how much?' '£40.'

£40 was a frightful amount of money in those days. To put things in perspective for the younger reader, my father's monthly salary, as a member of An Garda Síochána, was £28. And remember, we were just scraping by on my father's salary, we didn't have much to spare and we couldn't simply afford to lose a month and a bit.

Expensive though it was, I made a vow. I wanted to buy it for my mother and for my family. I was leaving for the States against their wishes, and I wanted to do this one thing before I packed my bags and left for pastures new.

That summer of 1959, I saved every last shilling I could. Most of my annual annuity from the FCÁ was already allocated to household expenses, so there wasn't much to be made there. As was any work I was doing for local farmers. The only way I could make some extra money was by selling turf, and that is what I did. In addition to the family's regular load of turf, I cut an additional load for sale, which I did in the autumn of that year. For my last summer in Ireland before emigrating, I went from neighbour to neighbour, with a little donkey and cart, selling surplus turf.

Coming towards Christmas 1959, I let my father in on the secret. I can still remember the smile on his face when I told him I was saving to buy Mam a cooker before I emigrated. I could see how proud of me he was. Yes, I was emigrating against their wishes, but he could see there was some good in me, and that I wanted to do a good deed before I left.

One evening, my father and I went to a small, quiet corner of the house, where he had his Garda black box. Every member of the Broy Harriers carried a black box, and my father still used it to store his private belongings. He also made use of it to keep my savings. Tipping the coins onto the table, we counted them together. Lo and behold, there was £40 in half-crowns in that small bag.

We were both elated! I had enough to buy the cooker! I left the house that day on my bike, with my head held high. I arrived at Costello's shop and handed Mr Costello my bag of half-crowns. A few days later, a new, sparkling gas cooker was delivered to my mother; a few days before Christmas.

That Christmas, the Kiely Christmas dinner was roasted in our new gas cooker. It tasted just as delicious, the only difference being the preparation wasn't as laborious as usual.

That year, the Kiely family, in our small lodging, were the beneficiaries of modern appliances. We were riding on the tide of progress that would sweep through Ireland in the coming decades, bringing much that was good and a little bad.

Charles Dickens once remarked 'It was the best of times, it was the worst of times,' and I feel similar about the Ireland I grew up in. I do think that little adventure of me buying the cooker for Mam, seeing the smile on her face when it arrived, and seeing how it made our lives at Christmas a little easier, may have impacted my later political beliefs; it illustrated to me how small signs of progress could have a positive and transformative effect on people's lives.

I emigrated to the United States on the 6th of January 1960, and politics and Ireland were far, far from my mind. That story would come later. All that was on my mind that day was New York City. I was a young man and I had a life for myself to make.

Young Kiely the Boxing Champ

One important part of my life, growing up, was a certain sport that I loved. If you saw me as a youngster, you really wouldn't think it. As I mentioned before, I was small for my age and unnaturally pale – despite my weekly pony of stout in The Ivy House.

Despite these disadvantages, I was handy at boxing. My right arm hooks were very good and I had sharp reflexes.

I made a bit of a stir initially, winning some fights, and many people in the village reckoned I was going places as a boxer.

For my interest in boxing, I owe a great debt to Garda Healy, who was a boxing coach and mentor to us boxers growing up in Tarbert. When Garda Healy found us, we were tough and full of enthusiasm, jumping around and swinging haymakers. More fighters than boxers.

Garda Healy helped us hone those raw skills and moulded us into disciplined boxers who could hold their own among the county and the province's best.

(A 'haymaker', for anyone not knowledgeable in boxing technicalities, is a wild swing of a right or left arm. It entails drawing your arm back and connecting with your opponent at an arc. It can be a mean punch, but one that should only be attempted when your opponent is weak and close to a knockout.)

Garda Healy was one of three guards stationed in Tarbert Garda station, the other two being my dad and the sergeant. Garda Healy would have us train in the small garden and courtyard attached to the barracks complex, the one our house also spilled onto. He would tie a large sack filled with old maize off the clothesline and had me and the others practise our jabs on it.

One day, Garda Healy was complaining about my coordination. We were practising combos on the maize sack. A sequence of five punches, two jabs, and a hook, before finishing with an uppercut. Our coach was happy with my speed and individual punches, but felt I was slow in the combination. I often got the order wrong and, on some occasions apparently, I hesitated.

Dan and Cormac pictured with their boxing coach Garda Healy. (L-r) Dan Kiely, Garda Healy and Cormac Hurley.

I didn't take too kindly to this criticism. I was taking my boxing very seriously at this time. I often dreamed of being a professional fighter and I was eager to grow and get better. I was slowly moving up the ranks. By this time, I had won a big fight in the County Boxing Championship in Tralee and, as a result, the following summer I was scheduled to compete in the Provincial Championship in Mallow, Co Cork. I knew that Garda Healy and the entire village had high hopes for me.

When he told me that my coordination was wrong, I was put out. I wanted to prove him wrong. I threw myself at the maize sack with venom, throwing out jabs and hooks like my life depended on it. When it came to the end of the combo, I threw an uppercut like I had never thrown one before.

I remember turning around to my coach and teammates, holding my head up high in triumph. Now, I thought to myself, what do ye think of that?

Then, I heard a loud thud! I turned around to discover a large pile of maize collapsed on the ground and the torn sack dangling over it.

I had a feeling of déjà vu. Having almost killed poor Johnny Coolahan playing hurling, now, I burst the punching bag and ruined my mother's and Mrs Healy's garden.

Lo and behold, both my mother and Mrs Healy, Garda Healy's wife, had heard the commotion and out they came to assess the damage. Both my mother and Mrs Healy looked at Garda Healy as if to say 'We told you so'. They never approved of us training in the garden, always predicting that something like this would happen. Garda Healy, to his credit, took my side. He accepted responsibility and told them he had fired me up. With a laugh and a shake of the head, he told the women we would clean up the mess and have the garden and quarters looking spick and span in no time.

I always appreciated Garda Healy for having my back, and it wasn't the last time he had it either. The next time, things were a lot more serious.

The following year, I was fighting in the County Championship in Tralee. In the weeks running up to it, I had been flaking that punching bag after being psyched up by my coach, Garda Healy.

When I arrived at the Desmond Boxing Club in Tralee, I was nervous. My opponent was a local lad, Tralee born and bred, and as I entered the small arena the crowd were cheering and chanting his name.

The first few rounds didn't go my way. My opponent was bursting with energy and he was connecting. By the time the ref drew the third round to a close, my nose was bleeding and my head was pounding.

As Garda Healy, pressing his fingers against my nostrils, held my head back, I could see stars and I seriously considered quitting, but the psyching from my team was too motivating. They really could fire me up they could: 'Go on now, Dan, my boy, do it for Tarbert, do it for all of us. Go on, Dan, my boy!'

The following rounds could not have been more different. I had a venomous right hook. Predictably, my opponent had expended far too much energy in the early stages of the fight, and by the fifth round he was very tired, failing to muster any defence to my hooks and combos. Late in the sixth round, I connected with a lovely left hook and he stumbled backwards, eventually collapsing on the floor. As the ref bent down to ask him if he was alright, asking him if he wanted to quit, I basked in the feeling of triumph.

To my opponent's credit, he got up and battled on. The last few rounds were more evenly matched, but he had no defence to my left and right hooks.

As the bell chimed to signal the close of the final round, me and my team were confident we were victorious. I remember Garda Healy smiled and struck a victory pose with his closed fist. It was going to be a victory; a victory for Tarbert, for Garda Healy, for the Kiely family, for my mam and dad, and for me. If I could only look back and see my expression at that moment, I must have been swimming in pride.

Then came the judges' decision: My opponent won! Myself, Garda Healy and all the Tarbert team were in shock. As the ref lifted my opponent's hand, the kid could hardly stand. He had two black eyes and he looked as if he hardly knew where he was or what was happening to him.

My first emotion was shock and disappointment. Being a kid, I respected the authority of the judges and immediately started to blame myself. Clearly, I thought to myself, I had not fought as well as I could have done.

Then I looked over at Garda Healy. He was enraged. But not at me, at the judges. He jumped out of the ring and ran over to confront them.

Garda Healy was older and wiser than the rest of us and he didn't naively accept the judges' decision. He knew I had been cheated of victory.

Later, it transpired that two of the judges were related to my opponent. Later in the dressing room, as I pressed a bag of ice against my nose, Garda Healy approached me.

Putting his arm around my shoulder, he told me he was proud of me and that I was the real winner. He told me I had been robbed by the judges.

This came as quite a shock to me and the whole incident proved to be quite the life lesson. Being still a boy, a part of me thought that adults were perfect, especially educated, important adults like the judges, and the world was basically fair. When of course nothing could be further from the truth; adults are far from perfect and the world is far from fair.

I was shattered and disappointed to lose a fight I deserved to win and, for a boy, it was a glimpse into how cruel, unfair and ruthless the world could be. It was a lesson I would take with me to America when I emigrated some years later.

Back to Kiskeam

Garda Healy would also play a part in another important event, one that proved to be my first introduction to the strange world of politics.

It all happened with the news. It came one evening after my father came home from work. Everything appeared normal. Dad was having a cup of tea by the open fire, and my mam was hanging up his wet clothes to dry. Suddenly, my father announced, in a low, solemn voice, that he was to be transferred and we all had to leave Tarbert.

Tarbert Garda station was to be reduced to a two-man station, and my father was being transferred to a barracks in Barraduff, a village outside Killarney, in South Kerry.

My mother couldn't contain herself. She started cursing the government and the Garda for being so insensitive, moving a large, young family from a place they had established themselves in, and plunging them into the unknown.

'Would you calm down, woman,' I remember my father saying. Even as a young boy, I could see my mother's point of view. Her children were settled in the local schools. While our lodging in the Garda barracks was modest, we had made improvements to it and, for a large family surviving mostly on one, modest wage, it was by no means the worst for the time. The house was relatively warm thanks to a blazing open fire, we had an outdoor toilet, and while our garden was officially part of the barracks complex, it was, for all intents and purposes, a nice garden.

By this time, we also had the holy grail of modern conveniences: running water. Our tap in the back kitchen was connected to the town mains, meaning water flowed. This made cooking, washing and laundering so much easier. It meant our family did not have to haul heavy buckets of water from the town well to the house on a daily basis, as I often did in the days before we got running water.

Despite my mam's concerns, she did finally agree, after arguing a bit with my father, to keep an open mind. The next weekend, the whole family visited the new house we were to be allocated in Barraduff.

My father was in two minds about the move. While he could see my mother's point of view, he liked the idea of being closer to his native parish. Barraduff was only a few miles from Kiskeam, the land he hailed from. Many from his extended family were still based there, like his brother, sisters, nieces and nephews. The prospect of playing in the local Kiely brass and reel band more regularly strongly appealed to him.

I know from my own life that as you get older you slowly find yourself being pulled in the direction of home. I was in America when I felt this longing, but my father, despite being located in North Kerry, only a matter of miles away from his home, felt it too.

That weekend, my father arranged for a hackney man to pick us up at Tarbert station and drive us to Barraduff. On the drive from Tarbert to Barraduff, I remember noticing the changing landscape. The farmlands, flat land and straighter roads of North Kerry were gradually replaced by a different, wilder landscape with mountains, trees and meandering roads. I know my father noticed it too, as he never took his eye away from the window. He was home, and part of him wanted to stay there, and he could hardly be blamed for that.

When we arrived at the house, we spent a few minutes walking around. I remember my mother looking at my father and shaking her head. Assessing the cottage was itself a struggle, as the small garden was overgrown with weeds and briars and, once inside, the sheer extent of the disrepair became apparent. There was no indoor or outdoor toilet, there was a hole in the roof, and it lacked running water. Barraduff was also very isolated, nestled deep in Kerry countryside and miles from any secondary school.

My father's transfer was a big episode in all our lives, growing up. After that visit, the weeks that followed were dominated by it. We all knew the decision to downgrade Tarbert station to a two-cop station came from above. However, my mother couldn't fathom why my father, who had a family of fourteen, would be selected for transfer ahead of Garda Healy, who only had one child at this time. My mam suspected it was because Garda Healy was involved in a lot of voluntary and community work at the time, and that had won him a lot of favour in the community, particularly with a local priest..

My father, in contrast, was a quiet man. When he came home from work, he preferred to play music and tell stories, rather than get involved in charitable activities and social events.

Then, one day, the plot thickened. As a child, I remember being mostly bewildered by the whole situation, my feelings lying somewhere between excitement and dread. But I was loyal to my mam, and when she asked me to do something I nearly always did it.

A few weeks after we visited the house in Barraduff, my mam came to me and said, 'Dan, I want you to do something for me.' 'Of course, Mam, whatever you say.' 'I want you to go to Dan Moloney's office in Listowel and hand him this letter; tell him your mother sent you.' (Dan Moloney was the local Fianna Fáil TD.)

My mother was a sharp woman and she could tell I was uncomfortable with what she had asked me to do. I was torn between loyalty to my mam and a desire not to upset my father. Noticing this, she added, 'If Dad asks you why you did it, say, "I only did what Mam asked me to do, and that you had no idea what was in the letter." Alright, Dan?' My mother suggested, winking at me.

While I was no academic high-flyer, I understood my mother's tactics; she had found a way for me to obey her while staying loyal to my father. I smiled at her, grabbed the letter and ran out the door. Outside, I saw a lorry leaving Tarbert Creamery and I hailed the driver down.

'Alright…jump in the back. AND DON'T DO ANYTHING TO THE MILK; IF A CONTAINER FALLS OUT OR IS OPENED, I KNOW WHO'S TO BLAME!' The driver said after I spent several minutes pleading my case.

I'm not sure if I believe in destiny, but there was certainly an air of destiny about that journey into Listowel.

I got a blessed view of the landscape and countryside between Tarbert and Listowel that morning: the bogs, pastures and foothills. I could see cattle grazing, men making their way towards the bogs, wild foxes out hunting, exploiting the dim twilight. When we sped past Lyon's Cross, I could see the sun rising on the horizon, covering the landscape with a beautiful orange light. Despite the fact I was freezing cold, crouched uncomfortably between big milk containers, I felt blessed to be alive. Every time the diver hit a pothole, the trailer would rock, the containers would bang off each other and I would be thrown forward, but I arrived in Market Street Listowel safely.

I thanked the creamery man and made straight for Dan Moloney's constituency clinic above his garage in Listowel.

I remember being apprehensive when I arrived at Dan's clinic. As I walked through the open door, the secretary and the five people waiting all stared at me. I walked slowly up to the secretary and handed her the small letter, explaining to her that my mother had sent me with the instruction to pass the letter on to Mr Dan Moloney TD.

Scowling, she took the letter and examined it. She then looked me up and down, taking the measure of me. Looking at my innocent face, and my clothes, dirtied from the grit of the milk lorry, I think she took pity on me. She smiled eventually, telling me to take a seat.

A man with a flat cap, who I could see had a lame step, also smiled warmly at me, patting me on the head as I went to take a seat.

I'm not sure what I was expecting, but I think I was worried that a constituency clinic would be quite a stiff and forbidding place. In contrast, the place was relaxed and friendly.

I immediately noticed the big, open fire. My hands were numb from the cold, and I splayed them in front of the flames. Soon, the secretary arrived with a pot of tea and a biscuit. The others laughed when I gulped back the tea, like 'twas porter', as one put it, and swallowed my biscuit whole. I was ravenous.

Eventually, my time came. The secretary stood up and said to me, 'Mr Moloney will see young Kiely now'.

Mr Moloney was busy with paperwork when I came in. He gestured for me to take a seat, without looking up. The two framed portraits behind Mr Moloney's back grabbed my attention. One was Éamon de Valera, the founder of Fianna Fáil, and leader of the anti-Treaty republicans during the Civil War. The other was of Pádraig Pearse, one of the executed republican leaders of the 1916 rebellion.

I have often wondered whether this, my first introduction to the world of constituency politics, to the life of a rural Fianna Fáil TD, had any bearing on my future decision to get involved in politics.

I did know, even at that young age, that my family were Fianna Fáil on account of my father's War of Independence and Civil War activities. The Anglo-Irish Treaty Michael Collins negotiated with the British in 1921 split Irish republicans in two; some accepted it, and some rejected it. The Treaty secured Ireland some degree of freedom, but it also entailed considerable concessions, including all Irish politicians being bound to swear an oath of allegiance to the British King, and the six counties of the north of Ireland remaining part of the United Kingdom. (I will write more about this political history in the pages to come.)

While I was far too young to have political views, or convictions of any kind, I was happy being in the presence of de Valera's portrait, as he was Dad's man, and I knew Dad was loyal to him. It eased any guilt I had for going behind his back.

When Mr Moloney finished his paperwork, he looked up, smiled at me, and said 'Alright young fella, what do we have here?'

He opened the letter and read it. Then he looked at me again, taking the measure of me, before quickly reading it for a second time.

'You're Dan Kiely's son, the Garda in Tarbert?' He said finally, having read the letter twice. I nodded and I was delighted by what followed. Mr Dan Moloney leaned back on his chair and began saying how my dad was doing such a good job as a guard, and we as a family should be proud of him. He also said something I had never heard before: he said my dad fought bravely during the War of Independence and we should be very proud of his military record.

That filled the fourteen-year-old boy sitting across from Dan Moloney with pride. My father's military exploits were never discussed in our house growing up, and for me, at the time a teenager with an inclination towards the military life, it was great to hear confirmation that my dad had been a good soldier, and had served his country in her hour of need.

'This will be sorted Dan.' Mr Moloney said to me as he picked up the old telephone that was on his desk. 'A guard with such a big family shouldn't be transferred. It's a disgrace, this carry on by that… of yours.' I thought Mr Moloney was about to reveal the person behind my father's transfer, but stopped himself out of tact.

After a few attempts, Mr Moloney eventually got through to a Mr Moylan. The name meant nothing to the fourteen-year-old boy sitting across from him, but now, years later, I can identify the man Dan Moloney was talking to on the telephone that day as being none other than Seán Moylan; a minister in the then Fianna Fáil government, and a republican veteran of the War of Independence.

I can still recall snippets of the conversation Mr Moloney had with Mr Moylan. Minister Moylan knew exactly who my father was, of course, my father having been a captain in his flying column, and they had served together in both the War of Independence and later the Civil War. I also recall him remarking how awful a scandal it was that a family with fourteen children was being uprooted and transferred, and I remember Minister Moylan seemed to agree. After Dan put the phone down, he winked at me. 'Go back to Tarbert son, and tell your mother that it will be sorted.'

'Oh, young man,' Mr Moloney said again, just as I was about to leave. 'Your mother will be over the moon about this, and women usually know best when it comes to these things.' He winked again. I smiled at him and left.

When I arrived home and told my mother, she was exactly as Dan Moloney predicted, 'over the moon'. My father's reaction, however, could not have been more different.

He arrived in as usual. My mother helped him remove his wet clothes and boots. As he dried his wet body by the fire, my sister handed him a mug of tea. Noticing the tension in the room, he asked, 'Well, you would swear it was a morgue I came home to. What ails ye?'

Nervously, my mother told him. He was angry, very angry. He was angry because a part of him wanted to return to his home parish. He was angry that my mother decided on a course of action without consulting him, but, more than anything, he was angry that she went public. My father was a proud and private man. The last thing he wanted was to have a politician involved in his personal affairs.

When I saw him sitting by the fire, shaking his head angrily, I said something I thought would comfort him: 'Dad, Mr Moloney told me you were a great soldier and you had served your country well.'

But he wasn't in the mood.

'Stop bothering me boy. Why don't you make yourself useful and do some chores around the house? What am I keeping all of ye for?'

Later, however, he returned from the local public house and he was in better form. Being a guard, my father couldn't be seen taking a drink, so a local publican he was friendly with allowed him to have a drink in the kitchen behind the bar.

When he walked into the small house, we were all quiet. 'Well young Dan, you want to be a soldier, do you?'

When I looked up at him, I could see he was smiling. 'Well young Dan, you want to fight for Irish freedom, do you?' Everyone in the household laughed. As he said it, he patted me on the head. It was a good end to a difficult day.

I know he said it to lighten the mood, let people know that everything was forgiven, but a part of me likes to think he was serious too, that he saw a bit of himself in me.

Unlike him, it was in business and politics, not the battlefield, where I did my bit for the country. But I always believed that, when it came to politics, if I had anything of my brave father in me, I would do all right.

Uncle Paddy's Home

'Oh, for goodness sake, I don't believe it. Dear God!' These were the words out of my mother's mouth, one fine September morning. She was at the door of our house, chatting to Garda Healy's wife and some other neighbours.

Me and my siblings were in the kitchen when we heard her let out that cry of shock: 'Dear God!' I immediately ran outside to see what all the commotion was about.

A small crowd had already gathered around the barracks to witness the spectacle. By the time we arrived, the motorbike had driven past the station and halted at the top of the road.

As I mentioned before, I only ever remember three cars in Tarbert village growing up: the priest's, the doctor's and the hackney's. So seeing a motorbike on those potholed, shabby roads, more accustomed to the beat of horses and traps, was quite the novelty.

I remember us kids jumping up so we could see the motorcycle in the distance. The driver got off the bike, removed his helmet and began waving.

'Mam, Mam, is he waving at us?'

My mother was too shocked to answer. She just stood there shaking her head.

The driver mounted the bike again and revved up the engine. Internal combustion engines were more primitive then, so it emitted a very loud, spluttering sound.

Dan Kiely Sr. (on the left), pictured with his brother Paddy Kiely. Two off-duty guards, and both former 'Broy Harriers'.

For the benefit of everyone assembled, the driver sped past the station and, at the end of the road, executed a U-turn. Everyone cheered and laughed. Then the surprise came.

As he removed his helmet, the cyclist's identity was slowly revealed.

It was our Uncle Paddy. My siblings and I ran towards him jumping with excitement.

Yes, the mystery motorcyclist was my Uncle Paddy. Paddy was more than an uncle to me growing up, he was my hero. I really looked up to him, and would look forward to his visits.

While we were all shocked when we discovered who the driver was, in retrospect, we should have known. Like my dad, Paddy was a guard, stationed in Waterford, but whereas my dad was shy and private, Paddy was sociable and gregarious. Loving danger and adventure, there was always a bit of mischief in Paddy.

While I might be flattering myself, I always thought Paddy had a soft spot for me. That day, he grabbed me and said, 'Alright young

Dan, your turn to drive now.' Nestled on his lap, I could reach the handlebars and pretend to drive the old-fashioned bike.

My mam warned Paddy not to 'let any of those rascals near that expensive machine,' but Paddy ignored her warning, and while he was inside having tea and sandwiches with my father, he permitted us to play with the bike and touch it.

My brothers and I took turns sitting on the leather upholstered seat. I remember the engine and the bike's internal mechanisms being exposed to view. We were all fascinated by the bike's various pipes and pistons, but half afraid to touch them, the vehicle being so magical and strange to us.

When Paddy came back out, we asked him if we could take turns sitting on his lap, and although he was tired, he eventually said, after pestering, 'Go on, sure, go on.' My mam shook her head, but Paddy ignored her again.

Paddy was a bachelor, never had kids of his own, and perhaps because of this was always a little more indulgent with us than our parents.

He would visit every year for the Listowel Races, a big racing meeting held in Listowel.

Paddy would usually cycle into Tarbert on a High Nelly bicycle, but I would still be sure to give him a hero's welcome. Whenever I heard he was on his way to Kerry, I would get a rush of excitement.

One races, I finally succeeded in pestering Paddy to allow me to accompany him into Listowel for 'the horses'. My mam said it was out of the question, insisting I had chores and farm work. Paddy eventually got around her though. Paddy's charm and ways worked on my mother too!

As I mentioned previously, both my father and Uncle Paddy served as special branch Garda until 1941, when their branch was disbanded. After leaving the special branch Paddy had a very distinguished career in the Gardaí. After leaving the Harriers, he was transferred to Dungarvan, Co Waterford, where he served as a guard until 1967 or 68 approximately. Despite his charm and good looks, Paddy was a lifetime bachelor; never marrying, despite plenty of interest. After retirement, he returned to Kiskeam to live in the old Kiely cottage by the lane. It was a famous landmark in Kiskeam because of its role as a 'republican house' during the War of Independence, meaning it functioned as an arms dump and safe house for the volunteers. When I bought the hotel in Youghal (which I will tell you about later), Paddy would act as manager for me during the summer, managing the bar and restaurant and handling receipts. He performed this role, very capably, until I sold it. During the winter months, I would always have him stay with us in Tarbert, which he loved and in his later years he stayed with us permanently, until his death.

I am very glad I treated him to a trip to America during his retirement, where he got an opportunity to meet his sisters, who he had not seen in many years. The sparkle on their faces when they saw each other, after being apart for years, made the trip worthwhile. I was very close to my Uncle Paddy, and gifting him the trip was the least I could do. As you will discover later, I know what it is like to be separated from family by the Atlantic, as I was an emigrant myself for many years.

Bound for Idlewild

The 6th of January 1960! It was a day I will never forget. One of the most important days of my life. It was the day I arrived at Shannon Airport, bound for the US, Idlewild Airport to be more precise.

While it was a day of considerable significance for me, the beginning was anti-climactic. My two older brothers, Tim and Pete, had emigrated to the United States and had been living there for some years by the time I emigrated. I had accompanied my parents to Shannon to see them off. Both Tim and Pete had worked in the airport, and, goodness me, the Shannon Airport staff gave them quite a send-off. As I mentioned before, both Tim and Pete worked in Shannon's catering department, helping prepare meals for transatlantic passengers. When he emigrated, it felt like the whole airport was there to give him a send-off. Glasses of lemonade and slices of cake were served, and a brass band temporarily took over Shannon's departure lounge.

I even remember Dad, Pete and I took turns playing the trumpet. I don't think I ever saw my brother Pete laugh as much as he strolled down the departure tunnel.

My experience could not have been more different. I arrived at Shannon on a freezing cold morning in January. It was almost colder inside the airport than outside. There was an open fire in the bar, but you had to buy a drink or dinner to be permitted to sit near it. I waited in the lobby, which was freezing, with my mother, father, two brothers and my two sisters.

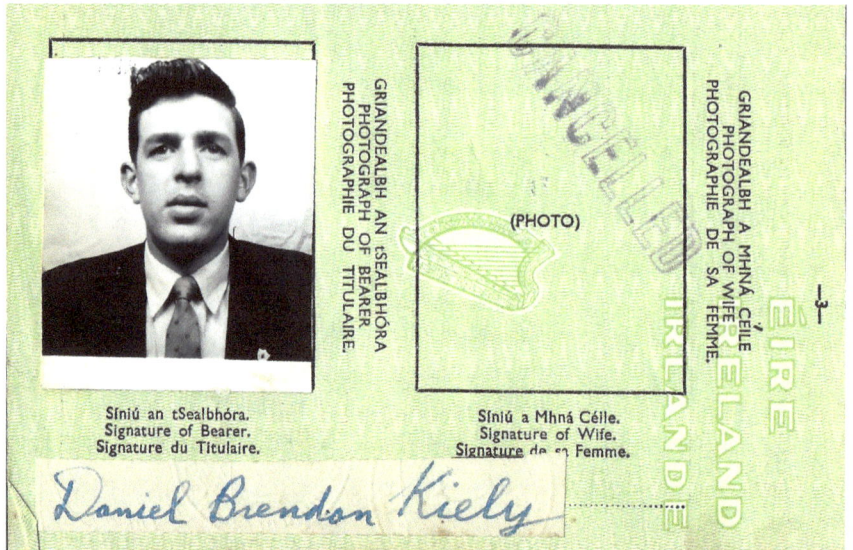

One of Dan Kiely's passports from the 1960s, during which time he made many trips to and from New York.

My father gave me a firm handshake and clasped my shoulder hard. He didn't cry, but I could tell he had love for me, and I could tell he was even a little proud. I was the third of his sons and the fifth of his children to spread their wings, and he was proud he reared plucky, enterprising children, willing to give it a go and try and make their way in the world.

'I will be back to buy you that car, Dad,' I remember saying to him. He didn't respond and I don't think he really believed me. My mother did cry and I don't think she had ever hugged me like the way she hugged me that morning. She held me for several minutes. It was hard leaving my parents and my brothers and sisters, but I took a deep breath and I did it. I walked down that departure tunnel and into the unknown.

While my memory is fuzzy, I think my initial feeling was apprehension and even a little melancholy. Thankfully, my nerves settled, and I can remember a pleasant enough flight.

Our first scheduled stop was at Gander Airport in Newfoundland. We also landed in Boston to allow passengers going to Boston off. We happened to land in Boston in the middle of a blizzard and, through my window, I could see large, mechanical snow ploughs, and men shovelling snow off the runway. This was my first sight of the United States of America, and I'm not sure what surprised me the most the snow ploughs, the sheer amount of people shovelling snow, or the snow itself. The whole airport was covered in a thick, white blanket of it.

Some hours later, we reached our destination. The plane landed. I had arrived. I was in New York City.

Don't forget that this was the early sixties and air travel was different back then. In those days, passengers would be forced to wait in the plane for some time before alighting. Once you were permitted to leave the plane, you had to wait in an airport cafe, where snacks and beverages were served, before customs officials called you for inspection.

I remember spending about an hour in the arrivals lounge cafe, before presenting my X-ray to customs officials and going through the various inspections. The airport I landed in, on that fateful day in January, was known as Idlewild Airport. It would be many years before it was renamed John F Kennedy Airport. The day I emigrated to America, the man the world would soon know as John Fitzgerald Kennedy was still a senator for Massachusetts in the United States Congress.

Then, my time came to leave the arrivals area. Little did I know, my biggest culture shock that day wasn't skyscrapers, bridges or highways, it was the door leaving the cafe.

As I approached the transparent glass door, I began looking for a door handle. Then, as the people behind brushed past me, to my utter amazement, the doors magically parted. I couldn't believe my eyes! I remember testing it with my foot. I nudged the doors with the sole of my shoe and watched them swoosh open. I remember flinching back in surprise.

I know now that there was nothing magical about the doors. They were sliding doors, triggered by motion sensors, but for a young kid from rural Ireland, these technological advancements were breathtaking.

If I was emotional by the time I arrived in the airport lobby, it was going to get a whole lot worse. Waiting for me were my brothers Tim and Pete, and another person who, I must admit, I didn't recognise at first. I shook hands with Pete, and when he said, 'Welcome to New York little brother' it made it all the more real.

I didn't recognise the woman standing beside him. She looked glamorous, with her blonde permed hair and fashionable hat. It was only after she hugged and kissed me on the cheek did I realise it was my sister, Cathy.

Any nerves I had melted away with Cathy's embrace. The role Cathy played in all our lives was immeasurable. She was the first one of us to emigrate to New York. Although she had left school at fourteen, she quickly got a job at an American telephone company, and quickly found her feet, building up a network of connections among the Irish American community in New York. She helped me with my application procedure and helped me with all the forms I had to fill out, as she had done previously for Tim and Pete. When I arrived, from the first day Cathy greeted me in Idlewild, she helped me every step of the way.

Outside the door, I heard a car horn, and someone shouted, 'OVER HERE'. I could see a man poking his head out the window of a car and waving at us. Cathy and Tim recognised him and ran towards the car. 'Come on Dan, follow us,' Cathy said.

I obeyed, but I couldn't take my eyes off the vehicle. Not since Uncle Paddy drove into Tarbert on a motorbike, had I been so transfixed by an automobile. I now know it was a Ford Mustang. To my naive eye, it looked like a spaceship, with its winged fenders and leather convertible roof.

'Let the new arrival sit in the front with me,' the driver said with a smile. I thought the man looked funny. Several buttons on his shirt were open, and he smelt of strong aftershave. Little did I know, I would have to get used to this. Over the coming days, months and years, I would see how big and strange a place the world really was; open collar shirts and Ford Mustangs were just the beginning.

Eventually, I realised I knew the man. His name was Finbar Carrig, a friend of my parents from Tarbert, and I had heard he was based in Rochester, upstate New York. He was one of the very few people in my family's network of friends who had a car, and he had kindly agreed to pick me up from the airport and drive me into the city. He had done the same for several other young immigrants.

The drive from the airport to our apartment in the Bronx, a central New York borough, popular with immigrants, took about an hour, and it was a very strange hour. Finbar, who had picked us up, wanted to talk about nothing else outside of the home country. He was desperate for me to give him news. He wanted to know who was dead; who had emigrated; who had married; any good, up-and-coming footballers from Tarbert; and who are these 'showbands' everyone was talking about – things of that kind. Despite the fashionable shirt, he had not lost the accent. He sounded like he had just returned from a hard day in the bog.

All I wanted to do, however, was look out the window, watch the sights as we drove by, which were as far from Tarbert and Kerry as I could ever imagine.

I can still remember driving across the Queensboro Bridge. I flinched back in my seat, almost with fright. The bridge's towers, constructed from steel girders, seemed to appear out of nowhere. I had never been anywhere before with so many traffic lanes, never mind traffic zooming from all sides at such speed. Nothing really prepared me for the Queensboro Bridge, and being blasted by the vista of the Manhattan skyline in the distance.

It is so long ago now, I can't remember exactly how I felt, but seeing those skyscrapers in the distance, piercing the heavens, was something you never really forget.

I also remember the driver getting a little frustrated. He wanted to hear all the news from home, but all I wanted to do was take in my new surroundings: the skyscrapers, the lights and the noise.

Eventually, the Mustang stopped next to a big, red brick apartment block. We were there, 1272 Nelson Avenue, The Bronx, New York City.

My first impression was it was nothing like anywhere I had lived before. Cathy and Tim said goodbye to Finbar, the man from Rochester, and presented him with a parcel my mother had given me for him. Tim opened the door, and with a mischievous smile, said, 'You first Dan.'

Like many young Irish immigrants to New York, particularly in those times before television, I assumed American apartments to be built from gold. Of course, that wasn't the case. The block's foyer was dark and dusty, and standing under the metal staircase that seemed to go on forever, I felt a little intimidated.

The apartment was modest, but I wasn't that hard to please. It had a gas cooker. I remember tuning the tap, and being happy to see freshwater bomb out; hot and cold. It also had a shower, another novelty for the boy from Ireland.

'Have a look at your room Dan, I made it up for you,' Cathy said.

It was a small storeroom converted into a bedroom, but there was a bed and a small bedside table, and what more did I need? I thought to myself. I remember touching the bed linen with my hand and telling Cathy it was perfect. I had slept on linen converted from recycled brown flour sacks, so my New York bed was luxurious.

We also had a window overlooking Nelson Avenue. It wasn't much of a view, but I could see the junction with West 169th Street, where there was a hub of people, lights and traffic.

I was understandably tired after the trip. I remember falling asleep on our small couch and waking up in my bed. One of my brothers must have lifted me into the bedroom after I fell asleep. I remember stepping out for a glass of water and discovering something on the kitchen table. The apartment was empty and everyone was out. It wasn't dark yet, and there was a flicker of light outside the window.

I was still tired so I went back to bed. I assumed everyone had gone out to have a few drinks in a bar, or to watch a showband in one of the nightclubs. I would turn out to be wrong. I was still new to this world. New York was different to Ireland and things were done differently.

I must have been asleep for another hour or two when I was awoken by a noise. It was more than a noise really; there was a chorus of people talking, laughing and chatting. When I walked out into the apartment, I couldn't believe my eyes. The small flat was full of people, many of whom I recognised from home, my cousins, neighbours, and friends that I had not seen in years. And it wasn't just the apartment itself that was crowded, some of them had spilled onto the landing and into neighbouring apartments. Our cousins from Kiskeam, who lived in a flat on the floor above us, had come down to join in.

The small table and chairs at the centre of the room had been cleared, and replaced by several people sitting on small stools and playing a series of brass instruments. One of them was my brother Pete, who, with the accordion resting on his knee, winked at me.

I remember when Pete, smiling mischievously, ordered his fellow musicians to stop playing. With the room hushed, he stood up and ceremonially handed the accordion to me.

'Alright brother, you are one of us now. Welcome to New York! Let's see what you have got, and make sure it's good, every new arrival has to bring something with them.'

The whole room burst out laughing as I, nervously, squatted down on the stool, and positioned my fingers over the treble keyboard.

Despite the nerves, I eventually found my rhythm. I managed to rattle off the first few notes of the 'Siege of Ennis', and my new bandmates, recognising it, quickly joined in. Before we knew it, a few people were dancing in front of us.

This, I was to discover, was how people spent their weekends in New York. In my first few months in America, I never visited a bar or nightclub. Instead, a large party of Irish immigrants, hailing from all corners of the country, would descend on the house or apartment of a new arrival, an Irish immigrant just off a plane from Dublin or Shannon. These parties would be a little wild and disorganised, full of music, chatter and bad dancing, but you got to know everyone; you would always see somebody you knew from home, no matter where the party was. This ritual was, most importantly, very helpful for new arrivals, it helped them feel at home.

The Kiely family getting some relaxation time in Coney Island, away from their busy jobs in New York city. The photo dates from the summer of 1961, from what was Dan Kiely's first holiday since arriving in America.

Goldman What?

The next morning, I was up early to catch the subway at West 168th Street. Cathy had a strong cup of coffee and a bowl of porridge waiting for me.

I soon discovered that Cathy was coming with me and, in truth, I was relieved. New York was a daunting place, so it was good to have the backup. Some hours later, we were exiting the Wall Street subway station together. The station is situated on a busy junction, where Wall Street meets Broadway. Although Cathy was with me, I still felt a little lost. The whole place was a hive of noise, energy and commotion. There were vendors selling newspapers and coffee, cab drivers shouting out their windows, and droves of people streaming in all directions.

Why was I there? I had an interview to get to. My destination was the offices of Goldman Sachs, which was located on Wall Street, and in the main complex of the New York Stock Exchange. Cathy was friendly with a Jewish lady called Ms Kosch, who worked as a secretary and manager on one of the Goldman trade floors. Cathy had met her quite randomly, while Mrs Kosch was out walking her dogs on Nelson Avenue. She had suggested that Cathy bring me down to meet her, as they had advertised for an office boy and secretarial assistant.

Finding Goldman Sachs' floor was our first task. Cathy was great with directions and was a naturalised New Yorker at that stage, but the New York Stock Exchange was busy that morning, with people rushing to and fro, and inside was a maze of offices and trade floors.

While Cathy searched for the right entrance, I couldn't take my eyes off the building itself. To this day, I think the New York Stock Exchange, also known as the 'Big Board', is one of Manhattan's most beautiful buildings. I love its grand Corinthian columns and the sight of the American flag flapping on the mast.

Eventually, we found where we needed to go. Ms Kosch, looking very stern, was waiting for us at the elevator door.

It turned out we were thirty seconds late, at least according to a large clock staring at us from the wall of the Goldman trade floor. 'You got to make sure the young squirt is on time Cathy, or I will get a talking to.' 'I know Ms Kosch, he will be on time every other day I promise,' Cathy replied, while giving me the eye.

We followed Ms Kosch through what was a busy, bustling trade floor. The energy was infectious. Secretaries were racing to and from offices, with bundles of files, and traders were shouting down their phones. IBM provided computer equipment and technology and I was fascinated by those strange machines from the first moment I saw them. I would soon discover that there was a whole floor designated to the IBM department, which contained some of the most complex computational technology in existence at that time.

Ms Kosch had a small office adjacent to the trade floor. It was insulated behind a glass partition, but it was still very noisy. We could hear traders shouting across the floor and holding animated conversations on their phones; there was a constant hum of ringing telephones and clicking of IBM machines.

Stock exchanges were noisy, energetic places, and they certainly were not places for people who wanted a quiet life. As for me however, from the moment I set foot inside the door, I was intrigued. I instantly warmed to this noisy, exciting and bustling environment, and I think Cathy realised this.

As Ms Kosch's assistant served coffee, I caught Cathy smiling. I think she knew she had made the right decision, and I would fit right in.

Inside the office, Ms Kosch's mood improved. She smiled as she explained my duties, which were extensive to say the least. I discovered the job I was being interviewed for was office boy, which didn't sound like much to me at the time, but was in fact quite important. I was to be an integral part of the running of the trade floor.

Today, Goldman Sachs is one of the largest investment banks and fund management agencies in the world, employing almost 50,000 people, with offices in such far-flung locations as Tokyo, Bangalore and Salt Lake City. Today it manages highly complex security and equity funds. In 1960, it was a far smaller operation, employing hundreds rather than tens of thousands, and its sole and exclusive premises was the New York Stock Exchange.

Although much smaller than it is today, the company I joined in 1960 was a leader and pioneer in the world of financial markets and equities. In the early 1930s, Sidney Weinberg and Gus Levy pioneered the process of block trading while they were Goldman directors. This meant bonds and securities could be sold as part of a package or 'block', as opposed to individually, which would eventually revolutionise the equity market. Goldman had also distinguished itself as one of the leading corporate underwriters on Wall Street, underwriting a $657 million bond issue for the Ford Motor Company in 1956, which would be $6.3 billion in today's money.

I wasn't long in the door, when I caught sight of Sidney Weinberg and Gus Levy's portraits, hanging proudly in the director's boardroom. They were very much revered figures on Wall Street!

As I mentioned, another big feature of life on Wall Street was the ubiquitous presence of IBM machines. IBM stands for International Business Machines, and their computer technology revolutionised American business in the sixties, and Wall Street did not go untouched.

However, manual filing and administration was still important, perhaps far more so than it is today, as computers have advanced considerably since those days.

A Kiely family reunion at a breakfast organsied by the Seán O'Ceallagh Na hÉireann society, the 'Old IRA of New York', in the Concourse Plaza Hotel, the Bronx, New York, on the anniversary of the 1916 Rising. Dan Kiely Sr. was a guest of honour of the society. Family members pictured include Dan Kiely, his mother Hannah Kiely, his wife Mary Kiely (née Keane), his brothers Tim and Michael, his sisters Aggie and Philomena, and his brother-in-law Mike Purtill. Also visible, in the foreground of the photo, are Dan Kiely's cousins from Kiskeam, Denis and Jerry Kiely.

In those early months, one of my jobs was to ensure everyone on my floor got their post. I would visit the main New York Stock Exchange posting depot every morning, and make sure everyone received their mail. I would often avail of a little Wall Street employee perk: postcards from the main postal depot could be mailed for free. I availed of the opportunity to mail some back home, never neglecting to mention where I was posting it from; great to give my mam something to boast about!

I was also responsible for passing messages between the various floors and offices, which was very important. Goldman ran a finely interconnected operation, and it was imperative that communication channels between the various floors and offices ran smoothly. I would also help the catering department during lunch breaks, by distributing coffees and pastries to the hardworking staff, which I was only happy to do.

Everyone worked hard at Goldman; that was something I realised very quickly. Stockbrokers and bankers were held to very strict deadlines, and every hour of their working day was an exhausting race to bring in revenue for the company.

Cathy left after ten minutes; she had work to go to, but I could tell she was very happy with how things had gone. After Cathy left, Ms Kosch showed me around the trade floor, explaining how everything worked. She introduced me to my new colleagues, most of whom were too busy to pay me the faintest bit of attention.

I enjoyed my time at Goldman. The work was important and laborious, and I was used to hard work! Every morning, there would be stacks of neatly folded stock receipts waiting for me on Ms Kosch's desk. I worked directly under her, and her management was hands-on. Her random spot checks were a frequent occurrence. She would often tell me off, but she would also occasionally compliment me for my efficiency. She once told me that I had an incredible 'work ethic' for a 'young squirt', and that I would 'go places'. I was tempted to reply,

'You have never cut turf in Tarbert, Ms Kosch,' but I checked myself. I just nodded and smiled at her.

It could occasionally be exhausting, but I enjoyed working at Goldman. Every so often, during breaks, I would steal a glance out the window at the busy streets below, Wall Street and Broad Street. And there was nothing quite like the skyscrapers of Manhattan.

I grew friendly with a stockbroker called Steve Knight, who took me under his wing. Steve was head of the IBM floor at Goldman, which quickly became my favourite floor. I was fascinated by the IBM machines, and how the cards were computed. Goldman was very advanced as a company at this time, as very little of the American economy was computerised. The IBM machines calculated the value of each share, and the dividend cheques sent to customers every month were based on these computerised valuations. The process intrigued me. Steve arranged for me to attend school in the evenings so I could learn the process. It worked! I would eventually become a supervisor on the IBM floor at Goldman.

Breaking Ball in New York

'Gaelic where?' I would have said words to that effect some months into my time in New York. I remember my sisters and brothers laughing at my innocence. Looking back, I find it hard not to laugh at myself. Gaelic Park was sacred ground for Irish immigrants in America. It was more than a sports stadium, it was the home of the Gaelic Athletic Association in America, and for Irish immigrants that turf in the Bronx had a deeply spiritual significance. It was a place where many of us congregated on a Sunday, a place that brought us together and helped us through the tough times. For me, personally, it was a place of enormous significance, and it became very central to my life in New York.

The pitch was small. The stands didn't have roofs so if it rained, you were either lucky enough to have an umbrella or raincoat, or you had to put up with it.

It was also adjacent to a subway depot, so matches would take place in the shadow of train carriages, but nobody seemed to mind and it added to the atmosphere. No one could ever deny you were in New York. What Gaelic Park lacked in modern conveniences (at the time), it more than made up for in atmosphere and intimacy. I don't think I have ever been in a stadium where the spectators roared and cheered more than they did in Gaelic Park.

During my first summer in New York, Cathy, Pete, Tim and I would often go to Gaelic Park on Sundays for a match. Cathy was eager for me to mingle and get to know my fellow Irish immigrants.

The games were messy, entertaining affairs, full of bad tackles, off-field scuffles and beautiful goals.

Being a Kerry man, my standards in football were high. Before I left for America, I had had trials with the Kerry Minors, and if I had not emigrated, who knows, I may have made it. I always loved the game as a sport, but after I emigrated to the United States, I learned to appreciate its immense cultural and social value.

A very prominent feature of Gaelic Park, in my day, were the visits to the beer stalls. You couldn't miss the stalls. They were situated near the pitch, and painted in big, red and white stripes. The barman, patiently handing out cool beers to the crowd, was always dressed smartly in a crisp white shirt and black dicky bow. Stripy beer stalls were a tradition imported from American football and baseball, and they created a unique fusion of the Irish and the American.

When I accompanied Cathy and my brothers to a game, I would often volunteer to go to the beer stalls at half-time, as you never knew who you would bump into en route, and that was always exciting. You could meet people from home who you hadn't seen in years, people you never realised had even emigrated to New York. The long queue for fresh, cold beer became an impromptu social gathering. Although, for us Kielys it was always sodas, many of us being incorruptible pioneers.

New York is famous for some fabulous stadiums. I was lucky enough to see the New York Polo Grounds before it was demolished. The famous stadium, situated in the middle of uptown Manhattan, was home to New York's baseball team, the Mets (the great rivals of the Yankees), and the American football team, the Giants.

The Polo Grounds was demolished in 1964 when stakeholders decided to sell the lucrative real estate and build grounds in cheaper locations with more space. The Mets built Shea Stadium in Queens, which I was also lucky enough to visit, and the Giants,

A young Dan Kiely serving behind the bar in the famous Gaelic Park, the Bronx, New York.

the American football team, moved to Giants Stadium, which was across the Hudson River in New Jersey.

The Polo Grounds had a special significance for Irish people. It was there, in 1947, that the first and only All-Ireland outside of Ireland was held; when the Polo Grounds hosted Kerry versus Cavan. Cavan famously defeated my county on that fateful day, thanks to a goal by Cavan's star centre forward, Peter Donohoe.

Many, many years later, in 1997, I, accompanied by several members of my family, attended a charity match between Cavan and Kerry in Downing Stadium on Randall's Island, celebrating the anniversary of the famous final played at the Polo Grounds. There was nothing at stake on that occasion of course, but I was glad to be a spectator. It was a great experience, to be there and witness Cavan and Kerry's footballers clash on the New York grass. Kerry won, thanks entirely to the genius of the wonderful Maurice Fitzgerald; he scored one goal and ten points that day, Kerry's entire score tally. What a graceful artisan that man was with a football!

Even though it was a charity match, both teams stood respectfully at the beginning, as an orchestra played a version of Amhrán na bhFiann. Tens of thousands of people across the stadium stood and began singing the anthem in unison. Some sang the words passionately, while others closed their eyes solemnly. Some placed their palms across their hearts in the American fashion. I had seen this at football games played in America before and I always found it a little strange, and wondered, were people taking themselves and football a little too seriously? However, in retrospect, I appreciate how important events of this kind were to the Irish American community. Being an immigrant in such a big, diverse city can be difficult, and football gave Irish immigrants an opportunity to come together as one, keeping the connection with their home country alive; that is why Amhrán na bhFiann was always sung with such gusto on American soil.

Taking to the Field

Sunday matches were not the only occasion I had to visit Gaelic Park that summer. I was persuaded by someone to trial for the Kerry Juniors. Therefore, on certain evenings during the week, I travelled to the park for training sessions.

One Sunday, on my way to the beer stalls to collect sodas, I bumped into somebody who recognised me from Tarbert. He remembered my footballing exploits back home and encouraged me to put myself into contention.

While Kerry was preeminent when it came to football, and frequently produced the best footballers, as a result of internal GAA politics, players from Kerry were rarely picked for the New York team. I didn't know this at the time, but this meant my chances of representing New York in the All-Ireland Championship were next to nothing, which was very unfortunate, as it would have been a great honour.

However, I felt that, at the very least, I was good enough to play for the Kerry Juniors, as I had watched them play Junior League games in Gaelic Park, and I wasn't terribly impressed. I knew well enough from my time playing with Tarbert, and from my trials with the minors in Ireland, that I could hold my own with the very best on the field. I was one of those players who had learned to use his relatively small height as an advantage. I was great at securing possession from kick-outs, and I was fast and aggressive with the ball. I also had imagination, so I was able to create opportunities out of nothing

The victorious Kerry, New York Juniors football team, winners of the 1963 NY Junior Championship. Dan Kiely is pictured first on the right in the front row. This Juniors team would go on to win three NY Junior Championships in a row.

for the forward line. During my time at Tarbert, I had the privilege of playing with some fantastic forwards, but as many great coaches have said, football matches are won in the middle of the park – and I agree with them.

I remember my first night, kitting out in the Gaelic Park dressing rooms, putting on shin pads and rolling up what were blue and black socks – they had run out of Kerry's distinctive green and gold socks, so our Junior team had to make do with socks borrowed from the Dublin kit. The indignity of it!

I remember the whole experience being more than a little surreal. There was so much about Gaelic Park and its environment that reminded me of Ireland – the dressing rooms in the park were, at least then, indistinguishable from what you would find in any GAA club in Ireland. When on the field, practising 45s, kick-outs, hand-passes, and other various footballing skills, you would almost forget where you were. I was surrounded by men with Kerry accents, kitted out in our wonderful green and gold (except for the socks on the first evening) playing the game we all love.

In the heat of the game, you would forget you were in New York, and for a split-second, you might fool yourself into thinking you were back in Ireland.

Playing in Gaelic Park with the Juniors during my first summer in New York was exciting, the memories of which I would not swap for the world, but it was strange.

After attending two or three training sessions, I wasn't sure what progress I was making, and whether I was impressing our trainers. It soon became apparent to me that junior football wasn't taken seriously in New York at all. We had a different trainer every week, and the Kerry Juniors had no settled fifteen, with players rotating on a weekly basis. The junior training sessions were more about giving fifteen young lads a run out on the field than training a disciplined football team that could compete in a recognised GAA tournament.

Don't get me wrong, I loved going to the park in the evening and playing a good, honest game of football. I played with some talented players, and there was nothing sweeter than running on the New York grass while wearing the 'green and gold' of my beloved home county; watching the ball float between the posts with the subway depot gleaming in the background.

However, I felt that the lack of discipline, and the lack of a clear training regime, was a shame, as we had some really talented players. I knew that the lack of proper training and instruction would have a detrimental effect on their development.

I was soon to learn I was not the only one who thought like this, and it was in fact a view shared by figures at the very highest level of the American branch of the GAA.

Occasionally, my brothers would point out John 'Kerry' O'Donnell for me, identify him as 'Mr Gaelic Park', the owner and manager of the grounds, and a central figure within the American branch of the GAA.

It would be no exaggeration to say John 'Kerry' was everywhere. On Sundays, one would see him walking around the stands and terraces, meeting and greeting spectators and slapping players on the back. He was always supervising the park's staff, ensuring that everything ran smoothly and efficiently. He was ever-present on training nights as well. When we left the dressing rooms for the field, he would be waiting outside with his arms folded, inspecting us with his hawk eyes. John 'Kerry' was a master tactician, but he had his limitations when it came to training, something that gradually became obvious to me.

One evening, I was in the dressing room in Gaelic Park, exhausted after a training game. I had taken a shower, and I was changing back into my normal clothes. One of the trainers, a man called Billy, told me the 'boss' wanted to see me. I wasn't immediately sure who he was referring to. I remember assuming the 'boss' was our usual trainer, Micko, who was changing with us, and I turned to face him. Micko laughed and said, 'Not me Dan, I'm nobody's "boss" around here, he means *thee boss*.'

A little perplexed, I followed Billy through the dressing room, through the main bar, and into a small office. When I came in, John 'Kerry' observed me for a few seconds, taking my measure. 'Take a seat there, young fella, I want to have a chat with you,' he said, and I obeyed. It was the first time John 'Kerry' had spoken so much as a word to me. He was softly spoken but he had a piercing stare; every time he looked at you, you couldn't help feeling you were being weighed up by a deep intelligence.

We were interrupted by Billy, the trainer, who came in carrying a pot of tea. I remember John 'Kerry' opening it and taking a sniff.

'DID YOU SCALD THE POT BILLY?' He shouted at the trainer, who had walked away.

'Of course I did. Jesus, you will be the death of me boss.' Not convinced, John 'Kerry' gave the tea a vigorous stir, before pouring us two mugs. He then looked at me and began:

'Dan, I have been watching you training. You have strong opinions about football, don't you? You are shouting orders left right and centre. If it ain't good enough for you, I'm sure you can find somewhere else that is more in keeping with your obviously high standards!'

I was a little intimidated by this and stared at him. I was eager to plead my innocence. The last thing I wanted was to get on the wrong side of such a powerful man.

'I just want the best for the team,' I said to him after a pause.

Finally, he smiled at me. I relaxed somewhat. For a second, I thought he had dragged me in to give me a 'going over', as they say.

'I know what you mean Dan. I was only fooling with you.'

'You were. Phew, you had me going there for a second, John "Kerry"!'

'So, Billy tells me you work on Wall Street?'

'Yes, I help out in the office there. Mr Steve Knight has really taken me under his wing. It is a great place, Goldman, John "Kerry".'

'It is, to be sure. Listen Dan, I was hoping you could help me, too. I have some work that needs doing.'

'Work! Sure thing, John "Kerry".'

'Well, I like your style. We need someone driven around here, who can whip these young fellas into a serious team. What would you say to helping train the Juniors?'

I paused for a second. I never dreamed he would ask me to do what he had just asked me. I was tempted to agree straight away; my only concern was that my time was limited. I had a full-time job at Goldman, and I had been looking for another, part-time job. I had made inquiries at construction sites and in Irish bars. I had come to New York to make a name for myself, to make a few bob, and get on in the world. I loved GAA, but training a team required time and effort and I wasn't sure that I had it to give. John 'Kerry' however, as I would discover, had 'been around the block', to use a phrase fashionable in New York in those days. He had his hawk eye on me.

'Listen Dan, I'll strike a deal with you?'

'Really, what?'

'You help train the juniors, and I will get you a job manning the beer stalls on Sundays.'

That was big! Serving at the stalls was very much prized! The pay was okay, and it was a great opportunity to meet new people and network. I smiled at John 'Kerry', and told him it was a deal. He even smiled back, something I would discover he rarely did.

Not for the last time, we both stood up and shook hands. John 'Kerry' and I would have many adventures together, and achieve some great things. We would go 'around the block' together!

Another photo of Dan and his Kerry Juniors teammates, the day of their victory in the NY Junior Football Championship.

A Car for Dad and a Trip for Cathy

The weeks following my meeting with John 'Kerry' should have been so happy for me, but Cathy was not herself. She spent a lot of time inside by herself, sitting at the kitchen table and brooding. Eventually, I discovered what was wrong with her: she was homesick. She had been in New York for six years at that point, and she wanted to visit Mam and Dad.

I was the plucky one in the family, and if there was an opportunity, I wanted to seize it. One day, while sitting at the kitchen table with Cathy, I told her she should go home for a visit. She shook her head and said, 'Come off it, Dan, I'm settled here now. I can't go traipsing back to Ireland, it could destroy everything we have built.'

I didn't agree. I felt she needed to get home, as it had been six years since she saw Mam and Dad. I reasoned with her that she was no good to anyone in New York if she was broody and homesick. If she visited Ireland, she would come back rejuvenated, a 'new woman'.

Cathy was stubborn when she wanted to be. Eventually, however, after persistent pestering by me, she began to warm to the idea of travelling home. After she agreed to visit Ireland, her attitude changed and I was in her 'good books' again. 'I have to thank my little brother … If you hadn't convinced me, I wouldn't be going.' She said to me some weeks before her scheduled trip. 'Don't mention it sis, although there is one little favour.'

'A LITTLE FAVOUR! … Oh, I see, I SHOULD HAVE KNOWN!'

After she had calmed down, I asked her to follow me into my small bedroom. Inside, I stooped down and pulled out a small, black case from under the bed. Cathy looked perplexed. I unlatched the case and opened it up for her. She blushed and looked at me strangely.

'Dan, what in the name of mercy is that?'

'Look at it, Cathy,' I said.

There was $900 in the case. It was money I had saved and saved over the previous year and a half I had spent in America. I had saved a little from my Goldman Sachs job every week, and when I got the job in the beer stalls, I saved almost all of it.

By this time, I was working seven days a week. I worked at Goldman Monday to Friday – and that was hard work, the longer I was there the more duties and responsibilities I was given. When I started working on the IBM floor, things got very hectic. Steve Knight was a good friend and mentor to me, but he didn't 'spare me'. The $900 was hard-earned! Cathy started grabbing bundles of it. She looked amazed.

'Now what on God's earth are you going to do with all this money?'

'You remember that promise I made to Dad?'

'Promise, what in the name of Jesus are you on about?'

'You know? I promised I would buy him a car when I got to America. You know how bad he has it, out in the flogging rain with those clothes. It's a thundering disgrace and I want to put it right.'

'Ah, I see your plan NOW,' Cathy butted in. 'YOU want to bring this back to Ireland! Well, you have another thing coming, my boy. I'm not traipsing around with a bag full of dirty money. DO YOU WANT ME TO BE MUGGED? READ MY LIPS DAN KIELY: NO!'

As often happened, 'NO' did not mean 'no'. I got around Cathy again. It took a while, but I got around her.

A week or so later, Cathy and I were sitting in the kitchen.

'Alright! … You win, give me the blasted money and I will buy our dad that car. You will be the death of me, Dan Kiely.'

My problems didn't end there. I also had to scramble together another $900, which would prove just as difficult. At that time, a car cost about £600, or $1,800. I started collecting. Tim, Pete and Cathy all contributed $300 each. They were all working hard and saving, just like me.

Around this time, we also got a new lodger in the flat. My younger sister, Mary Joe, arrived in New York. Cathy loved having her, as she always felt outnumbered by her brothers, and she was pleased to finally have a female ally. I didn't want to pester Mary Joe as she had just arrived.

In the end, I was bailed out by, yes, you guessed it, my older sister. Just before she was about to leave for Ireland, Cathy handed me a parcel. There was $900 inside. It meant we finally had enough money to buy Dad the car I always wanted to buy him.

When I woke up the day Cathy was to travel to Ireland, I couldn't help being a little worried for her security. As it happened, I did not need to be. I had underestimated my sister. When Cathy returned two weeks later, looking just as radiant and glamorous as the day she left, she had plenty of stories for all of us. One of the first things I remember asking her was how her trip through Idlewild Airport and customs went, and whether her handbag was ever in danger of being snatched. Not in the least apparently. She strolled through the lobby and security without a care in the world, the $1,800 safely cradled in her leather handbag. Far more interesting was what happened when she arrived back in Ireland.

Cathy being Cathy, didn't delay! On her first day back, she visited Dan Moloney in his garage in Listowel, as I had suggested. On arrival, she approached a young mechanic working in the yard. Adjusted to New York ways, Cathy hadn't dressed down for the occasion and was still attired in her feathered hat and blue dress! She asked the young mechanic if she could speak to a salesperson, as she was interested in buying a car. The young fella apparently had a good look at her, took the measure of her, and smiled. Cathy was about to take offence when the young man shouted to someone at the back of the store, 'She's here boss, she's here.'

A man in a suit came strolling out. He shook Cathy's hand and kissed her on the cheek.

'So, this is young Dan Kiely's sister? Well, pleased to meet you. Dan Moloney is the name.'

I had sent out word to my old friend Dan Moloney that Cathy was to pay him a visit and to expect her. Remarkably, after all those years, he still remembered me as the plucky young lad who arrived in his constituency office that day bearing that letter from my mother.

Dan apparently had about ten new cars and several second-hand ones on display that day. He personally walked Cathy through the garage, giving her the lowdown on the various models and designs. He paused by a small, used Vauxhall, and invited her to sit in, so she could 'get a feel for it,' as he phrased it. According to Cathy, Dan was desperate to sell her one of the second-hand cars he had in his lot. He jumped from one car to the next, explaining to her how great each one was, but Cathy wasn't having it.

'I'm under strict instructions to ONLY buy a new car. This is my brother's idea, and I better be said by him.' Mr Moloney tried to dissuade her. He said it was an awful amount of money to blow on a new car. He even suggested that Mikey, the mechanic who had greeted Cathy, would take her for a ride in the Vauxhall, just to prove that it was a fine, road worthy vehicle, but Cathy was having none of it. As I listened to her tell the story some weeks later, sitting in our Bronx apartment, I realised why asking her to buy the car was a good decision. Cathy could be as stubborn as I was, and just wouldn't take no for an answer.

Eventually, Dan relented and showed her the new Ford cars. It didn't take long for Cathy to spot the right one. We had discussed various makes and models before she left. We all agreed to prioritise getting an American car, not just because American automobile manufacturers were pre-eminent at that time, as they were with so many goods and products, but because we all thought the idea of buying our dad a new American car would be symbolic. It was in the United States where we had made a life for ourselves, and it was in the US we had made the money to buy the car.

She had been strolling for several minutes, when she spotted a beautiful, black Ford Anglia. Some months later, I would also return to Ireland for the first time in a while. Very few experiences compare to walking out of the airport and seeing the car there waiting for me. The Ford Anglia was small by today's standards, but it was a fabulous car, and a very special one considering how we had all clubbed together to pay for it.

I enjoyed listening to Cathy's stories about Ireland when she returned. Cathy had not been home for six years at that stage, and swapping the streets of New York for the villages of North Kerry was quite the cultural transition. She had plenty of interesting and funny stories as a result. She told me how she accompanied Dad, my brothers Denis and Pat and the Mackasseys to the bog one day, and how she had almost forgotten how hard it was.

Although, I was glad to hear that Cathy had some good memories of home, too. Listening to her describe hearing the cuckoos sing in the trees was funny, as it was obvious my sister had been away for quite a while, (she had forgotten the name of the birds!) but it raised my heart to no end.

Cathy also described what happened later that evening, when everyone had returned from the bog and it was time to present Dad with a certain gift.

After hauling the last batch of turf into the shed, my father wiped his hands and said to Cathy, who had just brought him a mug of tea, 'That is me done for the day daughter; I'm hitting the bed for myself. I won't see you in the morning. I'm on duty and…'

'We bought you a car Dad, and it's parked outside. It was Dan's idea and we all pitched in. We bought it for you because we couldn't bear to see you get drenched anymore.'

My father said nothing, initially. He stared at Cathy with a blank expression. Cathy then followed him out to the front of our house, where the new Ford Anglia was parked.

Cathy described watching him examine the car for several minutes. He tapped the tyres with the toe of his boot, and tapped the bonnet with his hand, as if he was trying to confirm that it was a real car, and we were not playing some trick on him.

I was a little apprehensive before Cathy left. I didn't know how my father would react. I still remember the day I went to Dan Moloney's office, and how furious he was afterwards. He was a proud, private man. He didn't want other people interfering in his affairs and he wanted to solve his own problems.

'Ye bought this Cathy?' he asked.

'Yes Dad, yesterday.'

'And how much did she cost?'

She told him. He rolled his eyes up to heaven and shook his head. Money was very valuable in our household. We got by with very little and 600 old Irish pounds was a frightful amount of money then.

'Well?'

'Well, Dad?' Cathy said, after a pause.

'Well, are you going to give me a drive of it or not? Sure, Jesus, you bought it for me,' he said finally, smiling at Cathy. Cathy told us that it was the first time he had smiled since she arrived home. They embraced after this, hugged and kissed. My mother had arrived at that stage, and she was smiling too.

With Dad at the wheel and Cathy in the passenger seat, Cathy described how he drove the Anglia through the narrow, bog-holed roads of Tarbert and the neighbouring parishes.

'You look impressed daughter,' my father said to Cathy with a smile.

'I am a bit, Dad.'

'Did you forget that I spent nine years in New York, driving buses on Fifth Avenue, and, as you well know, if you can drive on Fifth Avenue you can drive anywhere.'

The Girl with the Marilyn Monroe Hat

Everything was going well for me in New York at this time. I was enjoying training the Kerry Juniors in Gaelic Park. I discovered that I was a bit of a natural, and whereas before I would be shouting from the sidelines, I now had the opportunity to impose my strong opinions on how Gaelic football should be played, as an actual football trainer. Occasionally, John 'Kerry' would come and watch us train, always observing from afar as was his habit. He would often harangue me after training, to let me know if I had done anything wrong in his eyes. John 'Kerry' was a strong-willed character, and he never had any qualms about telling people exactly what he thought, but I grew to like him, and, as you will discover, I have many reasons to be grateful to him.

As I was, by then, a registered Gaelic football trainer, I was invited to attend some delegate meetings in Gaelic Park, initially as an observer, and I would often offer my views on the various issues being discussed. John 'Kerry' appreciated my contributions and, luckily for me, I more often than not agreed with his point of view.

I loved manning the Gaelic Park beer stalls, and it was great to watch the venue grow and diversify. Gaelic Park would be mobbed with Irish football and hurling supporters in the summer, and you wouldn't have a moment's peace, hurriedly dispensing beers and sodas to the thirsty spectators. Things got quieter in the winter, but there were still events, and eventually John 'Kerry' leased the Park out for Italian and Spanish soccer matches.

As much as I loved the stalls, what I really wanted to do was work behind the main bar. The Gaelic Park bar was tough work, mind you. The customers were more flush, and they often asked for 'small ones', so the work entailed mixing and shaking. There was also more pressure to be on time with their drinks. However, you had an opportunity to meet a greater range of people and the tips were much better.

When I asked John 'Kerry' if I could serve behind the bar, he was worried about my age. At that time, you had to be twenty-one to work in licensed premises, and I was still only eighteen. Everyone who worked in New York bars had to carry what they called a Cabaret Card (or the New York City Cabaret Identification Card to give it its full title) to confirm they were legally entitled to sell alcohol. It was a legacy from the old days of Prohibition, when the selling of alcohol was banned in the United States. It remained a requirement that all employees of nightclubs and bigger bars carry one until 1967.

I kept pestering John 'Kerry' until he eventually gave in. One day, after accompanying him to a delegate meeting in the Park, I decided to chance it. I could tell he was in good form. The board had voted in favour of two of his three proposals that day.

I still expected him to blast me to Kingdom come, as was his way, but I was in for a surprise. 'Alright, blast you Kiely, I know what you are going to ask. Go on, sure, I will see you next Saturday, we have a wedding. I will get you a Cabaret Card somehow. Jesus, ye young fellas will be the death of me yet.'

So, as often happened, I got my way in the end. I became a barman in the bar at Gaelic Park, and I was overjoyed.

I still remember the night before my first shift. I dragged out the iron and gave my white shirt a good press. I may have even worn a necktie. I also gelled back my hair in the New York fashion, as you can see from the photo of me serving in Gaelic Park.

It was a great bar. It was a big, loud, Irish bar, with a great view of the pitch. The walls were covered in GAA paraphernalia: framed jerseys, photos of victorious teams and other memorabilia.

It was a great place to meet people. In all my years working there, I must have shaken hands with hundreds, if not thousands, of people, from all walks of life.

Of all the people I met, however, there is one who stands out the most; one meeting I will never forget.

While I don't remember what exact day it was, I do remember it was the summer of 1962, and the sun was shining. Everyone was ordering either cold beers or Coca-Colas with ice. The 'locals' were sweating, rolling their sleeves up and badgering us to open the windows. I was nearly hyperventilating from running to and from the cellar, dragging buckets of ice.

I was at the bar when I noticed her come in. She was on her own, which was rare enough for a woman. She ordered off my fellow barman and sat on one of the armchairs by the window. I remember there was a group of young footballers sitting at the other corner of the bar, who couldn't take their eyes off her, and I didn't blame them, neither could I! She was radiant. Her hair was short and curly, and she was very fashionably dressed. Marilyn Monroe, the famous film actress, had died tragically that August, and there were pictures of her everywhere. I think Marilyn's style rubbed off on women, and the hat the lady wore that day reminded me of Marilyn Monroe. It was similar to the one she is wearing in the photo of us at the Seán O'Ceallagh Na hÉireann society's Communion Breakfast, celebrating the War of Independence volunteers of New York, which my father was an honorary guest at.

Eventually, she finished her soda and walked back to the bar. 'Will you have another?' I remember asking her.

'No, I thought someone would be here, but he isn't.'

Another photo from the breakfast organised by the Seán O'Ceallagh Na hÉireann society, in honour of Old IRA volunteers like Dan's father. It was held in the Concourse Plaza Hotel. Dan, his wife Mary, and other members of his family are visible in the right corner of the photo.

'Stood up?' I replied.

'No, not stood up! He obviously forgot!'

'Obviously,' I said with a smile.

We both looked at each for a minute or two. I could tell she was thinking what I was thinking.

'Have we met?'

I smiled and shrugged my shoulders.

'I don't know. I'm Dan Kiely from Tarbert, Kerry. Where are you from?'

Her lovely pretty face lit up. She smiled at me. Her name was Mary Keane, and she was from Ballylongford, another North Kerry village, and only a few miles west of where I grew up in Tarbert. She swore we had met before and I felt the same.

'You probably weren't wearing a hat like that in Bally, that's why I didn't recognise you!'

She laughed. We chatted for a few minutes. She was living with her mother in Little Neck on Long Island. That was disappointing. Long Island was miles away from me in the Bronx. Before she left, I kissed her on the cheek and got a whiff of her perfume. I was working, but I would have liked to have given her more than a kiss.

I didn't give her a second thought for the remainder of the day. It was only later that day when I was back in our flat in the Bronx that I thought of her again. 'Yes, blast it,' that is where I know her from, I thought to myself.

I remembered her from my days in the FCÁ. While serving in the FCÁ, we would be driven from the main barracks to open fields, where we would train and do target practice. The lorry would travel through the villages and towns of North Kerry, and my fellow recruits and I would look forward to it.

During the summer, we would be piled into a trailer hitched to the lorry, and we would all sit back and laugh and chat as the wind beat our faces.

We were young men, and we did what young men tended to do. Whenever we passed girls our own age, we would whistle at them and throw compliments. Some would cover their faces in embarrassment. Some would laugh, and either throw compliments back or make faces and insult us.

Our favourite village was Ballylongford. In Bally, there was a group of girls that would always wait for us at the petrol station, and whenever the lorry stopped for gas, we would have our sport. Those Bally girls were tough and more than a match for us, and one of them was a girl called Mary Keane. She looked very different that summer's day in Gaelic Park, from the girl I remembered in Ballylongford. New York had changed her, as it often did. She radiated class, confidence and elegance. I remember going to sleep that night hoping I would meet her again, just to tell her where we had met.

If someone had told me that night that Mary Keane would soon become my wife, I wouldn't have believed them. Marriage was the last thing on my mind. Although come to think of it, I think I might have liked the idea!

The Bishop with the Big Red Hat

Jumping ahead some years, many things changed in my life. I was still working at Goldman, but I had a better job. I was working on the IBM floor, responsible for computing the stocks and shares. All in all, I enjoyed it, and I was earning good money. When I started at Goldman, I was earning more than my father, a Garda of many years standing, and a veteran of Ireland's War of Independence. That caused me both pride and shame.

I continued working for John 'Kerry' at the bar, and I remained heavily involved in the GAA. By 1964, I had been nominated to represent Kerry as the Kerry GAA board delegate at the United States GAA, the 'USGAA' board, one of the county boards of the GAA.

The Kerry Juniors were faring better under my management. I eventually succeeded in moulding an undisciplined mob of talented young fellas into a decent football team, who wore the colours with pride and did their county proud.

I was massively helped by the fact that there were so many talented young players in New York at that time; immigration was so high, and so many were immigrating to the United States, we were destined to have talent. The Kerry Seniors were also doing mighty stuff at this time. When it came to selecting the New York team to compete for New York in the All-Ireland Championship however, I felt Kerry was overlooked, despite our domestic dominance. It was a bone of contention at GAA board meetings, and I often raised the issue on Kerry's behalf.

While Kerry was overlooked for political reasons, there were so many great and talented footballers and hurlers in the States at that time that the New York selectors had a hard job picking the final fifteen. There were the Turbridy brothers, Denis Bernard from Cork, and the Nolans and the Furlongs from Offaly, to name just a few sporting families. They were mighty talents, and it was a pleasure to see them play and to play against them.

It was interesting to read in the fantastic book *Tales of New York: A History of the GAA in America*, that the 1963 Junior Championship was a straight knockout competition; it had been so many years ago, I had forgotten. This was partially because more teams were competing at the junior level that year, which was positive. I was also glad to see Kerry seeded in division one, which was only right for a great footballing county like Kerry. The improvement in the Kerry Juniors was mainly due to the immense sporting talent we had at our disposal, but I would like to think my training methods also played a part.

In all my years of involvement with the GAA in the States, one project really stands out. It all started with a certain visitor with a big red hat.

It was a Saturday morning, and I remember it being a nice summer's day.

The sun had been a good omen for me in the past and it was that day too. I remember I was carrying a keg from the cellar into the main bar when I heard a noise. I walked out onto the stands to have a look. I remember seeing a big, black car. It looked like a limo from where I was standing.

The first thing I thought was, here is a bigshot politician visiting Gaelic Park for a photo opportunity. I hoped it was Senator Tip O'Neil or Senator Bobby Kennedy, both of whom I liked. They didn't hide their Irish heritage, and they often spoke on behalf of the Irish immigrant population in the States.

John 'Kerry' was waiting at the gates, with his hands behind his back and his back straight. He was wearing a three-piece tweed suit! I had never seen him dress like that before, for anyone!

The car stopped and a chauffeur, dressed in a dark suit and wearing sunglasses, got out and rushed to open the door. The person who emerged wasn't a politician, but a churchman of some description.

I wasn't good at distinguishing between various high-ranking clerics, but I knew he was high-ranking from how he was dressed. He wore a big red hat and his red soutane flapped in the breeze.

John 'Kerry' stooped to kiss his ring, but the priest brushed off such formalities. He slapped John 'Kerry' on the shoulder before they proceeded to chat like two old school friends.

I would later discover that the churchman was Cardinal Richard Cushing. He was then Archbishop of Boston and Cardinal, having been elevated to Cardinal in 1959. He was loved for his warm, hearty personality, and famous for his patronage of various churches, municipal buildings and charitable institutions, particularly in Boston.

The Cardinal and John 'Kerry' retreated into John 'Kerry's' office, where they talked for some time. Sometime after Cardinal Cushing left, John 'Kerry' visited me in the bar. He asked for a glass of lemonade with ice. He looked tired, and I could tell he was brooding over something. I poured him some strong tea, his favourite.

'I asked for a lemonade damn you young Kiely.'

'You look like you need it boss. Get that into you.'

John 'Kerry' smiled and took a sip. Having sipped the tea, he made a face and glared at me.

'Did you scald the pot Kiely?'

Red-faced, I took the mug back and threw it out. I made the tea again, making sure to scald the teapot with boiling water. Nothing in life seemed to irritate John 'Kerry' O'Donnell more than a pot not scalded. I had been working for him for two years at that stage, but we all make mistakes!

'Dan, I want you to work on something with me.'

I nodded at him. I was all ears!

'I want to bring a Kerry team over to New York for something, but I need the real cream. I want the bloody stars to show up, not just any old footballer. I want Tom Long, Mick O'Connell and Mick O'Dwyer.'

This was very much in keeping with John 'Kerry's' personality. When he wanted something, he told you straight. I knew exactly the three players he was referring to. They were the rising stars on the Senior Kerry team. I understood completely why John 'Kerry' was eager to bring them to New York. I was eager to learn more about John 'Kerry's' idea.

'The Cardinal wants me to organise a charity match, here in Gaelic Park. Kerry against New York. And he wants three from the All-Ireland winning Kerry team to take part. I have too much on, would you do it for me?'

We spent the next hour going through the possibilities. I threw some ideas John 'Kerry's' way, and he fired some back. I realised John 'Kerry' wanted to make the games happen, but saw the logistical difficulties. He liked the Cardinal, liked his passion for charity and Irish America, but, like many people, he thought he was a little impractical. He was worried that both he and Cardinal Cushing would lose money to the venture.

'I can't bring the whole damn team over here, Dan. The GAA wouldn't like it, wouldn't agree to it, because it would set a precedent and the cost… But it's a good idea. Could you pull it off?'

'Well, I could go over there personally and convince some of them to come. You wouldn't need the entire team for a charity match.'

John Kerry liked that idea, and it was agreed.

The day after I arrived in Shannon, my first time back in Ireland for three years, a lovely black Ford Anglia was waiting for me in the car park. Seeing it there gave me a fantastic feeling! I had arranged to meet Mick O'Dwyer, Mick O'Connell and Tom Long in a bar in Tralee. When I arrived, Tom Long and Mick O'Dwyer were there waiting for me, enjoying cold glasses of stout, and no doubt reflecting on their recent championship-winning exploits: Kerry had defeated Roscommon in the All-Ireland Championship final that September.

Both were happy to see me. One of them even offered to buy me a drink. The signs were good!

Neither man needed much persuasion. Both loved the idea of representing Kerry in New York. I was delighted. Both Mick O'Dwyer and Tom were fantastic talents, and their participation would add credibility to the charity games. As we got up to leave, I asked, almost forgetting, 'What about Mick O'Connell'? 'Oh, he is a little cool on the idea, Dan. You had better visit him yourself. He is down in Valentia this weekend.'

I was disappointed. Mick O'Connell was a great midfielder, one of the all-time greats of Kerry football. Like all midfield greats, he held teams together, but he also had an eye for a goal. I wasn't willing to give up on him.

The following day, I took the new car from Tralee to Cahersiveen, a small town deep in the West Kerry Gaeltacht, a mountainous part of the Iveragh Peninsula, Southwest Kerry. In Cahersiveen, I got directions to Valentia Island. To use an American expression popular in the clubs and nightclubs of New York at that time, Mick was playing 'hard to get'.

'I don't know, Dan, flying halfway across the world for a charity game! Flying isn't my thing,' Mick told me, as he flung a sod of turf into his open fire.

'What do you think?' I remember Mick asking his friend, a man by the name of Curtin, who was sitting across from him. Curtin shook his head. I told Mick that I understood his reservations about flying, but it would be a fantastic occasion to be part of. He could also help Kerry beat New York. I tried to tickle his ego. Without Mick O'Connell, the Americans had a much better chance of beating us, and every word I said was true. Mick O'Connell was a fantastic sporting talent, one of the finest footballers we have ever produced (and that is saying something), which is why I was so eager to persuade him to travel.

'Will JFK be there?' Mick asked. His friend laughed.

'He might be Mick.'

Eventually, Mick turned to me and said, 'Alright, I will go on one condition. That man there has been a good friend of mine over the years, and I would like him to come with me. If he isn't good enough for yer company, then neither am I.'

I had to think over the proposal. Bringing a fourth would add to the costs and, as John 'Kerry' had explained to me, keeping the costs down was imperative. There was also the small issue of who Mick's friend was. Mr Curtin was a republican and known in Kerry for his staunchly republican views.

In the end, I decided to give in to Mick's request. I had a good feeling about the Cardinal Cushing games. I thought they would be a success, and I was eager for them to go ahead. I was also the son of a War of Independence veteran, and I had republican and nationalist sympathies myself. As did John 'Kerry', to say the least! He was likely to be fine with Mick's choice of travel companion. I just hoped it would go down well in conservative and Catholic Irish America.

As it happened, it did! During half-time in one of the games, I even saw Curtin chatting with a senator's daughter!

All three players had a wonderful time and they all met Cardinal Cushing. I don't think I ever heard Gaelic Park roar like it did when that Kerry team walked onto the field for those two matches in 1962.

John 'Kerry' and I agreed to follow Cardinal Cushing's original format. Kerry, the reigning New York Champions, would be joined by three inter-county Kerry players, and play the New York select team three times. The opening game would be in New York, the follow-up in Boston, with the teams returning to New York for the final game. It was 'best of three', with the three scores forming an aggregate score, which determined the winner. In the end, such computing wasn't necessary, as Kerry won all three games convincingly.

I remember Mick O'Connell scored a fabulous goal in one of the games, and the crowd chanted his name.

That Kerry team was far and away the best football team in the country at that time. They were probably overshadowed by the later four in a row team, but they had some magical players, and we were lucky enough to host three of them in New York that year. The match attracted the biggest ever attendance for a GAA game in Gaelic Park.

I made sure my Kerry Juniors team were in the stands watching. Since John 'Kerry' asked me to manage them, I had taken it very seriously and wanted to show them how it was done. It worked! My Kerry Juniors team would go on to win three American Junior Championships in a row.

As the principal organiser of the games, I was beaming with pride. I remember meeting Cardinal Cushing as well. John 'Kerry' introduced me as the man who helped bring the Cardinal's ideas to fruition. He was exactly as I expected. He had a relaxed manner and he was bursting with energy. A very inspiring man, although, remarkably, he wasn't the person who made the biggest impression on me that day.

While enjoying a glass of Coca-Cola, I got talking to an American priest. I thought he was part of the Cardinal's entourage, but he introduced himself as a member of the Columban Brothers stationed in New York state. We chatted for some time. He congratulated me on the success of the Cushing games, and he asked after my family. Like so many of the Catholic clergy in America, he had Irish roots. We also discussed our mutual love of Gaelic football. I told him about my Junior team and the big plans I had for them.

I did mention how I would love to bring more footballers and hurlers over to America. It was a great opportunity to reward our fantastic athletes, and a great opportunity for Irish immigrants to watch them play. I also mentioned how expensive it was. Maybe I was canvassing a little, in preparation for my future career!

Before he left, he whispered into my ears, 'Have a look into chartered flights'. He winked at me and walked back to his friends.

I had never heard of chartered flights, but I did look into it, and I was more than happy with what I found, but you will have to wait a little longer for that story!

The fruits of our labour. A very proud John 'Kerry' O'Donnell pictured with three of the greatest footballers Kerry has ever produced, Tom Long, Mick O'Dwyer, and Mick O'Connell, who exhibited their skills in front of an American audience for the Cardinal Cushing charity games.

Leasing the Red Mill

'You did what!!' My brother Tim's jaw dropped when I told him. I was expecting it.

'Young Dan Kiely, my younger brother, have you lost all your feckin marbles?'

At this stage, I had been living in New York City for four years, and I had taken some risks, and carved open some opportunities for myself. They had, in the majority of cases, worked out.

I was probably the first Irish immigrant to secure employment at Goldman, and by the time I left, I had secured jobs for over forty Irish immigrants, including my brother Pete.

Pete had been working as a bellhop at a hotel in central Manhattan before I secured him a clerical job on the IBM floor at Goldman. He was initially paid less at the bank than he was in the hotel, but Pete gradually worked his way up the career ladder, eventually becoming a broker. His brief was to locate stocks and shares that had been concealed or hidden in clandestine accounts. It was important work and he loved it.

People scoffed at my interest in the GAA. They told me I was wasting my time and energy. They told me I should pour my enthusiasm and time into more profitable pursuits and that voluntary service to the GAA was thankless.

They were wrong. I have so many fond memories from my time working in Gaelic Park, and from my time as a trainer and later as a delegate with the GAA in America. The highlight out of all the many games I was privileged to watch in Gaelic Park, was perhaps the National Football League final between New York and Dublin in October 1964. That year, Dublin defeated Kerry by a single point in Croke Park, earning them a place in the final against Down, where they triumphed by a considerably higher margin: 2-9 to Down's 0-7. Dublin went on to face the New York All-Stars in the Bronx in what the GAA were billing as a 'World Championship' final, and it certainly felt like it, that October's day in Gaelic Park, as Ireland's National League Champions took to the field to face what was a very considerable New York side. New York was a force to be reckoned with in those days, and they beat Dublin by two points in a fierce game overshadowed by a bad-tempered brawl at the end.

It wasn't the outcome or the quality of the game that made it so memorable for me however. Robert F. Kennedy, or Bobby Kennedy as he was more commonly known, visited Gaelic Park for the occasion, and performed the ceremonial throwing up of the ball between the opposing players at the beginning. I remember him wading through a sea of spectators, shaking hands and posing for photographs. He even stood a few Guinnesses in the bar after the game. It was, of course, the last time Bobby Kennedy would throw the ball in for a game of football. He was dead by the summer of 1968, assassinated like his brother before him. His tragic death made his appearance at Gaelic Park that day all the more significant and poignant for the people lucky enough to witness it.

I was also enjoying my work with the Kerry Juniors. As I mentioned previously, we enjoyed some great successes, winning successive back-to-back Junior Championship titles three years in a row. I was lucky to have some wonderful players, including John Dalton and the Mitchells from Tralee, as well as the O'Driscolls from Camp. They were up there with the best of them. I have great memories of training John Dalton. What John lacked in physicality, he more than made up for in elegance and skill. He was a nimble, fleet-footed player in the Kerry tradition of great full-back. Give John the football beyond the opponent's 45, and he would do magical things with it.

I also took up the advice given to me by the Columban father who I met after the Cardinal Cushing charity game, and I began organising charter flights. My first charter flight was a Pan Am flight from New York to Shannon. It was a trip home for the Kerry Juniors team, newly crowned American Junior Champions, and it was nothing short of what they deserved. I will never forget the feeling I had taking off from Idlewild Airport for Shannon that day. The boy who had arrived in a snowy USA, several years earlier, awestruck by automatic doors, was leaving the runway in his own charted jet. The feeling was even greater when I saw the excitement on the players' faces. They had worn their county colours with pride, and the trip was their reward.

By 1965, I could afford to fly the Kerry Juniors around the country in chartered flights, to matches in Chicago, Boston and elsewhere. We also took weekend trips to Rochester and Syracuse, where we would go to the movies, visit zoos and other recreational parks. I loved those trips with the young players. Looking back, I think those trips embodied the GAA's founding principles, which were not simply to facilitate, grow and foster our traditional games, but also to build character and community.

The GAA was founded in 1884, in the shadow of the Great Famine (1845-49). Not only did millions of souls perish, but rural Irish society was ravaged. One of the founding purposes of the GAA was to revitalise the spirit of the Irish nation and renew Irish people's confidence. In my involvement with football, I took that mantle very seriously. We didn't just want good footballers and hurlers, we wanted good men and women who would acquire the confidence and character to succeed in life. Later, I remember listening to an interview with Breandán Mac Lua, a former executive officer of the GAA, and founder of the *Irish Post* newspaper in London, for the documentary film *The Rocky Road to Dublin*. On the subject of the GAA's founding principles, I was very struck by what Mac Lua said:

The Gaelic Athletic Association is much wider than a sports organisation. It was founded for the purpose of utilising sport to inject manhood and nationalism into Irish manhood at a period when the spirit of the Irish people was very low and very weak after the famine and centuries of persecution.

All the movements which have led to the establishment of the State, which we have, have drawn their members – be they fighting members or active political members – from the ranks of the Gaelic Athletic Association and as such it has been the reservoir of Irish manhood, who have played their part in the evolution of the State.

Despite the good things I was doing with the GAA, some people still found me impulsive. On that note, I had better tell you what I did that shocked my brother Tim so much. It is a long story, but it is, I guarantee you, an interesting one.

I met many fascinating people during my years in America, but one of the most interesting was a man by the name of Bill Fuller, my fellow Kerryman. Bill was a veteran of the nightclub and dancehall scene, his early ballrooms included a bustling Dublin venue, and the infamous Buffalo nightclub, located in Camden High Street in central London. Despite the Buffalo's reputation for excess and brawling, Bill took it over and revitalised it, turning it into a mecca for the Irish people in Britain. He would apply the same model to nightclubs in America. At his height, Bill managed clubs in Boston, New York, Chicago and San Francisco.

I met Bill for the first time in his New York ballroom, the City Centre Ballroom, located on West 55th Street, just off of 7th Avenue.

If you were Irish and in New York in the mid to late sixties, then the City Centre Ballroom on West 55th Street was where you had to be. All the more so if you were young and wanted to meet someone, then the advice was to take yourself to the City Centre.

It was a fantastic place if you liked the traditional Irish and ballroom dances. The music and entertainment nearly always consisted of a full orchestra. While some people found the style of entertainment reserved, there was nothing reserved about the courting going on; many a man or woman met their wife or husband at the City Centre. I wasn't surprised to read in our local paper, *The Kerryman*, many, many years later, that Bridie and Eddie O'Sullivan, owners of the Tatler Jack bar in Killarney, had met in Bill Fuller's ballroom.

Just like John 'Kerry', I struck up a friendship with Bill. I would often chat to him in the early hours of the morning, when the crowd had thinned out, and the staff would be clearing the ballroom floor.

I explained to Bill my views on the nightclub scene. All the New York ballrooms at this time, his included, had full orchestras and formal dance routines. While this was wonderful in its own way, I felt the showband craze was bound to take off in America. Having immigrated recently, I knew singers like Dickie Rock, Butch Moore and Brendan Bowyer were captivating audiences in Ireland.

The next generation of immigrants would be accustomed to this faster style of music and a more modern style of dancing and socialising. In short, I thought there was a niche for a new type of ballroom and concert venue.

I remember Bill smiling at me. He had left Kerry many years before then, but he still had the Kerry man's cute smile. He neither disagreed nor agreed with me.

Despite this, I was surprised when, in the coming months, Bill didn't make any changes to his set, to attract this new generation of immigrants, which I had warned him were coming. Bill seemed to me to be relaxed with the status quo. I would discover later that Bill in actual fact agreed with me 100%.

He was already signing showbands, and he was planning a string of new ballrooms and nightclubs to accommodate these new, youthful fashions and styles. Except, not in New York. Bill's eye was on Las Vegas, a new city built in the Nevada Desert, which was already famous for its casinos and wild party life.

Bill would eventually move his operations to Las Vegas and enjoy success there. However, with Bill concentrating on Las Vegas I felt a door had opened to me for some new blood.

I really felt there was a niche for a new type of club, a new type of nighttime recreation in New York, and you should know by now, that when I get an idea, I don't stop until it happens.

It was a dark, rainy weekday in winter. I had more free time during the winter, as Gaelic Park was not as busy, and there were fewer matches, weddings and functions. My destination that day was the Red Mill nightclub on Jerome Avenue, the Bronx, which was a short walk from our apartment on West 167th Street.

I had never been there before, but I had heard of the Red Mill, or the Moulin Rouge, to give it its official title. Everyone had. It was part of a string of Moulin Rouge cabaret bars, the most famous one being the Paris Moulin Rouge. There, in the nineteenth century, cabaret and unique dance routines like the can-can had been invented. I had seen photos of Frank Sinatra visiting the Paris Moulin Rouge in the *New York Post*, and I thought there was no reason why New York could not have something similar. I had big dreams when I left Kerry for New York, and during my time in America, they only got bigger.

Jerome Avenue was busy in the sixties, boasting several car hire and car repair businesses, although the Mill was the only club. I remember trying the front door, but there was no answer. I banged the door with my fist a few times and called the name I had been given, but nothing! I checked my watch. Had I got the day or time wrong?

Eventually, a man opened the door, smiled at me and asked me in. He directed me into the main ballroom and said the 'boss' would be with me soon.

Inside, I could hardly see anything. The air was stale. There was one large ballroom in the centre of the building, but it had been divided into small dance floors, sectioned by wooden partitions. The dance floors were crammed with red armchairs and couches with holes in the upholstery. This arrangement suited the cabaret style of entertainment. Rather than musical acts and performances, cabaret shows were fusions of theatre, drama, music and comedy.

I could see framed pictures of Frank Sinatra, Perry Como, and other legends from the glory days of American music, and I think seeing them convinced me to stay. 'Old blue-eyes', as Frank Sinatra was called, proved to be the inspiration.

I could see that the place had potential, but I also realised it needed a lot of work. The caretaker, Jimmy, had told me the boss would be with me in ten minutes. Twenty minutes passed and Jimmy finally came back. He told me the boss would be another twenty minutes, and handed me a cup of coffee.

Another ten, and then twenty minutes passed, and I had plenty

Dan pictured with the legendary country singer and guitarist Slim Whitman (Ottis Dewey Whitman Jr.). Slim Whitman was one of many sellout acts Dan hosted in his ballrooms and hotels in both New York and Ireland, including the Bronx's Red Mill.

of time to examine the room. I wasn't an expert in construction, but I had picked up a few things. I noticed the staff toilets were blocked and the sink in the bar had no running water. There was a hole in the roof behind the bar. Work was needed!

Eventually, the caretaker came back. I thought the worst when I saw he was carrying a pint of beer. The boss would apparently be another twenty minutes. I was getting frustrated at that point. I told the caretaker I didn't drink, and he brought me a cold glass of Coca-Cola instead, which I slugged down, and it was good – it needed to be; if it hadn't been I would have walked out the door.

Finally, almost an hour later, a tall man, wearing a Panama hat and chinos walked in. I explained to him I wanted it, but I needed to make some changes. He looked puzzled and asked me what changes. I told him I wanted one big ballroom floor, not all the sectioned cabaret malarkey. I also wanted new floorboards, as the existing ones were in bad shape. He wasn't too pleased with this, but he agreed. He told me there were two other people interested. I made a face at him. He assured me there were, but he wanted to give it to me, as he liked 'the look of me,' but only on one condition. I asked him what that was, and he said I had to sign the lease that day. He was heading back to Florida, and he needed it signed straight away. I looked at him and his Panama hat, and, not for the first time in my life, I made a quick decision.

I told him we had a deal and we shook on it. So, there I was, on Jerome Avenue, the Bronx, signing my first nightclub lease. My first of many! While I didn't know it at the time, I was to become the youngest ever holder of a nightclub license in New York State. As far as I know, I still hold the record. Not bad for a boy from Tarbert at twenty-one years of age.

Far From Run of the Mill

Renting the Red Mill wasn't my first, and it certainly wasn't my last risk, but, as was the case with many of them, it paid off. The nightclub on Jerome Avenue was a roaring success, and one of the best business ventures my brother and I went into.

My sister Philomena and her husband Mike Moynihan just so happened to run bars and nightclubs in New York, and their advice and experience was invaluable. Even outside of my connection with the Moynihans through Philomena, I knew the family from Gaelic football. When they heard we had leased premises in the Bronx they were interested in going into partnership with us. After negotiation, we agreed on a fifty-fifty split on all proceeds, which we thought was fair, considering their wealth of experience in the nightclub trade.

Our partnership with the Moynihans was also essential in keeping costs down. The premises needed extensive renovation, a new ballroom had to be laid, and the old, dusty cabaret furniture needed to be replaced. The Moynihans covered half of these costs, as well as offering their expertise.

When it came to the day-to-day running of the Mill, that task was left to Johnny Moynihan and me. I feel we did a great job. Having played with the Moynihans on the football field, the transition to ballroom management was seamless.

I had many late nights in the old office behind the main ballroom. I was on the phone cutting some last-minute deals with bands and performers. One minute I would be meeting a certain band's agent in one part of New York, then flying to another part to meet a promoter. It was hectic and fast-paced. It was the life of a New York nightclub owner and I loved it.

Our first job was to get the place renovated and up to spec. Converting an old cabaret bar into a modern nightclub wasn't easy, but I secured good tradesmen, and the place was looking much better in two weeks.

One big problem I didn't anticipate was the difficulty in recruiting staff. Staff costs were a major overhead. I didn't realise then, and I don't think people even really appreciate now how many people it takes to run a nightclub. When you hire new staff, you don't just have to consider wages, you have to consider your obligations towards them, what terms you will be employing them under and so forth.

Not for the first time, I was very privileged to be a member of the immigrant community. From the Kiely's own circle of friends and relatives, we knew so many people who were looking for work and who were happy to help out.

So many of my extended family ended up working in the Red Mill, including our cousins from Kiskeam who had been with us from the beginning, living in the flat above us on Nelson Avenue.

I remember I made an effort to arrive early that first Friday we opened. Things didn't get off to a good start however.

The ballroom was ready. We had knocked the wooden partitions that sectioned the ballroom and replaced it with one big dancefloor. We had a sparkling new wooden floor laid, and the stage was kitted out with new acoustics and equipment. I had booked a young, rising Irish showband called 'The High Spots' who had a few hits behind them in Ireland, and who were eager to break into the New York scene.

No sooner had I taken a moment to put my feet up, in comes Jimmy the caretaker to tell me he had found a new leak! There was a large hole in the ladies' restroom and rainwater was getting in. To add to our problems, a supplier who was to arrive with a lorry full of beverages was late.

I rushed into my small office and got going. I saw no point in procrastinating and feeling sorry for myself. There were problems that needed fixing, and I went at it. Lo and behold, by five that evening most of the problems were fixed.

I managed to persuade a tradesman to look at the restroom and plaster over the leak. An electrician sorted the lights, and my old friend Bill Fuller, who remained very friendly with me even after I went into the nightclub scene, and went into direct competition with him, did me a favour and he sold his alcohol stock at a cut-down price. As it turned out, and thanks in no small part to friends of mine like Bill, the night was a fantastic success and I never looked back.

We had some great years at the Red Mill and I have very fond memories of running it. We had over a thousand patrons for our opening night. I was very hands-on in my approach to running the nightclub. I would always be on the floor, running to and fro, making sure everything ran smoothly. The lifestyle also brushed off on me! Over my time running the Red Mill, I got to know so many interesting people in the music and entertainment industries. Some of Ireland's most popular entertainers and singers even slept in a house I bought in the Bronx. In my small office behind the ballroom, I entertained producers, managers and promoters. My connections in the industry grew, something that would prove very useful when we took over the Esplanade Hotel in Youghal and the Hibernian Ballroom in Ballybunion; ventures I will tell you about soon enough!

By 1966 things had taken a turn for the worse, however, as often happens in business. If there are any young people who are interested in business reading, they should take note: things always change.

When it came to the Red Mill it was more bad luck than anything else, and here is another lesson in business, it often is. The Irish economy was doing well in the sixties. Séan Leamass was

An image of the Esplanade Hotel, Youghal, Co Cork, the first hotel and ballroom Dan Kiely leased after he returned from New York.

elected leader of Fianna Fáil and subsequently Taoiseach in 1959, and began to introduce fresh, new ideas into Irish politics. He established the IDA, which encouraged multinational companies to invest in Ireland. He introduced free secondary level education, which meant Ireland would eventually have one of the most educated workforces in the world.

All these changes were good for Ireland, and when I entered politics in 1979 as a Fianna Fáil councillor, I was eager to continue this legacy of change, progress and development. However, there was one change introduced during that period that did not benefit me as a New York nightclub owner. That was the Irish policy to reduce Irish emigration to the United States.

The then Irish government was worried that too many people were leaving Ireland; that the country's youngest, brightest and best were emigrating to the United States, and thus depriving Ireland of talented young people. Ireland was not the only country to experience what is often referred to as a 'brain drain'. The government lobbied the American government to cap the number of Irish immigrants and eventually, in 1966, they got their way, with the American government agreeing to place a strict quota on the number of immigrants who could come from Ireland.

Our customer base was the immigrant community, particularly younger immigrants. When that community decreased in size, it wasn't good for us, and it was one of the major reasons why the fortunes of the Red Mill declined. We had done a roaring trade for so many years, with queues running down Jerome Avenue, but the quotas hit us hard.

I'm not in any way bitter about this. The Fianna Fáil government of the sixties was one of the most revolutionary, and most of the changes they introduced were positive.

There was another reason for the club's declining fortunes: weddings! When Mary and I got married we had our wedding reception in the Red Mill. It was a wonderful success and everyone in the family had a great time. Because of this, I decided to offer the Mill as a wedding venue.

In those days, in New York anyway, wedding receptions were very much an afternoon affair. People would attend the church ceremony in the morning before heading to the reception in the afternoon. I felt we could host receptions during the day and open the venue as a nightclub at night. Needless to say, it didn't work out, and in hindsight, I should have known why. Irish weddings are big parties; people love to mingle, chat and have the craic. Drink flows, and come the end of the evening people are often worse for wear.

One of the biggest challenges for anyone running licensed premises of any kind is how to handle people when they drink too much, and one of the big problems with hosting weddings in the afternoon is some of the guests would remain in the club after the reception was finished, waiting for the nightclub to open so they could have a few more! For some people, the more they drink, the more misbehaved they become.

Hosting weddings was a mistake. They proved to be more trouble than they were worth, but you always make some mistakes, nobody goes through life without making them.

From the Mill to the Hibernian

Throughout my life, I always relied on my good business sense, and come 1966, I sensed that the Red Mill's glory days were behind it. The restrictions on Irish immigration really damaged us, as we were the destination of choice for so many young Irish emigrants.

I eventually began spending more time in Ireland. For a number of years, I was over and back regularly, keeping the Red Mill going, while looking for a place to invest in at home. The Red Mill had some great years, so Timmy and I had a little capital built up, and we were both eager to 'give something back' as they say to find some establishment in Ireland to build up and develop.

I remember being told by a friend of mine, an old associate from the New York bar scene, that a fabulous, old Victorian hotel in Youghal, Co Cork, was up for sale. So I travelled to Cork to meet Mr and Mrs Hurley, the owners of the Esplanade, in Youghal. They took me around the town, showing me the famous Clock Gate Tower, an eighteenth century tower that was used to house prisoners during Ireland's 1798 rebellion, and we walked along the beach and harbour, which the hotel overlooked. The hotel itself was a little rundown, having been frequently damaged by floods. That said, the Esplanade was very advantageously located, overlooking the boardwalk and the beach, and I was particularly impressed by the ballroom.

When I was being shown around by Mr and Mrs Hurley, I remember admiring their Canadian Maple dancefloor. I could envisage the place teeming with people dancing and enjoying themselves. I didn't hesitate and I signed a lease with Mr and Mrs Hurley that day. The Esplanade Hotel in Youghal became the Kielys' first hotel in Ireland.

With the Red Mill quieter than usual, and Tim taking over the management of the Esplanade, I found myself with little to do for the first time in a while. So, I decided to do something I always said I would if the opportunity ever arose.

After getting involved in dancehall management in America, I always wanted to return to Ireland and manage an establishment closer to home. The Esplanade Hotel was a fine establishment, but I wanted something in North Kerry.

There is a little village west of Tarbert called Ballybunion. Situated on a small hill, it overlooks what must be one of the most unspoilt, spectacular beaches in Ireland.

As a child in school in Glin, I remember learning about Ballybunion's geography. Its beautiful granite cliffs, its 'blow hole' – or the 'Nine Daughters Hole' as we referred to it locally – is an enormous hole in the roof of a large cave, and it is quite an experience to peer into it from the top of the cliff.

I remember visiting Ballybunion as a child in the fifties with my mam and dad, and I loved running along the beach and walking along the cliffs. From the cliffs, you could look for miles into the wild Atlantic Ocean.

Back then, Ballybunion was just another village in Kerry. In the sixties however, it increasingly became a holiday destination, with hundreds and thousands of people from the surrounding towns and villages travelling there for the summer months.

When I visited Ballybunion in 1962, for the first time in some years, I noticed these changes. New businesses that weren't there before had suddenly sprung up. There were suddenly bed and breakfasts and guesthouses offering accommodation to couples and families from places like Limerick and Tralee. Shops sold buckets and spades, picnic baskets and other essential paraphernalia for a day at the beach, and vans dispensing ice creams and seagrass would be parked on the main street. It was more than new businesses however, there was a buzz and energy about the place. I really felt that Ballybunion was going places and I was desperate to be involved.

I remember asking around for quite a while, looking for a suitable location for a dance hall. When one could not be found, I was, not for the first or last time, forced to improvise. I eventually located a large, six acre site at Ahafona Cross. It was located in the centre of Ballybunion village, just before the junction with the main street, and most importantly, a five minute walk to the fabulous beach. It was perfect.

I remember the first day I viewed it with the auctioneer, walking around what was then a derelict site. I immediately saw the site's potential. Over the following weeks, I put all my focus into the site and began laying out the plans for what would eventually become the Hibernian Ballroom.

Drawing on the experience gained from running the Red Mill in New York, the Hibernian was very much a ballroom in the American mould. It was to have a max capacity of 3,000, and a wooden dance floor, which I felt suited the showband experience.

Again, drawing on my New York experience, I knew that sourcing the right quality wooden flooring was essential. I didn't want dancing feet to be tapping on substandard wood. I was impressed by the wood used in the Esplanade, a Canadian Maple, and I managed to secure a batch from the same supplier. We built a fine sunken dance floor, easily one of the best in the county, if not the country.

While today's bars and nightclubs are associated with the consumption of alcohol, and often copious amounts of it, back then, there were far more allowances made for pioneers, and abstinence from alcohol was far more common, with people eager to enjoy themselves and socialise without resorting to the bottle. In the Hibernian, I had two bars, one that served tea, coffee and sandwiches, and the other that served alcohol. I furnished both bars with foam mahogany seating, and both types of patrons were equally valued and equally essential to the success of the venture.

Originally, I wanted the Hibernian to be more than a dance hall. I was eager for it to be part of a much larger holiday camp complex, and I had big plans for the Ahafona site. In my initial three year plan for the project, I envisioned constructing a motel, three chalets, a tennis court, and a mini-golf course. I even toyed with the idea of constructing a swimming pool, in respect of which I was most certainly ahead of my time, as it would be exactly forty years later that Ballybunion would finally get this amenity, in the form of Ballybunion Health & Leisure Centre.

Recently, I located an article from *The Kerryman* newspaper, which featured the Hibernian, just when it was in the construction stage. It included a profile and a quote from me on the subject of my overall vision for the complex. Here is what I had to say about the Hibernian back in 1967:

'These innovations are the product of the fertile mind of the owner and contractor, Mr Dan Kiely of Tarbert. This dynamic young businessman has set about building himself a ballroom in ten weeks.... Dan is no stranger to the entertainment business and his ideas for the ballroom are not unambitious "This ballroom is something which was badly needed in Ballybunion" he said, "and I intend to run dances here for the twelve months of the year."'

Reading it again all those years later made me a little nostalgic. Our grand opening occurred the following week, with Dermot O'Brien and the Clubmen, one of the rising stars of the showband scene, putting on a fantastic show in front of thousands of dancing holidaymakers. I remember one local approaching me to thank me and tell me he had never seen the village dance so hard. That brought a smile to my face!

The Day That Was in It

1965 and '66 were big years for our family. Running the Esplanade and the Hibernian hotels were big enough ventures in themselves, but, believe it or not, they were not the only businesses we started in those years.

Tim and Pete remained in New York in '65, and '66, managing the Red Mill and some other establishments we had acquired, including two other bars in the Bronx. Back in Ireland, I had my hands full with both the Esplanade and the Hibernian in Ballybunion. The younger members of my family, including my younger brothers, Denis and Pat, were eager to get even more involved in our business activities. They remained involved until they emigrated to America in 1971, where they remained until they returned a number of years later to take up employment with the ESB in the power station in Tarbert.

While Ballybunion was only a few miles from Tarbert, I was always eager to have a business in Tarbert village itself. The picture of my mother and father walking to mass, or visiting the local grocer or butcher, and seeing the family name above a door, seeing a thriving, local establishment bearing the Kiely name, really appealed to me.

It will come as no surprise to anyone that when I eventually found a niche, it was directly connected with travel to America. During the early sixties, I would have travelled to and from New York and Shannon on countless occasions. I held conversations with several of my fellow passengers on those trips, both Irish emigrants going to and fro, and, in increasing numbers, American tourists and workers travelling to Ireland on holiday or on business.

I often offered people I met on the plane a lift if we were travelling in a similar direction. I did notice how costly hackney cabs were, particularly if you were travelling a good distance. I also noticed that there was a lack of car rental services, particularly reliable ones at an affordable price. It didn't take long for the idea to dawn on me.

A car rental service was desperately needed and I thought Tarbert would be an ideal location for one. Tarbert's location on the N69 road, the main national road from Limerick to Tralee and Killarney, made it an ideal location. This was outside of any sentimental reasons that I had to locate the business there. Tarbert was also very much an up-and-coming location at that time. Ferries from Tarbert to Killimer in Clare would begin operating two years later in 1969, further improving transportation links, and increasing Tarbert's significance as a transportation hub.

The following year, in 1970, the ESB would establish a power station in Tarbert, which remains, to this day, the main source of electricity generation in the region.

I remember meeting Tim and Pete in my old office in the Red Mill to discuss the idea. It was a little strange, discussing Tarbert and the future development of the village in New York, but that was what being a member of the Kiely family was like in the sixties; we were very much a transatlantic family. Tim and Pete both agreed with me that there was a niche for the service. They had, themselves, travelled to and from Ireland enough to know how horrendous the transportation options in Shannon were. They were worried as to whether we would generate enough revenue from it to make the business worthwhile.

I really believed in my brothers Denis and Pat. They reminded me a little of myself when I was their age. I could see they admired their older brothers and sisters and they were eager to get involved in the Kiely businesses. I felt both Denis and Pat could run the car rental service in Tarbert, while I concentrated on Ballybunion, where the Hibernian was flying (thanks in part to my siblings, including Denis and Pat).

My idea was for a comprehensive car rental and maintenance service. We would provide tourists with quality cars for rental, but we would also have a valeting and maintenance garage in Tarbert, which, in addition to maintaining the cars in our fleet, would double as a gas station and service garage for the surrounding area.

I think the technical name for this today is cross-selling, where a business provides the customer with a range of different services ancillary to its main service. I was really excited about the venture! I felt it would give the entire community a lift and bring a smile to our parents' faces. What more could we ask for?

I was not a car mechanic of course, so it was essential that I employ a good one. The last thing any of us wanted was for some American bigshot to rent a car from us in Shannon and for it to break down halfway to Killarney! The constant valeting and maintaining of the fleet was imperative.

The sixties were lucky times for us in many ways. So many of our business ventures worked, and both the Irish and American economies were doing reasonably well. I purchased a fleet of twenty-five self-drive cars ('self-drive' in the sense customers would drive the vehicles themselves, as opposed to being chauffeured). I also remember posting an ad for a mechanic, as we needed skilled personnel. I was lucky as two very capable people replied, Denis Mahony and Mike Lynch. They were also, I am happy to write, open to the bespoke arrangement I had in mind. Both agreed to provide maintenance services for the self-drive cars, in return for the use of the garage and pumps rent free. This arrangement allowed us to concentrate on the self-drive cars, while Mahony and Lynch took care of the garage and pumps.

The car rental business was, I am happy to say, a great success. *The Kerryman* also did a feature piece on 'Kiely Bros Service Station', to give it its full title. It is great to look back and see a photo of my brother, Denis, looking confident and proud with Tom Kissane, our trusty car wash attendant standing next to him.

1965 and '66 were indeed great years for us, starting so many new business ventures, and so many of them being fantastic successes. If truth be told, however, the most significant thing to happen to me in those two years had nothing to do with business. In 1966, our daughter Joan was born and I became a father for the first time. It was both a wonderful and slightly intimidating experience, as is often the case I am told when your first child is born.

I have nothing but good memories from the time, including rushing to the hospital to see Mary and holding the child in my arms. Joan is like me in so many respects and we have so many similar interests. It came as no surprise to me when, in 2019, she was nominated as Chairperson of the New York branch of the GAA. If someone had told me that, when I started working the beer stalls in Gaelic Park in 1961, that a son of mine would be running the place someday, I'm not sure I would have believed it, but a daughter! I'm not sure what I would have said, but I couldn't possibly be more proud of Joan. Joan is the first female head of the traditionally male-dominated organisation, and I'm sure she needed all her Kiely wits and guile to get her to where she is.

It was also around this time I got another opportunity to show my gratitude to my parents. My father was approaching retirement at this time, and my parents would therefore have to vacate what was the family home, the house attached to the Garda barracks, to make way for my father's replacement and his family. I noticed a suitable house for sale in Tarbert with an asking price of £600. I was eager to purchase it for my parents and gift them a house they could live out their remaining years in, although time was of the essence, as I knew the owners had received a bid of £530. Not to be defeated, I arranged to meet the auctioneer, a Mr O'Connell, and try to negotiate a sale. He told me the owners would accept the asking price. I didn't hesitate. I paid the £600, which was equivalent to $1,800, and my parents had a house to retire in.

They renovated and extended the house over the years and it became the Kiely base in Tarbert. My brother Denis lives in it today. I am very happy I paid my parents this compliment and gifted them a house that allowed them to live out their remaining years in safety and relative comfort. It was the least they deserved after so many years of hard work, of setting such a great example for us all.

Breaking Ball in Ireland

In 1970, I got an opportunity to do something I had always dreamed of doing. An opportunity arose for me to be the chairperson of the North Kerry Divisional Board of the GAA. Some county boards, Kerry included, are subdivided into smaller divisional boards, and the North Kerry Board encompassed not only Tarbert, my home village, but also Ballybunion, where we had the Hibernian Hotel and the new hotel in the East End.

The North Kerry Board had a special history. The board was founded in 1924, just after the independence struggle, by a postmaster and athletics enthusiast Maurice McGrath, and it was, therefore, a real honour to be nominated as chairperson.

I didn't have much time to settle into the job as the North Kerry Board was in dire financial trouble. Some years previous to when I took up the reins, a man had been refused entry to a match between two local clubs. He subsequently sued the board and won, being awarded £300 by way of compensation. £300 was a frightful amount of money in those days. To put things into perspective for younger readers, when I left for America in 1961, my father was earning £8 a week as a Garda. When I started working as an office assistant at Goldman Sachs, I earned $30 a week, the equivalent of £10. I considered this a good salary, and it was. It was after all £2 more than my father earned, and I was only a lad of seventeen at the time. My father's annual salary was £384. The board, therefore, owed the equivalent of what was the average annual salary at that time.

To make matters worse, the various clubs and organisations under the North Kerry Board's remit were desperately in need of funding. I was playing football again, proudly representing Tarbert, so I knew first-hand what a bad state the pitch was in. Having played in some fine sports fields in the United States, the contrast was stark. I thought the Tarbert pitch, in particular, was a safety hazard. I feared one of our players, or one from the opposing team, would break a leg or sustain some other career killing injury.

Despite the enormous debt hanging over us, I got to work generating funds to refurbish and modernise the various pitches and facilities in North Kerry. I arranged for the Tarbert pitch to be professionally drained and it worked; the improvement was massive. We extended the pitch in Ballybunion, which at the time was one of the smallest pitches in North Kerry. The pitches in Ballylongford and Listowel also required elaborate drainage, but we managed to generate the necessary funds.

This mantle would later be taken up by Bernie Callaghan, when he became chairperson of the Board, sometime after me. Bernie continued the refurbishing and modernising of pitches and facilities that I had started. Bernie would later become manager and owner of the Listowel Arms Hotel and the sports field in Listowel, the Frank Sheehy Park. It is now one of the finest pitches in the county. It was in a very different state when I became chairperson in 1970, so it is satisfying to see the fruits of our labour.

In my capacity as chairperson, I also attended County Board meetings as a delegate. County meetings were chaired by Dr Jim Brosnan, a medical doctor and former Kerry footballer. We were perhaps destined to hit it off, as Jim was a native of Moyvane, within the boundaries of the North Kerry Board, only five miles south of Tarbert.

Just as I had with John 'Kerry' O'Donnell in New York, I became friendly with Jim. I remember him approaching me after a board

The victorious Ballylongford football team, who defeated Tarbert in the final of the North Kerry Championship, 1970. Dan Kiely, who was Chairperson of the North Kerry Board at the time, is pictured first from left in the back row.

meeting in Austin Stack's and requesting I accompany him for tea and scones in one of the local hotels. I remember him being very eager to learn more about how the GAA was organised in America, and he was particularly impressed by the flights I had chartered.

By that time, I had organised charter flights to take the Kerry Juniors to and from Ireland and I had charted numerous domestic flights. They provided the players with an opportunity to see so much of America, and help them bond with Irish communities in other parts of the United States.

Jim was eager to restructure and reorganise club football in Kerry, and was receptive to fresh, new ideas on how we organised our games. He saw me as new blood, someone with fresh and innovative ideas. While the Kerry Club Championship, the Kerry Senior Football Championship, to give it its official title, dates from the 1880s, it was only in the 1970-71 season that the GAA trialled an All-Ireland Club Championship. The winners from the Kerry Club Championship would qualify to compete in the Munster Championship, with the winners of that competing in the All-Ireland Club Championship. Today, the final takes place in Croke Park on St Patrick's Day, in front of thousands of fans.

It was, and is a fantastic occasion, but it did have some drawbacks from a footballing and developmental perspective, in the respect that local clubs, on account of how it was organised and structured, only played against clubs from their own divisional board. Clubs like Brosna, Tarbert, Moyvane and Listowel therefore usually played against each other, depriving them of the experience of competing against talented teams from other parts of the county.

I suggested to Jim that we found a county league. This format would give our local clubs an opportunity to play clubs from other parts of the county, clubs like Tralee's Austin Stacks, Killarney's Dr Crokes and East Kerry, who would win the first All-Ireland Club Championship in 1970-71. This was very much in keeping with my overall vision for Gaelic games. In America, I had been eager for New York teams to compete against clubs from other parts of the United States, including Chicago, Boston, Philadelphia and Baltimore. This was positive from both a professional and a developmental perspective, as playing against a wide variety of talented individuals aided players' physical and mental development. In the United States, I felt it was also positive from a social perspective, as the games provided occasions for Irish communities from different parts of the United States to mingle and get to know each other.

I thought a league for Kerry clubs would have similar advantages, allowing talented players from across the county to grow together and learn from each other. The league format would bring additional benefits when it came to competing as a county. When the players played together at the inter-county level, togged out in Kerry's iconic green and gold, they would be familiar with each other, knowledgeable in each other's strengths and weaknesses, as they had competed against each other at club level.

Dennis took my advice and together we founded a Kerry club league. It was a fantastic success and it continues to function well up to this day, with a total of seventeen teams competing across six leagues.

In addition to being chairperson of the board and continuing to be involved with the training and the management of teams, an experience I will tell you about soon, I was also playing for my home town of Tarbert. I was overjoyed when I was first selected to play. Since I returned to Ireland from the United States, I was missing the football field, missing the thrill and glory of playing GAA.

I think playing a sport has enormous benefits when it comes to one's mental and physical health, and I was no different in that respect. I played for Tarbert in the maiden year of the county football league, which I had organised and established with Dr Brosnan, and we did remarkably well. The semi-final against Dr Crokes of Killarney was a highlight for me. I scored a goal and four points and I remember it as one of my best performances as a football player. Crokes were then, as they are now, a footballing force in Kerry. Founded in 1886, wearing their iconic black and amber, they hold the current record for the most Kerry club championships, thirteen triumphs, and they were fiercely competitive that day.

Beating them that day was exhilarating. Sadly, the exhilaration was short-lived. Some days later, I received some very disappointing news, although it was not entirely unexpected.

Ever since I had been nominated as chairperson, I could sense that some people were unhappy about it. Perhaps they saw me as something of an upstart, and I knew they resented my increasing influence in the county board, particularly my relationship with Dr Jim Brosnan. The county club league was not – as is often the case with new, fresh ideas – universally welcomed, and some people were hostile to it.

In the days after our semi-final win, I was informed that I was not going to be selected for the final. It broke my heart. The semifinal against Killarney was perhaps my best performance in a Tarbert shirt, and I had a goal and four points to prove it. According to the selectors, I was ineligible for selection as Tarbert was not my official place of residence – Mary, young Joan and I were living in Ballybunion at the time. They claimed this was the GAA's policy and that they were simply applying it.

I checked the GAA's official rule book however, and I could see that this was simply not the case. The GAA's rule was that you were entitled to be considered for a club if you either lived within the club's designated boundaries *or your place of employment* was within those boundaries. Kiely and Bros, our car rental and car maintenance service, was my place of employment at that time, and clearly within Tarbert's designated boundaries, it was situated in Main Street Tarbert! I was therefore eligible for selection, according to the GAA's official rules.

It was a cruel thing to do to me, and it gave me an insight into how cut-throat people could be when matters of power and influence were at stake. It was an early taster of what was to come when I became actively involved in politics in the years that followed.

My brothers refused to play in the final. I also think the selector's treatment of me had an effect on player morale. Unsurprisingly, we were beaten in the final.

So Near, Yet So Far

I didn't allow this bad experience as a player to deter me from continuing to be involved in the GAA, however. When the opportunity arose to train the Kerry Minors in 1970, I enthusiastically embraced it. I felt I had finally entered the big league when it came to football management and training. Ever since John 'Kerry' asked me to train the Kerry Juniors in New York, I had loved this side of the sport!

I also had a good feeling about some of the young players I was managing. They impressed me throughout our training sessions, and I remember discussing their potential with Dr Jim Brosnan. My view was that we had several potential All-Ireland winners in our ranks. Young Ger O'Keeffe, who played with Austin Stack's in Tralee, really impressed me in the early months, and he was certainly one of the most exceptional fullbacks I have ever managed. We had three fantastic young forwards in our ranks, John Egan from Sneem, young Mickey 'Ned' O'Sullivan from Kenmare and Ger Power. They were fantastic, and I knew they would terrorise back-lines if managed and trained correctly.

We played Cork in the final of the Munster Minor Championship, and nobody thought we had a chance. We trashed Cork 4-9 to 1-11, and the exhilaration I felt after the game was unforgettable. Nobody fancied us, but we managed to defy the odds, and the faith I had placed in our team had paid off.

We beat Derry in the semi-final in August, 2-10 to 0-11, and perhaps my most significant memory from that game is the fact that

Derry fielded a young player called Martin O'Neill. All the Derry lads played well that day, but I remember Martin because he would go on to become a world class soccer player and future manager of the Republic of Ireland soccer team. It is a 'small country' as they say.

Our reward was a clash with Connacht champions Galway, who, similarly to ourselves, had defied expectations to triumph against Dublin in their semi.

Played on the 27th of September, I remember the final as a nervy, scrappy affair, and certainly not the exhibition of young footballing prowess we all wanted. I don't blame either set of players for that, however. There were 71,725 in Croke Park that day, and I can only imagine how daunting it was for our players on the field, contesting a final in front of such an audience.

As I wrote previously, the GAA is more than simply a sporting organisation, it very much embodies the spirit of the Irish nation. In the United States, I witnessed how football could unite the Irish community, and in Ireland, Croke Park is very much the spiritual home of the GAA. As the Artane Boys Band played the opening bars of Amhrán na bhFiann, the emotion on the players' faces was palpable. I can't blame them for being a little cagey!

The match ended in a draw, 1-08 to 2-05, with the replay scheduled for late October. Unlike the first game, the replay was a fantastic spectacle. The only downside was that my team was not victorious. Galway beat us by a single point, 1-11 to 1-10. I think the journalist Jarlath Burke's report on the game for *The Tuam Herald* captures my feelings and memories perfectly, and his words are worth quoting in full:

Magnificent minors from Galway and Kerry made Gaelic football sparkle in the October drizzle at Croke Park, where they mastered dismal conditions to make this replay not merely the highlight of the Minor Championship but the greatest Minor final for many years.

And it was a tremendously exciting finish to a razor-edge game that started at a breakneck pace, slowed down a little, and then accelerated almost to the limit of endurance. These lads gave everything they had in a battle royale for the All-Ireland crown.

The difference being Jarlath Burke, as a Galway man, had very different feelings to mine come the final whistle. Though I was disappointed, I was enormously proud of what we had achieved, and in the coming years, I would see many of my predictions regarding the players' potential come true. We not only had a few future All-Ireland winners in our midst, but seven! Seven players from the 1970 minor team would go to enjoy All-Ireland senior glory: Paudie O'Mahony, Mickey 'Ned' O'Sullivan, Ger O'Keeffe, Jimmy Deenihan, Paudie Lynch, Ger Power, and John Egan all won Senior All-Ireland medals for Kerry. Some of them would become integral parts of Kerry's famous four-in-a-row winning team, which won four consecutive All-Ireland senior titles between the years 1978 and 1981. Some of the players I trained, including Paudie O'Mahony, a wonderful goalkeeper from the Dingle Peninsula, and Jimmy Deenihan, the sole North Kerry representative on my minor team, would go on to win five All-Ireland senior medals.

Despite my success as a manager and chairperson, there was still the small matter of the £300 debt. Since I became chairperson, I had brainstormed various ways to clear the debt. It was a frightful amount of money and it inhibited our development as a divisional board.

To help, I decided to utilise my various contacts in the United States. I had built up an extensive network of contacts from my time running the Red Mill. Whenever I hosted a big, showband star in the Bronx, be it Brendan Boyer or Dickie Rock, I often arranged for them to play in other venues across the United States. In addition to managing the Mill, I eventually doubled as a showband tour manager, liaising with other ballroom owners in cities across the United States, in locations as far-flung as Cleveland, Detroit, Washington,

D.C. and Philadelphia. I could, for example, be hosting Dickie Rock in the Mill one weekend, arranging for him to play in Buffalo, New York the next weekend, Boston the weekend after that, and so on.

I had, as a result, a good working relationship with the Irish ballroom owners in most of the bigger American cities, and I decided to use this to our advantage. The idea was to arrange a series of club football matches in locations across the United States. We would take a Kerry club 'All-Star', comprising of one star player from each of the Kerry clubs, and arrange matches against some of the top GAA clubs in America. In addition to the North Kerry Board receiving a percentage from the takings at the gate, the ticket sales from each match, I intended to arrange for showbands to play in local venues on the night of each game.

It necessitated a lot of organising and planning and as I was also running the Hibernian and Kiely and Bros Garage at this time, I remember being very busy for a few months. We were also of course taking a financial risk. While I felt both the games and the concerts would be a success, flying the teams over to America and flying them onto the various cities for the games would come at a considerable expense.

Flying a player from Shannon to New York could have cost us £60, and therefore the cost of flying the entire All-Star team would exceed the actual debt.

I had chartered jets successfully in the past however, and I explored the possibility of flying the team to America on a chartered flight. It paid off! I charted a flight from Shannon to New York through Pan Am, and it helped make the project financially feasible. One of the great advantages of charting a jet is it reduces the per head cost considerably. Charting your own flights, as opposed to booking on a standard commercial flight, does require additional organisation and planning, however. I was filling out forms and liaising between staff at Shannon and New York airports for weeks, but it was worth it. When the various costs were broken down, it transpired that we actually flew the 'Kerry Clubs All-Star' team to America for free!

When I first suggested chartering flights to and from America, while I was managing the Kerry Juniors, people laughed at me. I had the last laugh, however. Chartering flights turned out to be a great success and I created opportunities for people to fly to and from Ireland at a reduced cost.

Having flown teams via charter jet previously, including the New York Kerry Juniors, I was eager to do something similar with the Kerry club players, who had contributed so much to football in the county. Each club in North Kerry could nominate two players they had deemed to have made an invaluable contribution.

The chartering option worked to great effect for the Kerry Club 'All Stars'. Our flights from Shannon to New York and back were both chartered and for the various domestic flights I purchased a 'Discover America' ticket, which enabled me to get a reduced rate per head. I flew the team to play games in locations across the United States, places like Buffalo, Boston, Cleveland and Washington, D.C.. I also arranged for the players to stay with Irish-American families in the various cities, and that provided more opportunities for the different Irish communities to bond and to get to know each other.

The games sold well, and the ballrooms those nights after the games were full. People had doubted me when I was unexpectedly nominated as chairperson, largely on account of my young age, but I had exceeded their expectations.

The takings from the All-Star games were more than enough to clear our debt, and we even had a little to spare! We invested the extra money into refurbishing and modernising our facilities. At the time, many of our clubs didn't have proper facilities and dressing rooms. Some of our players had to suffer the indignity of changing in their cars before matches and I hated the sight of it. I thought it was a disgrace and vowed to change it when I became chairperson, and I did.

The Kerry All-Stars before boarding their chartered flight in JFK Airport, New York. The team would play in stadiums in locations such as Buffalo New York, Boston, Cleveland, Washington D.C. and Chicago. The photo is courtesy of Pan American World Airways.

We organised the American trips again the following year, with each Kerry club nominating two star players to represent them. The following year I arranged for Nita Norry, a famous showband singer, to accompany us on our tour, and she sold out crowds in ballrooms across the United States. This helped cover the costs of the trip.

Another initiative of mine while chairperson was the establishment of a juvenile board. I really felt the GAA was not providing enough opportunities for very young kids to play. I always felt that allowing kids to play football and hurling as part of a disciplined team with regular training and practice sessions would have enormous benefits for both them and the GAA as they grew up. Other sports had under-16 and under-14 levels, and I couldn't see why the GAA should be any different.

Luckily for me, Fr Linnane, an enthusiastic and forward-thinking priest, became chairperson of the newly established Juvenile Board and he shared my views on the matter. The Kerry Juvenile Board, which had responsibility for arranging matches at under-16 and under-14 levels. I followed suit and established the North Kerry Juvenile Board with his brother, Joe Linnane.

Looking back, it is remarkable how many people commented to me that I was being a little too ahead of our time, and the idea may never catch on. My response was that we were in actual fact twenty years behind. Other sports saw the potential in juvenile leagues and competitions, particularly soccer, which would provide stiff competition for the GAA in the coming years and decades. I'm happy to say that I was proved right in that assessment as, today, juvenile football and hurling flourishes in Kerry and other parts of the country.

Managing the Kerry Minors and chartering the Kerry All-Stars team to America for a series of exhibition games was perhaps the peak of my time with the GAA. It was also, unfortunately, my undoing. Far from silencing my critics, it only incensed them. The success of the Kerry All-Stars games caused some influential people to become even more resentful of me.

I wanted to continue and expand on the chartered flights venture, taking more teams and players to America. It had been a great success on all accounts, it helped generate funds and it helped create some fantastic sporting and cultural events. The GAA top brass was opposed to the idea, however, and sought to develop their own All-Stars format. In the years that followed, I got the distinct impression that I was no longer wanted, and I made the difficult decision to end my involvement with the GAA.

While this was a sad moment for me personally, I have no

The wonderful Nita Norry, showband singer. Nita accompanied the Kerry All-Stars on their tour of the United States, performing sellout concerts in locations such as Boston, Cleveland and Chicago which were staged after the GAA games.

regrets. Ever since the day I arrived in Gaelic Park to train for the Kerry Juniors, I had loved every minute of it. I had achieved so much, trained future All-Ireland winners, and I worked with some fantastic individuals: John 'Kerry' O'Donnell, Dr Jim Brosnan and Mick O'Connell, to name but three.

I am also happy to say that while I parted company with the GAA, other members of my family continued to be actively involved. Around this time my two brothers, Pat and Denis, had emigrated to New York and were competing in football matches over there; Denis played for Kerry under-21s, and Pat with the Kerry Juniors. They were both fine footballers and it came as no surprise to me that they remained actively involved with the GAA in the coming years. Denis would later become chairman of Tarbert football club, and Pat would enjoy success as a player for Tarbert.

It was disappointing to end my involvement in football, but I still had hunger in my belly. The economic situation changed for the worse in the seventies unfortunately, and I therefore had plenty to occupy myself with.

Dublin Bound

The seventies hit me hard, financially. As I have written previously, the American and Irish government's mutual decision to cap Irish immigration into the United States had a devastating impact on the nightclub scene across the Atlantic. By the early seventies, I had left the nightclub and entertainment business in America entirely. My brother Tim remained involved somewhat, but I took a step back to concentrate on our businesses in Ireland. All was not well on the Irish front either.

Ballybunion continued to develop into the seventies, with its beautiful beaches and scenic walks attracting holidaymakers from Kerry, Limerick and further afield, but it was a very seasonal trade from a business perspective. I closed my hotel, the Hibernian Hotel on Main Street Ballybunion, for the winter months, as it was impossible to make a good trade.

Then tragedy struck! The Hibernian Ballroom went up in flames. It was an accidental fire, but it was a terrible end to a venture I had invested so much time and energy into. I would rebuild the ballroom later, and while it wasn't entirely a success the second time around, I am glad I rebuilt it after the fire. It showed resilience and toughness. Character traits I have valued throughout my life.

During this time, an opportunity arose for managing another ballroom. A friend of mine called Oliver Barry suggested I inquire into leasing a certain ballroom on Camden Street in Dublin. I made an appointment to see the owner of the said ballroom, a man by the name of Tom Ivory.

I remember the first day I met Tom. It was a cold winter's day in Dublin. Tom greeted me outside the door and invited me in. It was some contrast to my initial reception at the Red Mill. In Dublin, I received some Irish hospitality. I followed Tom into a kitchen area, where tea, sandwiches and cake were laid out.

Tom, dressed in a long tweed coat, didn't look like a Dublin man, and I told him as much. It transpired he was from Wexford, which proved to be a good conversation starter. Tom was very much involved in his local hurling club in Wexford and had a deep love of the game. He was very interested in my various activities with the GAA, particularly my management of the New York Kerry Juniors in 1970. Wexford had lost the Senior Hurling All-Ireland Championship final in 1970, and I could see Tom was still sore over it.

After tea, he offered to show me around. I felt things were going very well, and I was impressed by what I saw of the venue. I did think it needed a paint job, and the stage needed to be extended to accommodate my needs, but other than that I was very much impressed. I was particularly impressed by the ballroom floor. I stomped on it to check for its quality; something I always did when viewing potential premises to lease.

Tom laughed when I insisted on viewing every toilet and outhouse in the building. I explained how I had been in the nightclub game for many years, and that I had learned one or two things about leasing nightclubs. I had rented nightclubs in the United States only to lose money when structural problems were identified after I signed the lease.

The ballroom was operational at the time, with Tom opening it on both weeknights and weekends. From what I could gather, he did a reasonably good trade. He hosted agricultural events on Wednesday nights and Garda dances on Sunday nights. At the time I visited, the two prime weekend slots, Friday and Saturday nights, were vacant.

I was very interested in leasing the ballroom from him for both Friday and Saturday nights. Tom explained he was eager to host a nurses' dance on Friday nights, following a similar format to the already successful Garda dance, but he was willing to lease the ballroom to me on Saturday night.

I told him I wanted it, but Tom, I was to discover, drove a hard bargain. He was willing to lease the ballroom to me, but on terms and conditions I didn't like.

Joe Dolan was one of the most innovative and beloved of showband singers, achieving both national and international acclaim. Dan was proud to host Joe at both his Dublin and Ballybunion ballrooms. Joe also serenaded fans in Dan Kiely's lively New York ballroom, the Red Mill.

I explained to him that I wanted to host some of the top singers and showbands in the country. I wanted household names like Dickie Rock, Tom McBride ('Big Tom') and Joe Dolan. It was a big venue situated in the heart of Dublin's south city centre. I felt we needed big names to fill it. Tom's method of working was to pay performers a set fee, rather than a percentage of the takings at the door, which was usually their favoured method of payment. I explained to Tom why these terms really didn't work for me. The kind of singers and performers I wanted to attract, would almost certainly insist on a percentage of the takings.

Tom was stubborn, however, and he refused to change how he remunerated the performers and singers. I suggested that he continue with his method of payment for the nights he operated the venue, which would have been every night except Saturday, and I have my own method of payment for the nights I lease the ballroom. I thought it was a reasonable suggestion, especially as I would be the leaseholder and manager for that Saturday night, and therefore accepting all liabilities for that night.

Tom Ivory was a stubborn Wicklow man, however, and while I got on great with him, and we became great friends, he was a tough man to bargain with.

When I sat in my car, I was convinced the ballroom was a good prospect, but I hadn't reached an agreement with Tom. During our conversation, I had passed a remark about Tom's long, tweed coat, and in response, he mentioned that he was interested in hunting.

This was something we had in common. My love for hunting had started early. Growing up in Tarbert, accompanied by my two friends Cormac and Johnny, I would chase wild rabbits with our terrier and a hound borrowed from one of our neighbours. The taste for the sport stayed with me into adulthood and when I returned from the United States, I took up pheasant shooting. I found it very enjoyable, and it provided a welcome distraction from the often stressful life of running various ballrooms and businesses.

It just so happened that Tom Ivory was involved with a hunting syndicate in Wexford, and one of his favourite pastimes was pheasant hunting. While we had not been able to reach any agreement over the leasing of the ballroom, we had got on very well, and I wasn't surprised when he suggested I visit him in Wexford for some pheasant hunting.

I took him up on his offer some weeks later. I accompanied his syndicate on a hunting trip through the hills around Mount Leinster, situated on the Wexford/Carlow border. I was fitted out with a long, tweed coat for the occasion, and I got on very well with all the syndicate members, Tom included. I returned the favour by inviting Tom on a hunting trip to Kerry, which he accepted.

We hosted Tom in the Ballybunion hotel, and like many people visiting the Kerry seaside town for the first time, he was very much struck by its beauty. To this day, I think Ballybunion Beach is one of the most fabulous beaches in the entire country, and it is no surprise it has become such a celebrated holiday destination.

Over a dinner of locally caught salmon in the Hibernian, I remember trying to twist Tom's arm when it came to his terms and conditions, but the man was not for turning! I eventually gave in and agreed to lease the ballroom on his terms and conditions, that each singer or band I contracted to perform would be paid a set, advanced fee.

Looking back, I think I should have bargained harder or refused his offer outright, but, as I have said, the seventies were economically tough. I had a growing family and I needed an extra source of income. Tom and I shook on it that night, and Camden Street was about to get the Dan Kiely treatment.

For much of the coming year, I was commuting from Kerry to Dublin regularly, and I poured all my energy into making a success of Tom Ivory's ballroom. Tom did permit me to make the necessary renovations. We gave the inside a lick of paint, and I extended and re-floored the stage. Observing the new stage after its completion, I remember thinking, yes, it was finally fit to host some of the biggest names in the showband world.

As I had feared, however, Tom's terms were a real impediment in securing the big names. One of the first performers I approached was Dickie Rock. I had hosted Dickie Rock and the Miami Showband in the Red Mill in the Bronx when they were not an established name stateside. To return the favour, they performed for me in the Hibernian Hotel and the Hibernian Ballroom in Ballybunion. By the time I leased the Camden Street venue in the early seventies, Dickie Rock and the Miami Showband were massive household names, with many of their most famous songs loved and celebrated in houses up and down the country. These included 'Come Back to Stay', which Dickie sang at the Eurovision in 1966, and 'Every Step of the Way', which saw Dickie Rock and the Miami Showband become the first Irish artists to go straight to number one in the UK and Ireland.

The Final Count

Having hosted Dickie Rock in both Ballybunion and the Bronx, I knew the amount of excitement and enthusiasm he could generate. I had seen him dance and sing on stage in front of thousands of screaming and screeching fans. People often talk of 'Beatlemania', referring to the kind of hysteria generated by the pop group, the Beatles. Well, in the Ireland of the sixties and seventies, there was certainly Dickie-Mania!

It would, of course, be wrong to mention my associations with the Miami Showband without mentioning the tragedy that befell them. In 1975, while returning to Dublin from a concert in Northern Ireland, their bus was stopped by armed members of the UVF, the Ulster Volunteer Force, a paramilitary organisation. Three members of the Miami Showband were killed. The atrocity scarred the nation.

Dickie Rock had actually parted ways from the Miami Showband in 1973, two years before the terrible atrocity. By the time I contacted Dickie, inquiring as to whether he would perform for me in Camden Street, he was performing and touring as a solo singer. As it happened, Dickie turned me down after I made several attempts to persuade him to perform, and for exactly the reason I feared, he wanted a percentage of the takings. All the major singers and performers' agents insisted on those terms.

English comedian and actor Richard ('Dick') Emery was one of the most famous and crowd-pleasing acts Dan brought to Ballybunion.

I also remember contacting Joe Dolan, who I had a great relationship with. Joe Dolan and The Drifters had performed in the Red Mill for their maiden tour of America in 1965. Joe Dolan's 'Make Me an Island' was one of the biggest and most loved songs in Ireland during the early seventies. I would have given anything to hear Joe's beautiful voice in my Camden Street ballroom. I got in touch with Joe's agent, but, unfortunately, I received the same answer I had from Dickie Rock's representatives: receiving a percentage of the takings was a non-negotiable condition.

This, unsurprisingly, had an impact on takings, as I was limited to small up-and-coming bands. I struggled for the first few months, attracting crowds of about 600 or thereabouts, and that was in a venue with a maximum capacity of 2,000. In the beginning, I was really only managing to break even. As the rent was £200, when bills, wages and other expenses including the band's fee were included, I didn't have a whole pile left over.

The one thing going for me was that Kerry was enjoying success in the All-Ireland Football Championship during this period. Kerry people would therefore descend on Dublin in droves for the All-Ireland semi-finals and finals. As many were familiar with me from Ballybunion, many were eager to give me a turn and knew I would put on a good show. For one All-Ireland Sunday, I had managed to finally persuade Dickie Rock to play. After years of haggling over the terms and conditions, he agreed to perform for me. I was very excited and I knew having him perform on the night of the All-Ireland would make for a fantastic occasion.

Three weeks before his scheduled appearance however, I got a call from one of his representatives. He had pulled out, and to add to the indignity of it, he had agreed to perform for a competitor of mine on the very same night, the night Kerry was playing in the All-Ireland final, a competitor who was just down the road from me.

It was humiliating. I am not one to wallow in my sorrows, however, and I went about arranging an alternative.

After some consideration, I decided to take a risk. Life is full of risks after all, and I was never afraid to try my luck. I decided to contact the Mulcahy brothers. Founded in Mitchelstown, Cork by Maurice Mulcahy in 1952, the Maurice Mulcahy Band was a traditional orchestral octet. The main members were brothers Maurice, Mike and Joe Mulcahy, who played the trumpet, the baritone saxophone and the clarinet respectively.

They were one of the first internationally recognised dance bands to play in Ballybunion, being a regular feature in the Central Ballroom in Ballybunion in the 1950s. They toured extensively in England, playing in locations such as Kentish Town, Fulham Broadway and The Shamrock in Birmingham. My old friend Bill Fuller was very familiar with them, having hosted them in his Buffalo nightclub in Camden High Street, and it may well have been Bill who initially introduced me to Maurice Mulcahy. Maurice died tragically in 1963, but Joe, Mike and the other members of the Mulcahy family continued to perform and play. They had a very different style of music compared to showbands like the Miami Showband. Their music had more in common with traditional orchestral music, with baritones and trumpets, although they had their own unique sound, blending different variations of dance music. The band's official website describes their music as:

The type of sound produced by the band would consist of several sounds in the course of one dance, containing Glen Miller, Latin America and Dixieland music.

More importantly, from my perspective at the time, was the fact that they were enormously popular throughout Munster, particularly in North Kerry and Ballybunion, where their performances in the

Central Ballroom and later, my Hibernian Ballroom, were legendary. The risk was, they did not have a very big following in Dublin, but as it was All-Ireland Sunday, and I predicted my patrons would largely be Kerry people, I decided to take a punt on them.

I was nervous that Saturday, and I had every reason to be. I will never forget walking up Camden Street at seven o'clock that evening and seeing a long queue outside my competitor's ballroom, where Dickie Rock was scheduled to play. When I went to check on how things were progressing in my own ballroom, my heart sank. There was no one waiting outside and inside it was virtually empty.

It had been a hard few years, with my Hibernian Ballroom going up in smoke, and the economic downturn affecting my other businesses. I spoke too soon however, because when I left the bar and returned to the nightclub, I was delighted to see that a large crowd had formed outside the venue.

It didn't stop there, either, the people kept trickling in. My risk had paid off. I had bargained on them to attract their loyal Munster following and I was right. One thing all my years in the nightclub business has taught me is: you have to know the needs of your patrons and customers, you have to give them what they want. That particular night I guessed right, and it didn't come too soon, I was due a little luck. For my next business venture, I very much had to make my own luck.

Running with the Hounds

In 1976, I saw another business opportunity and decided to try my luck. Like many of my business ventures through the years, it grew out of a pastime. I have already mentioned how Tom Ivory and I shared a passion for hunting, pheasant hunting in particular. If we didn't have that pastime in common, we may never have had the positive working relationship we had at the Olympic Ballroom. Hunting already, by '76, opened opportunities for me, and it was about to do so again.

Kerry and West Limerick are ideal hunting grounds, largely because of their large, wild pheasant population. The hunting season began in November, and extended into the year, which meant that just before Christmas and after, my friends and I would hit for the glens and hills of North Kerry on pheasant hunting expeditions. It was a fantastic sport and, as I mentioned previously, a much needed distraction from all the pressures of business.

I always preferred to hunt pheasants that had been reared in the wild, as opposed to those bred in sporting estates, like the one Tom Ivory's hunting syndicate was affiliated to. In the seventies however, the pheasant population began to decline dramatically, on account of the birds being hunted by foxes.

Many felt that the local fox population needed to be culled, and so we began hunting more of them in an effort to reduce their numbers. There are about 200,000 wild foxes currently in Ireland, and I would hazard a guess that there were even more of them back then, so the prospect of foxes going extinct was never even a remote possibility.

I was a pretty adept hunter at that stage, and having rubbed shoulders with some very proficient hunters over the years, I had learned some advanced techniques. I had, for example, a small sound device which could be used to lure foxes towards the traps. I had been introduced to it by the Burnham brothers in Marble Falls, Texas, and we used it to great effect when hunting in Kerry. The device released a similar sound to that of the rabbit or hare and lured the foxes towards the snares we had set for them.

It was while hunting foxes that the thought occurred to me that there must be a market for fox furs and pelts. After killing the foxes, we would load them into a trailer, and from there they would be transported to an incinerator. It dawned on me what a terrible waste this was, as foxes have such beautiful, colourful pelts, and I often thought to myself that surely there must be a market somewhere for fox pelts.

I did a little research, and I discovered that there was indeed a high demand for fox furs, particularly in countries like Sweden and Norway, countries with long winters where the wearing of fur was a practical necessity.

I got in touch with an Englishman by the name of Jeffery King, who had a tanning operation in England. He was excited about the prospect of working with me. He explained to me that his expertise lay in the tanning of pelts, and he struggled to find good, reliable suppliers. I explained to him the situation in Ireland, where we had a large wild fox population, and I suggested he buy a batch from me. He agreed and I got to work.

I soon discovered that skinning foxes is actually quite an elaborate process, requiring no small measure of skill and ingenuity. Luckily for me, I managed to source a local man by the name of Patrick O'Sullivan, who was interested in getting involved in the business with me. With the assistance of Jeffery in England, Patrick and I learned

Dan pictured with his business partner Jeffery King, behind a pile of 'sleeved' fox furs.

the technique together. After I delivered a batch of carcasses, Patrick and I would get to work. We used a process known as 'sleeving', which entailed making large incisions on certain points of the pelt, before slipping the fur off the animal while keeping the fur intact. Patrick and I needed several practice runs to get it right, as it entailed making a series of very precise incisions and manoeuvres. In order to remove the pelt from around the face, for example, we would have to make two triangular cuts on either side of the jawline. The fur around the tail would have to be removed with two sticks.

After the pelt was removed, Patrick would remove the flesh from the underside of the pelt with a small, sharp instrument known as a tanning brush. We would then peg the pelt to a board, and it was only then that we could begin the drying process. It was essential to dry the pelt as quickly as possible to avoid putrefaction.

After the pelts were dried thoroughly, I would arrange for them to be mailed and delivered to Jeffery in England. When Jeffery received the pelt, he would begin the tanning process, which was another elaborate and painstaking procedure. It involved dousing the pelts in large tanning baths, before drying and conditioning them, after which they were finally ready to be delivered to the furriers in Norway and Sweden, where they would be made into fur coats and other clothing accessories.

The first step in the process was salting. But then we ran into difficulties. The pelts began leaking in the post! Whatever way we were salting the furs the residue was leaking through the packaging, which was, understandably, causing difficulties for the people delivering them. The postal service eventually refused to deliver the furs unless I rectified the problem. This came as a disappointment to all of us involved, Jeffery King included, as he saw me as one of his best and most reliable suppliers.

Jeffery decided to visit us in Kerry to help find a solution. I met my business partner for the first time when I collected him from Shannon Airport, and when I saw him strolling through the arrivals lounge, I remember thinking to myself, here is a man who looks the part. Jeffery was big and imposing, boasted an English moustache, and, true to form, he arrived wearing a long fur coat. The clothes he is wearing in the photo reproduced here, where he is pictured with me next to a batch of skinned pelts, was exactly how he was dressed when he arrived off the plane, and he made a distinct impression on everyone in Kerry. He was loud, hearty and passionate about the fur trade.

His solution to our leaking problem did not really work for me, however. He showed me an alternative way of salting the pelts. Rather than massaging the salt over the inside of the pelt, his solution was to inset them into large, wooden barrels, and leave them stew in the salt. I didn't like this method, however. Having a barrel for each pelt would be expensive, not to mention the fact it would add to storage and maintenance costs. While the fox pelts were a viable business, the margins were not wide enough to carry additional cleaning, maintenance and storage costs, which would be necessary if I followed Jeffery's methods.

When Jeffery returned to England, I explored other solutions. I decided against using this method of salting, opting instead to dry the pelts thoroughly. I built an extension in the back garden of my house, purposely for the drying of the pelts. After Patrick had them skinned, we pegged them to large boards and sorted them overnight in the extension, where they were thoroughly dried by electric fans. The method worked. The leakages stopped. The postal service was happy to deliver my pelts again and Jeffery received them in perfect condition.

By that time, several of my friends and extended family members were involved in the business, and all of them were needed.

I still have fond memories of our hunting expeditions, which nearly always took place at night, as foxes are nocturnal animals. When business was good, I could afford to pay people £3 per fox, and our average kill was thirty foxes per night. This was a great wage for a night's work, especially since I also covered any additional expenses, including transport and ammunition.

I did very well out of the fox fur business, particularly in the mid to late seventies, after I had established myself in the trade, and found the most effective method for skinning and preserving the pelts.

In the mid to late seventies, I typically got about £20 per fox pelt, and since I was selling between 10,000 and 15,000 pelts per year, it was a good return. I eventually had enough knowledge of the industry to make it worth my while to buy already dried pelts from other fox traders in Ireland, which I would then auction through the Hudson Bay Company in England. In the eighties however, the demand for fur decreased on account of a combination of various factors, including growing awareness of animal rights.

By 1984, I had left the fox fur business. By that time, I had entered an entirely different line of work. For some, fox fur trading is a grisly business, but, take it from me, it has nothing on Irish politics.

The Best of Times
& the Worst of Times

I had my hands full with the Olympic Ballroom, but believe it or not, it wasn't the only ballroom I ran in the seventies. The fire at the Hibernian Ballroom was a travesty, but I wasn't about to give up on Ballybunion. The beauty of its natural landscapes and the buzz of the town in the summer made it a special place. Other businesses of mine were going well, including Arthur's nightclub in Tralee, which my brother Tim managed and ran in the winter when I was concentrating on the fox fur business, while I ran it in the summer. It did a great trade during both seasons.

I was delighted when an opportunity arose to get back into the ballroom business in Ballybunion. I had heard that Tommy Horan, owner of the Atlantic Hotel, was eager to lease the hotel's sizeable and popular ballroom. I was lucky in the respect that I had always enjoyed a good, working relationship with my fellow hoteliers and business people in Ballybunion, and Tommy and I were therefore able to come to a good arrangement. Tommy would continue operating the hotel, while I would take over the managing and operation of the ballroom, similar to the arrangement I had with Tom Ivory at the Olympic.

Staying true to form, I went about making the necessary changes and renovations to the building, extending the dance floor and ensuring everything was in working order before the summer holidaymakers came swarming in.

By the time I took over the Atlantic, I had many years of experience in the management and running of ballrooms and nightclubs under my belt, and my approach was more refined as a result. I was also blessed at this point, in having a good relationship with some of Ireland's best and most loved bands and performers. This was another reason why Tommy was so eager to lease the Atlantic Ballroom to me.

He was particularly eager for me to secure a deal with a one man band called Johnny Barrett, and I didn't blame him. Johnny is perhaps no longer a household name, but he was much loved in the Ballybunion of the sixties and seventies.

Johnny Barrett's story illustrates just how important the ballroom business was for Ireland's performers and entertainers. It not only provided them with a platform through which they could reach thousands of adoring fans, but also a means of earning a living from their music.

When I first met the great Johnny Barrett, he was juggling live performances with his job in Cork County Council. He was making about six or seven pounds a week in his county council position, and on a good night in the Hibernian or the Atlantic, I could afford to pay Johnny six or seven times that amount, freeing him to concentrate more on his music and his live performances, which he eventually did.

Johnny's musical hero was Elvis Presley, and he would often play some of Elvis' hits on requests, which always proved to be great crowd pleasers. Hits like 'Are You Lonesome Tonight?' and 'Can't Help Falling in Love with You' would go down a treat with counting couples that would come to the Hibernian, and later the Atlantic, to dance and enjoy the summer.

I think Johnny even modelled himself on his mentor, particularly the outrageous dress sense. He would often arrive at the Hibernian or the Atlantic wearing colourful shirts and flipped up collars, he may have even sported a pair of blue suede shoes on occasion. This all added to the excitement and the atmosphere, and I think it probably contributed to Johnny's immense popularity.

I am very happy to write that not only did Johnny work for me, but I took over the complete management of his career. I secured him concerts and opportunities in America, as I did for other artists, including the likes of Butch Moore, Danny Doyle and Dermot Henry.

Charles Dickens famously said, 'It was the best of times, it was the worst of times'. That line really resonates with me when I think back on my life in the seventies. I certainly had my ups and downs, and many of the fantastic performers and singers I worked with had similarly mixed fortunes.

I was so happy to see Johnny's career take off after I gave him his initial break in Ballybunion. Tragedy, however, would strike Johnny and his wife Ann when their young son Pat died from cancer. Pat was Johnny and Ann's only child, and he was just beginning to emulate his father in pursuing an interest in music and performing. It was a dreadful tragedy to happen to such a wonderful man.

It wasn't of course the only tragedy to befall some of the musicians and performers I had worked with. I have already mentioned the terrible killings of the Miami Showband members in 1975, who, along with their lead singer Dickie Rock, frequently performed in ballrooms I managed.

There was another great singer and musician I hosted in Ballybunion who was struck by tragedy, but before I tell you about that, let me tell you a little bit about him. Roy Orbison is today considered one of America's greatest singers, songwriters

Considered one of the godfathers of rock and roll, and one of America's most innovative entertainers, Roy Orbison performed to sellout crowds in Dan's Hibernian Ballroom twice in 1968.

and live performers, and, along with Chuck Berry and Elvis Presley, a leading pioneer of 'rock n roll' music.

Believe it or not, I was honoured to host him in Ballybunion, not once, but twice! It might be surreal for some to imagine Roy Orbison, dressed in black and sporting his distinctive Fender guitar, performing songs like 'Only the Lonely', 'In Dreams', and 'Crying' in front of thousands of fans in my Hibernian Ballroom, but in the summer of 1968, that is precisely what happened. Like many of the greats of American music however, his life was touched by tragedy. It was an awful tragedy and, looking back at my life of hosting and managing bands and performers, I can't help feeling sometimes that perhaps the music business was cursed.

His wife Claudette had died in a motorbike accident some years before he visited us, and in September of the year he visited, only months after performing for us, he received the news that his two eldest sons had died in a house fire.

My story doesn't end there, however. While it must have been hard to find any reason to live after such a terrible tragedy, Roy Orbison, I am happy to say, taught me something about human nature. I only met the man twice, but I have very fond memories of our meetings. He taught me something about resilience, and how the human spirit can fight on despite some awful setbacks. Two years later, in 1970, much to my shock, I heard that Roy Orbison was touring Ireland and Britain again. I couldn't believe it. I thought such a tragedy would knock a man out. To this day, I still find Orbison's resilience remarkable. He returned to the Hibernian that summer of 1970, and played one of the best shows I ever had the honour of hosting. People remember that tour from something he did some weeks after he left Ballybunion. He played in two different venues on the same night: pleasing fans in Granemore Carnival in Co Armagh, in the evening, before crossing the border into the twenty-six counties, to play in the Adelphi Theatre in Dundalk. He was a remarkably spirited man, and certainly an inspiration to anyone who faces tragedy in their lives; a reminder that there is always light at the end of the tunnel, no matter how dark things may seem.

It was fitting perhaps that many of the people I worked with encountered tragedy in one form or another. I also faced some personal difficulties in the seventies, and just like Roy Orbison, while away on business I got some awful news. I remember being in London, arranging for the sale of fox pelts through the Hudson Bay company, when I heard 'phone call for Mr Dan Kiely' on the intercom.

It concerned my wife, Mary. She had just suffered a massive brain haemorrhage and was in intensive care. I rushed back to Ireland as quickly as I could. It was an enormously stressful time. I was worried for the welfare of my wife, but I was also worried for my children.

Mary and I had three children at that stage, and my wife was pregnant with our fourth. When I arrived back, I insisted that Mary be transferred to Richmond Hospital. I remember spending many agonising hours in the hospital waiting room, patiently waiting while the consultants examined Mary. When the doctor finally called me in I could tell from his face that things were not good.

'Tell me straight now doctor, no beating around the bush.' That was always how I liked things done. I preferred people to be honest and upfront in difficult times. If things were bad, I needed to hear the unvarnished truth. To his credit, the consultant was upfront with me. An angiogram revealed Mary had a growth in her brain and he recommended surgery. He explained that Mary's chances were fifty-fifty. If they didn't operate, she could die, and would almost certainly be left with permanent brain damage; while if they did operate there was a risk of death. It was a terrible choice.

The growth was apparently the size of a half-crown, but as small as it was, it was endangering the life of both my wife and our young child she was carrying, so I decided to consent to the procedure. The odds were not good, but I felt that Mary had the best doctors , and that was the course they were advising. They operated on Mary that night. After another agonising wait, they finally returned and the news was mixed. The operation had been a success, but Mary had suffered significant, albeit temporary, memory loss. She was also going to be immobilised for a considerable period of time. Mary had a long road to recovery ahead of her, but I knew my wife was strong.

The years immediately following the procedure were difficult for my wife and for us as a family. She eventually recovered most of her memory, but she would be tormented by seizures. With my wife recuperating from her injuries, my next dilemma was how to look after my children. During those years I was allotted the role of single father. My various business interests were still taking up so much of my time. Between the fox fur business and managing the various clubs and ballrooms, I was already very stretched. Yet, not one to complain, I got down to it and I looked after my children while my wife recovered.

After the operation, Mary gave birth to our fourth child, our daughter, Eileen, and that helped raise all our spirits. As had happened on many previous occasions in my life, I was lucky to have the support of my family and friends. In hindsight, I don't think I could have survived that turbulent period without them by my side.

I am particularly indebted to a cousin of ours, a wonderful, selfless woman called Kathleen O'Brien, from Ballylongford. I would be away most weekends, driving to Dublin to manage the Olympic Ballroom. Whenever I returned, Kathleen would always have the place spotless. All the beds would be made and the washing was done. She also helped look after our children while I was away until I eventually hired a full-time housekeeper to take care of the house and care for our children. I don't think I would have survived those years without Kathleen. Despite Kathleen's, and later the housekeeper's, very best efforts, however, there is no doubt I was needed more at home while Mary was recovering.

I had a young daughter to look after and, as anyone who has young children will know, they consume all of your time, God bless them! I was forced to settle into the role of the full-time Dad.

In retrospect, I do wonder what effect being without the support of her mother had on my youngest daughter. It would have been obvious to everyone, even from the way her hair was parted at school, that it was her dad rather than her mam who was on parental duties, washing her face and dressing her for school. It was a difficult time for all of us, but perhaps my youngest daughter felt it the most.

I'm very happy to write that Eileen is now the leasee and manager of a thriving cafe in Ballybunion, called The Coast Cafe. Her first years in life were hard, being without her mam, but it didn't hold her back. She has managed to put her Kiely business genes to good use! I am very proud of her, as I am of all our other children. I have already mentioned my daughter Joan's considerable achievements. Noelle is running her own business in Lanzarote; another daughter who inherited those Kiely business genes. Donal worked for me for many years in my business in Lisselton Country Club, and kept the show on the road. Before his recent retirement, he had a very important role in the ESB power station in Tarbert.

To quote Dickens again, the seventies were the worst of times and the best of times. I went through difficulties, as you always do in life, just as many of the singers and performers I worked with were forced to grapple with tragedies of their own. I will never forget the quiet resolve of Roy Orbison. I found him a remarkably humble man and I found his decision to persevere with performing and writing music after going through so many difficulties, inspirational.

I had of course gone through difficulties of my own. The fire that claimed the Hibernian Ballroom and my wife's illness. Many more difficulties were to come, but, like Roy Orbison, I persevered. I still had a fire in my belly and ideas for more business ventures. Another American singer, Hoyt Curtin, sang about the 'gay old times'. Well, I thought it was time to bring the gay old times to Ballybunion!

Gay Old Times

Most people have heard of the Rose of Tralee, the international beauty pageant held annually in Tralee. Some people might be surprised to discover that we hosted an annual pageant in Ballybunion every year, from 1970, up until the early years of this century.

It was a different kind of pageant. Rather than beautiful young women competing for the crown of 'The Rose of Tralee', it was virile young men competing against each other, young bachelors. In 1970, I along with Joe O'Sullivan, Brian Walsh and others founded Ballybunion's International Gay Bachelor Festival.

Every year, a panel of judges would decide who from a group of young, single men was Ireland's most eligible and 'gayest' bachelor. The annual, winning bachelor exemplified the 'best attitude, personality, and broadest outlook on life', but, somewhat like the Rose of Tralee, we wanted, more than anything, our festival to be fun and light-hearted. We wanted people to come to Ballybunion to enjoy themselves, appreciate our beautiful scenery and enjoy a unique, local festival, and I think that is exactly what we provided them with.

Naming the Ballybunion Gay Bachelor of the Year was the climax of the festival, and that usually took place on the final day, in either my Hibernian Ballroom or the Central Ballroom. In addition to the main contests, however, we had various ancillary events and contests, and these proved to be real crowd pleasers.

The maestro in action. Dan Kiely presenting the Ballybunion Gay Bachelor Festival.

Bachelors would compete in tugs of war, donkey races and periwinkle eating contests. Over the years, the periwinkle eating contests generated a lot of publicity, largely because many of our American, British, and Dublin visitors did not know what a periwinkle was, and what exactly we were asking our poor bachelors to consume.

For the benefit of any reader who isn't familiar, periwinkles are small, edible crustaceans, popular in North Kerry. There has been some speculation over the years that they enhance virility, but I will leave you to be the judge of that.

Our bachelors were drawn from across Ireland, and looking back, I am enormously grateful to all of them; they all participated in good sport.

Due to the success of the early festivals, we eventually secured a sponsorship deal with the Guinness Group, and we were then in a position to be more generous with the prize money. An Irish Army Lieutenant called Tommy Kiely (no relation) was the victor in 1973, receiving £500, with an extra £100 bonus being awarded if he succeeded in finding himself a wife within a year.

As well as being more generous, we could afford to be more ambitious as a result of the Guinness Group deal. As with everything I

Legendary broadcaster Gay Byrne presented the awards ceremony at the Ballybunion Bachelor Festival one year. He is pictured here with Dan Kiely, Dan's parents, Dan Sr. and Hannah, and Gay Bryne's wife, broadcaster and harpist Katheleen Watkins.

put my hand to, I was eager for the festival to spread its wings and attract contestants from other parts of the world.

In 1975, my friend and fellow committee member, Kevin Harty, travelled with me to the United States with the intention of attracting more American contestants. Utilising my contacts, we visited cities like New York, Chicago and Pittsburgh. I also arranged the printing of 100,000 brochures, which we distributed across the United States, and it was a very successful trip on all counts.

In the following years, we succeeded in attracting more visitors and contestants from the United States, and just like the Rose of Tralee, the Gay Bachelor Festival became a celebration of the connections between the two countries. To give you an example of just how successful that venture was, when I took over as chairman again in 1983, we had two bachelors from the United States, two from Britain and one from Australia. We also succeeded in attracting contestants from even more far-flung locations. In 1978, for example, we had a bachelor from Luxembourg of all places, and he thoroughly enjoyed himself, excelling in our annual Bachelor Pram Race!

By 1983, we had secured sponsorship from Harp Lager, and that allowed us to take the festival to new heights. Harp was eager for us to expand the 'pram racing', and I could see why. It was different and unique, and certainly something you would be hard-pressed to find anywhere else in the world. The format was bachelors would take turns carrying each other in prams, racing from bar to bar through the village, the winner being the first bachelor pair to have successfully manoeuvred through the various bars and arrived at the finish line.

It may sound a little strange to some readers, but it was tremendous fun, and Harp's patronage meant we could award more generous prizes. In addition to the main prize fund, the winners of the pram racing got a lovely piece of Waterford Crystal.

I was always eager to promote the festival, always looking for new ways to secure national and international publicity. Looking back, I am particularly proud of the fact I secured slots for us on The Late Late Show. It was, and still is, the flagship chat show of RTÉ, Ireland's national broadcaster, and being featured on The Late Late Show gave both the town and the festival a real boost. This was thanks in no small part to the show's presenter, Gay Byrne, who not only agreed to feature us on the show, but agreed to be MC at one of our annual festivals, interviewing the respective bachelors and presenting the winner with his prize.

The photo reproduced here, which features Gay and his wife Kathleen Watkins, with my parents and me, was a proud moment for me. Gay genuinely loved our festival, and I wasn't surprised. All of Kerry's successful festivals, whether it is the Rose of Tralee, Killorglin's Puck Fair, Listowel Writers' Week or Ballybunion's Gay Bachelor Festival when it was at its height, attracted tens of thousands of visitors, precisely because it was unique; you will find nothing like them in any part of the world. Where else other than in Ballybunion, for that one week in June, would you have found young men competing in pram races and periwinkle contests? The answer is nowhere, and many of our visitors, Gay Byrne included, were charmed and intrigued by the novelty of it.

It wasn't all plain sailing of course, it never is. While I got on very well with Gay Byrne, I was at loggerheads with another famous RTÉ presenter, which I will tell you about in a bit. First, to our trip to America, and what happened after we returned. Our trip was a great success. We succeeded in raising the festival's profile in the United States and attracting some American contestants.

In the months and years after Kevin and I returned, however, we began receiving these strange letters from people in America and Europe, accusing me and the committee of promoting homosexuality, an immoral sexual act as they saw it. I was a bit perplexed, until I discovered why. They had misunderstood our use of the word 'Gay' in 'Gay Bachelor Festival'. Gay, to our understanding, which was the most common understanding of the word in Ireland in those days, meant happy and jolly, which was a perfectly apt name for our festival, as we wanted people to come to Ballybunion and enjoy themselves.

Desperate to minimise the bad publicity, we agreed to drop the word 'Gay' and rename the festival The International Ballybunion Bachelor Festival, although it is hard not to laugh when looking back.

Now, to a certain RTÉ television presenter. In addition to promoting the festival in the United States, I was also eager to promote it in Dublin. I was very eager for us to have a float in Dublin's St Patrick's Day parade, and when an opportunity arose, I seized it with both hands. I'm happy to say our St Patrick's Day parade float became a recurring feature, and by 1983, after we had secured sponsorship from Harp. I was eager to do something that little bit special, introduce our city cousins to some good, Kerry humour. I wanted something funny and outrageous that would generate publicity and bring a smile to the faces of children and adults alike.

The winning bachelor receives his prize on RTÉ's The Late Late Show, presented by Gay Byrne.

The committee eventually settled on the idea of having a baby elephant accompany the Ballybunion float, with a sign hanging from its neck that read, 'I Enjoyed my Holiday in Ballybunion'. Having children of my own, I knew the kids would love it, and I also felt adults would appreciate our quirky, Kerry sense of humour.

Arranging to hire an exotic animal is no mean feat, and I remember me and my fellow committee members being forced to fill out endless forms and make endless telephone calls. We eventually struck a deal with Duffy's Circus, where they agreed to lease a baby elephant in their possession. The poor thing died in the months leading up to the parade however, leaving me and the committee in a fix. I tried to arrange a replacement with both Duffy's and Dublin Zoo, but they claimed to have none available.

All through this period I and the festival committee were the subject of jokes from a certain RTÉ radio host by the name of Mike Murphy. On the airwaves, he mocked us poor culchies down in Kerry, particularly over our struggles to secure a baby elephant. At one point he even suggested we paint a cow and attach a petrol pump to its head so that it would resemble an elephant. I remember giving an angry interview to the *Irish Independent* at the time, stating that we were all very offended down in Ballybunion. We had taken it all in good sport, and I am happy to say, we cordially invited Mike Murphy to attend the 1983 Bachelor Festival, which he graciously accepted, and, by all accounts, had a wonderful time.

I have very fond memories of that particular year in fact, as it was the first year of our lucrative sponsorship agreement with Harp. The fabulous Ellen O'Brien presented the trophy to the winning bachelor, and we were also joined by Frank Hall, Joe Cuddy and of course Mike Murphy.

In the years and decades that followed, the festival faded, which was very unfortunate, as I thought we could have created an international festival equal in stature to the Rose of Tralee. Luck was not on our side, however. While it's sad to dwell on what could have been, I am very proud of our achievements as a committee, and I couldn't have achieved what I did achieve without the help of my fellow committee members, including Nuala and Joe Costello, Brian Walsh, Kevin Harty and his daughters, Tim and Pat Buckley, Joe O'Sullivan, Jackie Hourigan, Mariá Finucan and others.

Putting My Hat in the Ring

Some people have told me that fox hunting makes them squeamish. This is unsurprising, it is a 'blood sport' after all. Well, I can tell you that fox hunting is mild compared to what politics in Kerry was like in the seventies and eighties, which certainly was a 'blood sport'.

I initially got involved in politics in the seventies. Between running and managing my various bars and hotels, the car hire business, and the fox pelts operation, I knew first-hand the kind of challenges facing the region. As I have written previously, my father, Dan Kiely Sr was a War of Independence veteran. He was a captain in the Seán Moylan Flying Column, (whose exploits have been immortalised in the book *Kiskeam Versus the Empire*). His brother, and my uncle, Denis Kiely, was also actively involved in the independence struggle during this period and served as a quartermaster for the Seán Moylan Column. Both sided with de Valera and the anti-treaty republicans when Civil War broke out. When de Valera founded Fianna Fáil in 1926, they both transferred their support to the new party.

Fianna Fáil had always been the political home of the Kielys, for as long as I could remember. When my mother asked me as a young fella to approach a politician about my father's transfer, it was to the local Fianna Fáil politician, Dan Moloney, she sent me.

Fianna Fáil was therefore the natural choice for me. Even outside of family loyalties, I felt the issues I was passionate about were Fianna Fáil issues. Having run successful businesses in the North

Dan Kiely, ready to throw his hat into the political ring.

Kerry region, I was eager to see the region industrialised and developed. North Kerry had great potential. Its proximity to the Shannon Estuary made it an ideal location for industries and factories, and I felt that we were not getting the kind of investment we needed and deserved.

Attracting development and creating employment had always been signature Fianna Fáil policies and I felt it was the natural political home for me, or so I thought!

I was also impressed with the North Kerry Fianna Fáil structures on the ground. Everything appeared to work well. The local *cumanns* (the small, grassroots organisations) were very committed and hardworking, and North Kerry's *Comhairle Dáil Ceantair* (the main constituency branch, made up of all the smaller *cumanns* and an executive council) also worked well.

The Fianna Fáil organisation in Kerry was a well-oiled machine, and the results spoke for themselves. In the 1977 general election for example, we polled over 20,000 first preference votes, which was almost sixty percent of all votes cast, which was sufficient to elect two candidates. Kit Ahern and Tom McEllistrim Jr Fine Gael in comparison, (who ran two candidates, Ger Lynch and John Blennerhassett), polled a paltry 8,000 votes.

I soon discovered that not everything was as well as it seemed. I would discover that the hard work and dedication of many good, loyal Fianna Fáil members was being destroyed by petty in-fighting, incompetence, and incorrect use of party funds.

I first ran for a seat in Kerry County Council in 1974, as one of five Fianna Fáil candidates from the Listowel electoral area. Having watched from the sidelines for years, it was great to be involved. I canvassed extensively across the length and breadth of the Listowel electoral area.

Canvassing can give one great insight into how constituents actually think. I wasn't surprised to hear my own fears and worries for the North Kerry region shared by people on the doorsteps. People felt we desperately needed more employment opportunities for young people. They were worried about the scale of emigration to Britain and the United States in particular, and how the young people who did emigrate were not being looked after when they arrived. Another thing that struck me on the canvassing trail was how neglected and abandoned people in the region felt.

There hadn't been, by the time I ran for the council, a Fianna Fáil TD from Listowel and North Kerry for some time, and it showed. Having a local TD is very important in Ireland, as a region inevitably gets more attention and focus from Dublin when it has a sitting TD, and preferably a good one.

I was unsuccessful in my attempt to win a seat on that occasion however. I polled 758 first preference votes and hung on until the seventh count. (For readers unfamiliar, Ireland has what they call a 'proportional representation' electoral system, which means voters vote for several candidates in order of their preference, rather than for one single candidate, as they do in some jurisdictions. For example, a voter gives their first preference to their most preferred candidate, their second to their second, and so on down the list. If there are, for example, twelve candidates on the ballot, it is possible to enter up to twelve preferences. After the counting of the first preferences, if a required number of candidates have not reached the 'quota', [the number necessary to secure election], voters' second preferences are distributed.)

Surviving until the seventh count gave me a first-hand glimpse of the drama and intrigue of our peculiar electoral system. Rather than being turned off, I found the buzz and atmosphere of the counting centres, with tally men going to and fro between boxes, exhilarating. After the election, I was already looking ahead to the local elections of 1979, where I was eager to avoid the mistakes I had made in my first election campaign.

For the 1979 election, I decided to change tactics somewhat. By that stage, I was convinced that the Listowel and North Kerry region was being neglected. Some of it was down to boundaries. The way the North Kerry constituency boundaries were drawn were not favourable to us in the Listowel area. They controversially included Tralee, the largest town. The McEllistrim family had dominated Fianna Fáil politics in the constituency for years, having topped the poll in '61, '65, '69, and '73 (they were to top it again in the '77 and '81 elections). Their heartland was Castleisland in the east of the county, which was regionally and economically far closer to Tralee in the middle of Kerry, than Listowel in the north.

People in the north were therefore neglected. We were lucky in the 1977 general election, as Kit Ahern, a hardworking Fianna Fáil representative from Ballybunion was elected, helping in some way to correct the regional imbalance.

I still felt I had a big role to play. I decided to be a little bit tougher, even if that meant going up against one of the county's most enduring political dynasties, the McEllistrims. I felt that if Listowel and North Kerry didn't fight their corner, they would be bullied. I ran the campaign very much on the issue of roads. I highlighted the fact that other electoral areas in Kerry were receiving far greater amounts of money for the paving and maintenance of roads. This upset a few of my Fianna Fáil colleagues in county buildings in Tralee. They saw my comments as an attack on them, although that is not what I intended. I was drawing people's attention to a fact, an obvious unfairness in the allocation of funds, standing up for my constituents, just as they stood up for theirs. I thought the fact that other parts of Kerry were advantaged in funding was a compliment to them, to their hard work, yet another reason why North Kerry needed better and stronger representation. Many of them did not see it like that and dismissed me as an 'upstart'. They had forgotten the wise, old saying, 'what's good for the goose is good for the gander'.

Dan Kiely pictured with his mother, Mrs Hannah Kiely, while Chairperson of the General Council of County Councils. Dan remains the only politician to hold the position for two consecutive terms.

While my campaign message may not have won me many friends in county buildings in Tralee, it clearly resonated with my North Kerry constituents. I was elected to Kerry County Council. I was also nominated that year to sit on the board of the GCCC, (The General Council of County Councils) an organisation through which I would achieve many things.

In many respects, it was an ideal time to be in politics, as the eighties would prove to be a tough decade for Ireland, and strong, dynamic leadership was more important than ever. In other respects, it was the worst time to be in politics, as the political situation in Dublin was so unstable. In the early eighties it proved almost impossible for any party to form a stable government. There were three general elections in the space of eighteen months: June 1981, February 1982, and November 1982.

Kit Ahern, the Fianna Fáil TD from Ballybunion, was nominated to contest the June 1981 election. I poured all my energy into Kit's campaign, believing that electing her would massively advantage Listowel and North Kerry.

Kit fought hard, but it was a tough battle. As well as contending with the McEllistrim dynasty, she also had more competition in the form of Denis Foley, a young county councillor, whom she had defeated in the '77 election, but who, in the intervening years, had established a large base in Tralee.

She failed to retain her seat unfortunately. She was nominated by the party to run for the Seanad through the Labour Panel, but she decided not to run. I saw my chance!

I didn't know much about Seanad Éireann at the time. I knew it was the upper house in the Irish parliamentary system. Senators (or *seanadóirí* to use the official Irish term) could debate legislation, sit on committees (where laws and policies were formed and discussed) and table amendments to bills passed by the lower house, the Dáil. Unlike upper houses in some jurisdictions, the Irish Seanad's power was confined to delaying, rather than rejecting bills passed by the Dáil.

Despite its constitutional limitations, I felt it was the ideal role for me at that time. It would provide a national platform through which I could raise, debate, and discuss the kind of issues I had been championing in Kerry: industrial development, regional funding, and rural depopulation and emigration. Some discouraged me from running, arguing that I was still too inexperienced on the national stage. It wasn't the first time I had heard that, nor was it the last. I ignored their advice, and, as things transpired, I was right to do so.

I was elected as a senator through the Labour Panel in August 1981, securing 60,000 first preference votes. I still remember the night I returned home after being sworn in as a senator for the first time. My family and some of my loyal supporters greeted me at the Limerick border, just outside Tarbert, with a cavalcade of cars. As we drove through Tarbert, hooting the horns, supporters came out to wave at us, and I could see a bonfire blazing in the distance.

We put on quite a show that night. I had always been eager to inject a little American style razzmatazz into Kerry politics. People in Kerry associated me with my ballrooms and nightclubs, as well as the Gay Bachelor Festival, and they knew I had a reputation for putting on a 'big show'. Politics is a show business as well, and I think my experience of running for the Senate really illustrated that for me.

My elation proved to be short-lived however. The Fine Gael and Labour government formed after the election proved to be one of the shortest in the country's history. It collapsed after the Fine Gael Minister for Finance John Bruton introduced a VAT (value added tax) on children's shoes, something some of the socialist TDs supporting the coalition couldn't support, and it was hard to blame them!

As I was a sitting senator, and Kit Ahern had decided not to run, I was nominated by the party to contest the general election in the North Kerry constituency, along with Tom McEllistrim Jr and Denis Foley. Tom McEllistrim Jr (who had replaced his father) and Dick Spring, who was to be elected leader of the Irish Labour Party that year, had built up considerable support, and were considered shoe-ins by the bookies, but I felt I could take the third seat. Kit Ahern had secured over 4,000 first preferences in the June election, and I felt I could improve on that. I felt that Ms Ahern's loyal support base would transfer to me, as I was the local candidate, and I felt I could also attract new supporters. I had been running businesses in North Kerry for many years at that stage, and I had built up a considerable network of friends and colleagues.

Confidence was high in my camp as we approached the election date, but it soon became clear that my opponents were 'feeling the heat' as they say.

I was soon informed that Fianna Fáil had received complaints, from both the Foley and McEllistrim camps, that I was distributing leaflets and flyers without requesting voters give their second and third preferences to McEllistrim and Foley. In Irish politics, when more than one candidate from the same party contests an election, it is party policy for the candidate to request in their promotional material that voters 'continue their preference' for their party colleagues running in the same constituency. As far as I am aware I followed this rule to a T, and, as I said to the press at the time, neither the Foley nor the McEllistrim camps provided any concrete evidence to the contrary. Jack Lawlor, Fianna Fáil's director of elections in Kerry at that time, gave a statement to *The Kerryman* on the matter, which was embarrassing and unfair.[1]

I took all this as more evidence that politics in Kerry was a tough business, and I had to fight my corner. The election did not go my way, unfortunately, but I am incredibly proud of the effort put in by my team, my friends, family and canvassers, who knocked on doors for me up and down the constituency in the middle of winter.

I lost to Denis Foley by about 300 first preference votes. We also succeeded in eating into Tom McEllistrim's vote share, with his share of first preference votes reduced by almost 1,500.

It was what happened after the election that illustrated to me just how ruthless politics could be. Following the Irish Constitution, the Seanad was dissolved with the Dáil, so a Seanad election immediately followed the Dáil election. While running for the Dáil was draining, particularly in a cold February, I decided to run to retain my seat on the Seanad. I was hotly tipped to succeed, having won 60,000 first preference votes in August.

It was clear at this stage, however, that both the Foley and McEllistrim camps saw me as a rival. They pressured Noel Brassil, a councillor from the North Kerry area, to run for the Seanad through the Labour Panel. Brassil didn't have a hope of being elected; the only possible result of him entering the race was a splitting of the

---

[1] *The Kerryman*, February 12th, 1982

vote, us both being from the same constituency, representing similar interests, and running through the same panel. That is exactly what happened. I lost my Seanad seat through an act of backstabbing within the Fianna Fáil ranks.

Little did I know at the time due to the political instability in the country, I would have fought two more gruelling elections before the year was out. By November of that year, the Fianna Fáil government had collapsed. In similar circumstances to what befell the previous Fine Gael one, socialist TD, Tony Gregory withdrew his support in protest over public spending reform, proposed by the then Minister for Finance, Bertie Ahern.

I ran my campaign very much on the issues of generating employment and industrial development. At our first press conference in Tralee, in October 1982, I outlined my ideas for agriculture, which were very much consistent with Fianna Fáil thinking at the time. I felt that our agricultural sector needed to be revitalised, as it was the backbone of rural Ireland, and we imported too much agricultural produce.

In 1982 for example, we imported over thirteen million pounds worth of eggs. I proposed we introduce a system of guaranteed pricing, where the farmer would receive a guaranteed price for his produce. This would incentivise farmers to produce more, and it would end our reliance on imported foods. I still think to this day that we rely too much on food imports, to the detriment of our domestic agricultural sector. For a country blessed with such high quality, cultivated farmland, it's an embarrassment.

I also campaigned for the industrialisation of the Shannon Estuary. This had been one of my priorities for some time. I also thought that excess revenues from any new Shannon development should be reinvested into the local region. At the time, Aran Energy was considering developing an oil refinery in the Estuary, a development that we calculated would provide £4.5 million Irish punts in shipping traffic rates and other charges. (Aran would eventually purchase land between Ballylongford and Tarbert, although the major infrastructural project never materialised, sadly. It was something I never stopped fighting for, right up to the later years of my political career.)

I was also passionate about establishing a separate North Kerry harbour authority, to examine and lobby for the development and industrialisation of harbours in North Kerry. The opposition at the time, Fine Gael, favoured a national harbour authority, which was a bad idea, as a national authority would inevitably concentrate on the bigger regions, and regions like Listowel and North Kerry would be overlooked.

Throughout my campaign that November, I remained proud to be a Fianna Fáil candidate, and I remained steadfastly loyal to the party. While I sparred with my constituency colleagues, Foley and McEllistrim, this is not unusual in Irish politics, or politics anywhere for that matter; politics is a highly competitive sport.

I believed the Taoiseach at the time, Charlie Haughey, was the best man to run the country, and I was very eager for us to win the election. While the country was in a deep recession that November, there were some positive signs. The Fianna Fáil government had been the shortest in the history of the state, but they did introduce some positive changes in the short time they had been in office. Interest rates on Ireland's borrowing were dropping, and this was a sign of returning confidence in Ireland and the Irish economy's capacity to recover. We had a young, brilliant and dynamic Minister for Finance at the time, Bertie Ahern, who would later lead the country through a period of unprecedented growth and development, the 'Celtic Tiger' years.

Speaking of unprecedented, my campaign tactics were also, I am happy to say, a tad unconventional.

Inspired by my successful Seanad bid in '81, I decided to inject a little razzmatazz into the election. As I mentioned previously, politics is like show business, and it is a great way of generating interest and momentum, putting a smile on people's faces in what were difficult times for many. I remember we flew a hot air balloon over the constituency in an attempt to generate awareness and spread the word. I also remember driving through Tralee in an open top car. Our plan was to cause a stir, and we succeeded.

My unconventional campaign tactics caught the attention of both the local and the national press. The article below, by Donal Hickey, which appeared in the *Irish Examiner* in the run-up to the February election (when I was a senator), testifies as to how my campaign tactics were ruffling feathers.

'People know I'm a good man' says Fianna Fáil candidate, Senator Dan Kiely, whose brash, high-powered campaign has added a colourful dimension to the election in this widely-scattered constituency.

In conservative North Kerry, they're not used to American-style electioneering. So, when Kiely staged an assault in Tralee on Saturday with a long, noisy motorcade led by the man himself in an open-roofed car, people took notice.

"Never again will you see three TDs in Tralee. I'm optimistic that I can win a seat for the northern part of the constituency this time," said the Tarbert auctioneer and businessman who is being quoted by the bookmakers at 4/5 to be successful.

This is a rather unusual situation in this three-seater in that all its deputies - Tom McEllistrim and Denis Foley, both Fianna Fáil., and Dick Spring, Labour - are based in Tralee …

You won't find a bookmaker in Tralee that will take a bet on Tom McEllistrim, who is regarded as a 'banker', and Dick Spring, Minister of State for Justice, is odds on to hold a seat that has been in the family since 1943.

Dan Kiely, a man with a name for springing surprises in elections, is depending greatly on Mrs. Ahern, who polled 4,158 first preference votes in June, for support.

The Final Count

The crunch in the Foley v Kiely affair will come in the first count. Whoever is ahead at that stage will almost certainly carry the day.

I failed to win a seat, unfortunately, although the result was even closer than the February election. As we expected, Dick Spring and Tom McEllistrim Jr were both elected. I beat Denis Foley on first preferences, polling fifty seven more than him , but he overtook me in transfers, securing a third seat after a long night of counting. I also ran for the Seanad the following month, although I was also unsuccessful on that occasion, which was disappointing, but unsurprising, as I had run in two general elections and three Seanad elections in the span of eighteen months.

Despite the pain of defeat, I wasn't ready to leave politics. I had what they call the 'political bug' and the issues I had campaigned on were not going away; lack of investment in North Kerry and the Shannon Estuary, high emigration, and lack of quality employment opportunities for young people.

Unlike its predecessors, the Fine Gael and Labour government formed after that election lasted the whole five year term. There wasn't another general election until 1987. It was also one of the worst governments in the history of the state, however (in my view), so the problems I highlighted certainly didn't go away, and only got worse in many cases.

I spent the five years that followed in the political wilderness. However, and let this be a lesson to any young readers, particularly ones interested in politics, it is remarkable what one can achieve in the wilderness.

In the Wilderness

Thus began a period in the political wilderness for me. Fighting two back-to-back Seanad and Dáil elections that November, and narrowly missing out on both, was tough, but I wasn't prepared to abandon my political career just yet. I remained a councillor in Kerry County Council, which I considered a very important job. It was a good platform through which I could represent my constituents and highlight the issues that were important to them.

In some respects, I probably did as much to advance those issues during my years in the wilderness, between '82 and '87, as I did at any point in my career.

I did consider leaving politics after my unsuccessful run for the Dáil and Seanad in the winter of 1982. Ireland was mired in recession, and the government that was elected after the November election, a Fine Gael Labour coalition with Garrett Fitzgerald as Taoiseach, would make the situation a lot worse, in my opinion.

I had a young family at the time, and my wife had still not fully recovered from her brain haemorrhage, but a part of me felt that the right thing to do was to concentrate on business and work. The fox fur trade had dried up by the eighties, and it was not a fortuitous time to be running nightclubs and bars, with emigration to the United States and Britain being so high. I therefore considered leaving politics to concentrate on my businesses, but in the end, I decided not to, and

I'm glad I made that decision. I still had so much to achieve, and I would go on to achieve many things.

In hindsight, I think two elections saved me. There was a European Parliament election scheduled for June 1984, and I decided to run for a Fianna Fáil nomination. This was only the second time in history that representation in the European parliament was decided by popular vote, the first being in 1979. The EU, then ECC, was an organisation growing in power and stature, and I felt the European Parliament would be an ideal platform for me.

When it comes to European elections, Ireland is broken up into four constituencies: Connaught, Ulster, Leinster, and Munster and Dublin. At the time, there were fifteen seats up for grabs. Fianna Fáil

Dan's mother, Mrs Hannah Kiely, standing next to her son's General Election poster.

was planning to run three candidates in the Munster constituency with a target of two seats.

I did ask supporters and canvassers in my own constituency, the people who had supported me right through my career, for their opinion on whether I should run or not. I was pleasantly surprised to discover that the majority were enthusiastic about the prospect of me running. They commented on the fact that Kerry was at that stage unrepresented at the European level. Having heard the views of my supporters and canvassers, I was heartened, and I began to take the idea more seriously.

The European Munster constituency is massive, comprising the counties Cork, Kerry, Tipperary, Limerick, Waterford and Clare. The quota at the time was almost 60,000. This didn't intimidate me, as I had contested gruelling and difficult elections before. Seanad elections are particularly difficult in this respect. In some respects, getting elected to the Seanad is tougher than getting elected to the Dáil. In the Dáil, you are confined to a single constituency. My own North Kerry constituency was tough, but it was relatively small. For the Seanad, however, you are forced to canvass up and down the country, with the various panels representing people from all corners of Ireland, which makes campaigning all the more difficult. As I had previous experience with elections of this kind, I was up for it!

My first task was securing the nomination. Noel Davern and Gene Fitzgerald, former Ministers for Education and Finance respectively, were considered 'shoe-ins'. The fact that Davern was from Tipperary, and Fitzgerald from Cork, meant they could rely on large amounts of support from those two counties (or so they thought). My rival for the third and final nomination was therefore Sylvester Barrett, a sitting TD from Clare. The bookies and the press considered Barrett to have the upper hand, as he had been the former Minister for Defence and the Environment.

A regional balance should be a major priority for political parties when selecting candidates. Candidates should be evenly spread out across the constituency. I had seen the devastating effects of regional imbalance in my own constituency of North Kerry, where Listowel and North Kerry were deprived of a local TD for years. It came as no surprise to me that I would encounter a similar problem when I ran for Europe.

When I initially sought the nomination, Fianna Fáil argued that Kerry was geographically too close to Cork, Gene Fitzgerald's constituency. Sylvester Barrett, so went the party thinking, would therefore be a better choice, as he was based in Ennis, Co Clare, in the North of the Munster constituency. Clare, Cork and Tipperary were considered more regionally balanced, than Kerry, Cork and Tipperary – which would be the make up if Fitzgerald, Davern, and I were nominated.

I argued, on the contrary, that my location in Tarbert, at the border between North Kerry, West Limerick and Clare, was the ideal location for a Munster MEP, being geographically close to all three counties; Tarbert is on the Limerick-Kerry border, and Clare was a ferry ride across the Shannon. The geniuses of 'regional balance' in Fianna Fáil's Dublin HQ didn't factor this in, unsurprisingly. When they saw I was a Kerry politician, they assumed I was miles from the Limerick border.

The nomination process took place at a convention in Cork City Hall in March 1984. I remember being received warmly by my fellow members, and I was also delighted with the support I received from Cork. Even though Gene Fitzgerald was the local Cork candidate, the fact both of my parents hailed from the rebel county really stood to me. I picked up a great Cork vote.

I wasn't successful, unfortunately. Fitzgerald, Davern and Barrett secured the nomination, with Fitzgerald and Barrett winning seats for Fianna Fáil in the subsequent election. While I didn't win, I took great heart in the fact that so many loyal people and canvassers supported me. It was the first big election I had run in since my Dáil and Seanad bids of November '82. My enthusiasm for politics was back.

Dan delivers an address to the General Council of County Councils' conference. The conference was held in the Golf Hotel (then the 'Ambassador') in Ballybunion. To Dan Kiely's right is Pat Coffey, then Vice Chairperson of the GCCC, and to his left, Seamus Dooley, former County Manager of Kerry County Council.

I was involved in another big election the following year. In August 1985, I was elected chairperson of the General Council of County Councils (GCCC), a large, influential, representative body. With a national assembly of sixty-five sitting county councillors, and a ten person executive board, its remit was to represent the various county councils across Ireland. It was a great achievement, and for the first time since I lost my Senate seat, I had a national platform.

The following year, in August 1986, I became the first person in history (and the only person in history) to be re-elected as chairperson of the GCCC. I took satisfaction in the fact that I had defied the bookies yet again! They had wrongly written me off on so many occasions, and they were wrong about my GCCC prospects too. I beat the favourite, former Minister of State, Ger Connolly, to the chairmanship.

HE Margaret Heckler (née O'Shaughnessy), former United States Ambassador to Ireland, standing outside the Ronald Reagan Lounge, Ballyporeen, Co Tipperary. Dan had accompanied the Ambassador on her visit to Ballyporeen.

I took the position of chairperson very seriously, and I was proactive throughout my tenure, introducing policies and actions aimed at making councils more effective and more accountable to voters. While I was chairperson, we introduced a system of block grants for county councils. This allowed for more autonomy when it came to funding and budgets. Previously, county councils were constrained by government directives when it came to the allocation of funding, after our reform, they could allocate funding to the areas where it was needed the most. This was important, as local councils were best positioned to know where precisely funding and investment was needed. I couldn't for the life of me fathom how a civil servant or government minister in Dublin could know what roads in Kerry needed maintenance, or what GAA club or voluntary organisation needed support. It was a very good reform and it led to more effective and accountable county councils.

Being elected chairperson of the GCCC also raised my standing within the party, and in that respect, it couldn't have come at a better time.

Those two elections played a part in why I decided to continue in politics and ultimately decided to contest the election when it came in 1987. There was another factor in my decision to remain in politics, however, and that was Charles J Haughey, then leader of Fianna Fáil, and at the time leader of the opposition.

I can't recall when I first met 'Charlie', as he was known to his droves of loyal supporters, but I enjoyed a very warm relationship with him throughout my career. During those years in the political wilderness, he supported and encouraged me; he liked my approach to politics and my overall worldview, including the importance of investment, and revitalising the rural, agricultural economy.

He owned an island off the Kerry coast, Inishvickillane, and I remember him visiting me once in Tarbert. He was very eager for me to run in 1987, something I was hesitant about at the time, since Foley and McEllistrim had very much consolidated their support at that stage.

While Charlie Haughey was very much a controversial figure, in my own experience I found him loyal and honourable. I think his governments, some of which I was proud to be part of, laid the foundations for the successes the country would enjoy in the 1990s and 2000s, under Bertie Ahern, the man known as his 'apprentice'. The pro-business, pro-investment policies of those years were laid in 1987, when Charlie Haughey returned as Taoiseach, as I will discuss in the next section. He was also very much the man who initiated the peace process, encouraging dialogue between John Hume and Gerry Adams.

One of my most abiding memories of Charlie from that time was of him accompanying me on a pheasant hunt. As far as I can recall, the former Taoiseach was quite adept with a shotgun!

What perhaps persuaded me to stay in politics more than anything, however, was the fact that the problems I had been highlighting throughout my career remained, and in many cases, the Fine Gael Labour coalition government were making them worse.

To give just one example, I have written previously about how eager I was to establish a separate industrial authority for the Shannon Estuary. I felt the Estuary had been underutilised, with great opportunities for employment being lost. A single Shannon Estuary authority would have been in a position to put forward an action plan aimed at encouraging investment and development. It would have been a 'game-changer' for the region, raising living standards and providing opportunities for young people.

The Fine Gael minister over ports and estuaries at the time was Jim Mitchell, who opposed regional port authorities. He advocated for a central port authority, based in Dublin, which would monitor and manage the development of all of Ireland's ports and estuaries. Regional port authorities would, according to Mitchell, lead to a 'fragmentation of development'.

He was wrong. A central port authority would repeat exactly the same problems I had seen at the council level when it came to the allocation of funds. Under Mitchell's plan, I felt estuaries like the Shannon Estuary would continue to decline through neglect and lack of investment. To this day I feel the Estuary's potential has not been fully realised.

My years of fighting did bear some fruit, however. In December 1985, The Mid-West Regional Development Board published a brochure entitled, *The Shannon Estuary – Europe's Choicest Deepwater Industrial Location*. Even with its publication, I feared that Foynes and Limerick, rather than my constituents in North Kerry, would be the biggest beneficiaries, on account of the lack of separate port authority for the region. I feel history proved me right on that score.

Another issue close to my heart was emigration. This was understandable of course, as I had been one myself, emigrating from Ireland to the United States in 1960. I knew the difficulties faced by young emigrants first-hand, and I also knew that emigrating to America was much harder than it had been in my day.

When I emigrated in 1960, the US-Irish immigrant community was remarkably close-knit and loyal; they would always have your back, and they would do anything for you. New arrivals would be collected at the airport and lodgings and a job would be ready for you when you arrived. The party my sister Cathy organised in my honour was a common occurrence for new arrivals from Ireland in those days, an important rite of passage that provided immigrants with an opportunity to meet and mingle with their fellow Irish.

The Irish community was still close-knit in the eighties, but New York had become a bigger, more complicated place, with a high crime rate. There were temptations for the new Irish that just weren't there in my day.

I wanted to do something to help the situation. Becoming chairperson of the General Council of County Councils two years in a

Dan Kiely pictured with other members of the Limerick Harbour Board. The board was eventually disbanded and amalgamated into the Foynes Harbour Board.

row had increased my political clout, and afforded me access I hadn't previously enjoyed.

I got in touch with my old friend John 'Kerry' O'Donnell. He was still running Gaelic Park, still very much 'Mr GAA'. I was eager for him to establish an information centre in the Park. It would be a place new immigrants could go to get information on accommodation and jobs and be directed towards the various resources available for them.

Having lived in America, I knew how important Gaelic Park was to the Irish community. Outside of the significance of Gaelic games, it had always been the place where immigrants could meet their fellow Irish, learn about new jobs and opportunities, and advance in society. A small information centre there would have been an invaluable resource for them.

For one reason or another, the information centre never materialised, but I am happy with the way Gaelic Park has developed and evolved since that day. The new Gaelic Park redevelopment plan includes the construction of new, state-of-the-art facilities. The plan was spearheaded by my daughter, Joan Kiely Henchy, chairperson of New York GAA. It will give the Irish and Irish American communities in the United States the centre they deserve.

I am happy to say I had more success with Bord Fáilte, the Irish tourist board, and Aer Lingus, the Irish state airline. I wanted them to become directly involved in providing information and assistance to new Irish immigrants into the US, link them with other members of the wider diaspora, and provide them with information on the resources that were available to them. Many members of the Irish community in America also deserve credit. Tommy Hennessy, for example, a building contractor and union boss, was very supportive of my efforts to help immigrants.

One of the greatest assets to Irish immigrants at this time wasn't an Irish person at all, but an Irish American called Margaret Heckler.

Margaret Heckler was appointed by Ronald Reagan as American Ambassador to Ireland in January 1986.

I met her for the first time that year, at an event in the American Embassy in Ballsbridge, Dublin. I am happy to say I enjoyed a warm working relationship with her during her tenure as Ambassador, and we became friends. I relayed to her the difficulties faced by the Irish immigrating to the United States, and she was very receptive, promising to do what she could to alleviate the problem.

Before I discuss that, however, I would like to write something about Margaret Heckler herself, as she is a woman not enough has been written about. Her achievements have been forgotten to an extent, which is unfortunate.

Born Margaret Mary O'Shaughnessy in Flushing, New York, she excelled academically from a young age, graduating from the Jesuit run Boston College with an LLB. She was appointed Health Secretary by President Ronald Reagan in 1983, where she had many notable achievements, including the 'Heckler Report', a report on the disproportionately poor health outcomes for ethnic minorities in the United States. For the Irish reader, her greatest achievement as secretary was the International Fund for Ireland. The fund was a giant venture by the British, Irish and American governments, established to promote peace and dialogue on the island of Ireland. While she was the health secretary, Margaret managed to raise $120 million in donations to the fund, an awfully large amount of money at that time, and a major boost to the peace process. With regard to American ambassadors to Ireland in the twentieth century, I think perhaps only her and Jean Kennedy Smith did more to advance the cause of peace on the island.

Our greatest achievement together was Ronald Reagan's visit to Ballyporeen. President Reagan visited the Tipperary village on the 3rd of June 1984 (the birthplace of his great-grandfather Michael). I had taken Ambassador Heckler on a visit to the village, where she was struck by the warmth of the people, and their eagerness for their famous son to visit them. The photo of her reproduced in this book is from that visit, with Margaret pictured in front of the Ronald Reagan Lounge in Ballyporeen. President Reagan's visit was symbolic of course, but if my years in politics taught me anything, it was that symbolism and public perception matter.

The visit was a personal triumph for me. I had played a small, but significant part in Ronald Reagan's visit to Ireland, and I think the work I did helped Irish immigrants in America, constituents who were, unsurprisingly, close to my heart, as I had been one of them myself. It wasn't the last thing I would do for immigrants while in politics, not by a long shot. I was reelected to the Seanad in 1987 (the conclusion to two more gruelling, back-to-back election campaigns) which I will tell you about in the next chapter. I wasn't long in the door of the Seanad when I heard about a certain visa problem. I remember thinking at the time, 'this is a job for Dan Kiely'.

More Ups and Downs

D-day finally came, the day of the general election of 1987. The election was set for February of that year, and in the end I decided to run. Politics can be addictive and the more I saw of public life, the more obvious it seemed that the kind of issues I had been championing were not being taken seriously. I had received a decent 2,000 votes in the council election of 1985, which led me to believe that I still had a strong support base in North Kerry. Being nominated as chairman of the GCCC (the General Council of County Councils) for two consecutive years running (and the first person in history to do so) revitalised me, and restored my political confidence.

It also gave me a unique insight into what was happening to the country at that time. In hindsight, the level of resistance I received was remarkable. John Boland, the Fine Gael Minister for the Environment, was a real thorn in my side. My attempts to make county councils more answerable to people, particularly when it came to funds, were strongly resisted by him and others. The Fine Gael Labour government wanted everything based in Dublin and they showed a dismissive attitude towards rural Ireland.

I announced my intention to run in early '86. I wrote to the national executive of Fianna Fáil stating my intention to seek a nomination from the party. North Kerry had two sitting TDs at the time, Tom McEllistrim and Denis Foley, but Listowel and the north of the county had no strong local representative. Constituents felt abandoned, and

Best of friends, best of enemies. Pictured (l-r) is Dan Kiely, former Taoiseach Charlie Haughey, Tom McEllistrim, former Minister for State in the Department of Defence, and Tommy Foley, Tom McEllistrim's former Campaign Manager.

investment opportunities were being lost. The election, when it did happen, would, sadly, prove me right on that score.

My campaign had barely started when I realised my two rivals, Tom McEllistrim and Denis Foley, were up to their old tricks. As it had been five years since I ran in a national election – the last one being the Seanad election of November '82 – the Kiely political machine was a little rusty.

Political campaigns are gruelling, expensive, and you need a large number of supporters and canvassers to give you a chance of success. I was therefore very eager for the party to convene an early convention where I would be formally nominated. I had been given private assurances, including one from the party leader Charlie Haughey, that I would be nominated. Foley and McEllistrim had also indicated to the press that they considered my nomination a 'formality'. Assurances are not the same as formal ratification, however. Anything can happen in the run-up to a general election, and especially at conventions where emotions are high. I was desperate for the party to formally ratify me as the nominee, to allow my campaign time to prepare and focus on the job at hand.

When I started preparing and planning my campaign in the summer of '86, neither I nor any of my supporters were even sure if I would be nominated. It is hard to prepare yourself for something that may not even happen.

As the party had provided assurances, I didn't think organising an early convention would be a problem. So, at a meeting of the Dáil Ceantair in Tralee, I proposed an early convention. It was defeated by nine votes to seven! Both Foley and McEllistrim, my main rivals for the seats, voted against my motion, despite the fact that they had said my nomination was assured. The chairperson of the Dáil Ceantair also voted against the motion. I tabled this motion in December 1986, and the election had been scheduled for '87. I went into the new year without knowing whether I would be nominated by Fianna Fáil at all.

Outside of robbing my campaign of momentum, it also cost me financially. Political campaigns are very expensive. I was left with the dilemma of whether or not to invest money into an election I may not even be running in.

There is a possibility that Foley and McEllistrim intentionally delayed the procedure. I can understand why they would do this. Fianna Fáil was very unlikely to win three seats, despite the sitting government's unpopularity (Fianna Fáil had never won three seats in the constituency's history). If I did win a seat, it would have been at the expense of one of the other TDs.

I still found their attitude unsporting, and not in Fianna Fáil's interest. The sporting thing to do would have been to allow the nomination procedure to progress, and have all three of us on the ticket, and let the people of Kerry decide. Being incumbent TDs, with large bases of support in Tralee and beyond, meant they already had an advantage over me. Their shenanigans about the nomination disadvantaged me further. I made my feelings at the time known to the press:

'... At the moment I can't say if I'm a candidate in the event of an election or not. It is certainly giving the two TDs an unfair advantage over me. If they are interested in the party rather than themselves then there should be an early convention,' said Councillor Kiely. He added that a convention would kill speculation which is rife at present that the party was going to opt for a two-candidate strategy in North Kerry, or that there would be serious opposition to Councillor Kiely for the nomination.

"I want to know what the two TDs are afraid of. If these boys are going to continue their antics I will have to go back and seriously consider my position ..." Councillor Kiely added.

(The Kerryman, Friday, December 12th, 1986)

The convention eventually took place in January, in Horan's Hotel in Tralee, where I was formally nominated to contest the North Kerry constituency for Fianna Fáil, along with Foley and McEllistrim. This was only a month before the election, however, and the delayed nomination hampered me.

Come election day, I was still mildly optimistic. I was lucky in having a loyal, committed team behind me. I had people knocking on doors up and down the county for me, just as they had done in the early eighties. Knocking doors on what was a cold, dreary February – the worst time of the year to have an election.

I also fought the campaign my way, as I had done throughout my political life. We flew a small plane over Listowel, with a banner 'VOTE NUMBER ONE FOR DAN' trailing after it, just in time to catch the mass-goers coming out of St Mary's Church. It caused a stir and further cemented my reputation for electoral theatrics. Ger Colleran, a reporter for *The Kerryman*, remarked on my 'brash electioneering', to which I now reply: running in Kerry, up against who I was up against, who could blame me?

Despite our best efforts, I was not successful. I polled a disappointing 2,939 first preference votes, in what was a disappointing election for Fianna Fáil, and one that resulted in a hung parliament nationally.

Denis Foley did manage to improve on his first preference take from November '82, and secured the second seat. Much to everyone's surprise, Tom McEllistrim lost his seat. He lost the third seat to Labour's Dick Spring by four votes after a long night of counting; thus ending a long, unbroken succession of McEllistrim TDs in Kerry. After the election, the blame game started within the party ranks, and emotions were high. While they had not tipped me to be elected, they had hoped my surplus votes (my excess votes distributed as part of the proportional representation system) would get Foley and McEllistrim elected, as had happened in the two previous elections. They blamed me for a supposed collapse of support in the county.

Soldiers of Destiny. Dan Kiely with the faithful on a canvas in rural Kerry.

This was nonsense of course. It is an awful shame that these Fianna Fáil bigwigs, with all their expertise, can't count! Party support in the county had dropped considerably in the intervening years. Fianna Fáil's combined first preference share in Nov '82 was 17,168, shared between McEllistrim, Foley and myself, while in Feb '87 it was 16,711, shared between the same three candidates. That accounted for a drop of 457, a sizeable number, but not enough on its own to explain how we had lost a seat.

The reason we had lost the seat lay in the disastrous vote management in the county. I had been highlighting this for years. I had been telling the party repeatedly, at *ardfheiseanna*, conventions, *cumann* meetings, Dáil Ceantair meetings and more, that the people of Listowel felt abandoned. That February election proved me right.

Fine Gael had spotted our weakness and exploited it. Their candidate, Jimmy Dennihan, was from North Kerry. As Fianna Fáil had no Oireachtas member from the north of the county, Dennihan was free to build up a large base. He polled 10,118, a consistency record at the time for a share of first preference votes.

There was also something else hanging over me. In August of the previous year, I was involved in an unfortunate incident at my bar and lounge, the Lisselton Country Club. I had gone into the election with the issue hanging over me, and it was generating bad publicity.

In retrospect, I accept responsibility for it, although, in many respects, I feel I have been hard done by, so this is an opportunity to set the record straight. To provide some context to the incident, my father, Dan Kiely Sr, died in 1983, at the age of eighty-three. As the reader will know by now, I was very close to my father. His death had a massive impact on me. On the fateful day, I had been in Listowel on some business. When I finished in Listowel, I went back to Lisselton in order to attend a funeral. On my way to the funeral, I stopped off at my bar, the Lisselton Country Club, which I ran and managed with my brother Tim and my son Donal. Walking in the door, I saw that my bouncer, Sean Kissane, a decent local man who had never given me an ounce of bother, was in a heated argument with two men. I thought nothing of it and walked off. Sean was a good bouncer and I was happy to leave the situation in his capable hands.

The funeral was a difficult one, as far as I can remember, and it brought back memories of my father's bereavement. The deceased man had been a good friend of my father's. When I returned later that night the bar was busy, as we were hosting a twenty-first birthday party. Revellers had taken to the floor and the drink was flowing, which was always a good sign, or so I thought.

I did notice that Sean Kissane was missing – he wasn't manning the door as I had asked him to. I eventually found him just outside the door, in another heated argument with the same two men I had seen earlier. I could tell the situation was getting worse. What happened next has been disputed, and would be disputed forcefully in the months to come, both in the district court in Listowel and the circuit court in Tralee.

Some people alleged that I produced a pool cue and struck the two men with it, injuring them. This is untrue. I never touched a pool cue that night. I did intervene, however. I could see the situation was getting worse, and I wanted it resolved. I didn't want a brawl outside my bar. My intention was entirely peaceful. I intervened to assist Sean control what was a worsening situation. I did lose my cool. I will admit that. I did something I shouldn't have done, namely getting entangled in a violent skirmish.

I do, however, have a valid explanation, if not an excuse. One of the men insulted my father. This hurt me. I could understand why they would feel entitled to throw abuse at me. I was a county councillor and a former senator and exposing yourself to abuse and ridicule is part and parcel of public life, but why throw abuse at my father? Why make a nasty, totally untrue and disparaging remark about him? It was uncalled for.

My father did so much with his life, he served his country bravely, both as a War of Independence veteran and later as a member of the Guards. He worked every day God sent him, so his fourteen children could have a decent life. Memories of him coming home in his wet clothes after a day on the beat, came flooding back to me. In the end, my emotions got the better of me.

It didn't warrant the charge of assault, as I was acting in self-defence. The two men were in the wrong. They had been fairly ejected from the premises and were refusing to leave. I fought the assault charges with everything I had. Unfortunately, I was convicted of two counts of assault the following November. When the election happened in February, I had merely been charged with the two counts, and not yet convicted. My solicitor Louis O'Connell had the case adjourned until after the election. Any talk of me being disbarred from running was therefore nonsense.

By the time I was convicted, however, I was a serving senator again, so it was, of course, difficult. While I had not been charged at the time of the election, it was still a terrible distraction. Rumours about the incident, as well as exaggerations and misinformation, were spreading, and it was the last thing I needed.

I cannot say how many votes the sorry incident cost me. As I wrote previously, I feel it was Fianna Fáil's neglect of the constituency that cost us, both me personally and the party more generally.

Come April 1987, the toll was beginning to show. I gave a downbeat interview to *The Kerryman*, where I vowed never to run for the Dáil again. Having been written off several times in my career by others, I was writing myself off. I would, however, prove myself wrong on that score, as you shall see.

Then the prospect of running for the Senate arose. Initially, I dismissed the idea. The general election campaign had been gruelling, and my assault case was weighing on me. I didn't put my name forward for a Senate nomination when the Kerry Dáil Ceantair convened after the election; partially because I didn't want it, and partially because I felt Tom McEllistrim, having lost his seat, was a certainty. I was right on that score. McEllistrim was nominated unanimously to run.

I was stopped outside the by journalists, who asked me if I was intending to run. I said I wasn't. In the weeks that followed, however, I reconsidered my position. Politics were proving to be a habit that was hard to kick. I think the fact Charlie Haughey became Taoiseach in March of that year (albeit as leader of a minority government), helped persuade me to give it another go. The prospect of being an Oireachtas member of a Fianna Fáil government appealed to me. I felt I still had something to offer.

I decided to seek a nomination through the Administration Panel, through the GCCC (The General Council of County Councils), the organisation I had run for two years. It was a close run contest, but, unfortunately, I came up short. After failing to secure the GCCC's nomination, I felt deflated and wondered to myself whether perhaps that was that. As had often happened in my career, however, that wasn't the case.

In hindsight, failing to win the GCCC nomination was actually a saving grace, and saved me from defeat in another expensive election. The GCCC nominated candidates for the Seanad through the Administration Panel. However, my old rival Tom McEllistrim had been nominated, by Fianna Fáil in Kerry, to run through the same panel. If both of us had run it would have split the vote. It would have been a repeat of my disastrous '82 Seanad run, where Noel Brassil, nominated by the McEllistrims, cost me a Senate seat.

I had one card left to play. Much to everyone's surprise, I sought the nomination of the ICPSA. The ICPSA, or the Irish Conference of Professional and Service Association, was an alliance of various trade unions and representative bodies, representing professionals. Their members included powerful groups, such as the Association of Garda Sergeants and Inspectors, the Association of Garda Superintendents, and various bodies representing financial services, including the Citibank Staff Association and the Financial Services Union. They were often called the 'white collar union', in reference to the fact that they represented higher paid professionals. They nominated five candidates to run through the Labour Panel for the Seanad. They traditionally nominated two Fianna Fáil candidates, two Fine Gael, and one independent, to ensure they wouldn't be perceived as being biased towards either one of the two larger parties.

I approached the ICPSA to seek their nomination and much to my surprise, I received it. It was a much needed boost, both personally and politically. I also received support (for my Seanad bid) from Fianna Fáil's national executive, which also buoyed my confidence. I interpreted it as a vote of confidence from Charlie Haughey himself.

I was successfully elected to the eighteenth Seanad Eireann. It was a great personal triumph, and the bonfires were lit again in Tarbert that night. Being nominated by the ICPSA brought me great satisfaction and I saw it as a personal vindication.

In the end, it was the guards that got me elected, as Garda representative bodies made up a large chunk of the ICPSA. This surprised some people, as I had the assault charges hanging over me.

It didn't surprise me, however. I had always enjoyed a good relationship with the guards, and I had always fought their corner. The photo reproduced in this book is one of my favourites from my long political career. Pictured are me along with senior members of the Garda Representative Association, leading a long line of rank-in-file Gardaí up O'Connell Street. We were marching for better pay and working conditions.

I was the son of a guard, and I knew how hard a job it was. It was therefore a great personal triumph for me. I am not a saint, and I never claimed to be, but I am my father's son, and I hope I did him proud.

With all this going on, you are probably wondering how I found time to do anything as a senator. You will be happy to hear that I did indeed find the time. I was lucky and privileged to be in the Oireachtas during a very crucial time in Irish political history, and in the history of Fianna Fáil. Despite being a minority government, that Fianna Fáil government was quite radical, with Bertie Ahern, our dynamic Minister for Finance, laying the foundations for what would become the 'Celtic Tiger'. I would also witness many of the leadership struggle to dominate the party in those years, Albert Reynolds replacing Charlie Haughey in '92, and Bertie Ahern replacing Albert in '94. I will tell you all about them in the next section.

My biggest political achievement as a senator in those days, however, had nothing to do with grand visions or leadership challenges. It is, perhaps, more modest than that, but it meant a lot to me and to the people I helped. It was something I did to help Irish people emigrate to America.

I have written previously about the warm working relationship I had with former Ambassador Margaret Heckley, and how we together helped Irish immigrants in the United States. I have written previously about how, in many respects, life was tougher for the Irish in the US in the eighties, than it had been for us in my day, the sixties. They had perils and temptations to contend with that we didn't have, such as crime, drugs and community breakdown. When I became a senator, I got to know a dynamic United States congressman called Brian J Donnelly.

When I was elected to the Seanad in '87, I reached out to Irish America and used the extensive connections I had in that country. I really felt this was somewhere I could be of use, and not just to Fianna Fáil, but to Ireland more generally. The Irish-American relationship was very strong at the time. Ronald Regan, whose visit to his ancestral home of Ballyporeen I had helped organise with Margaret Heckler, was very passionate about the bond between the two countries. The annual St Patrick's Day custom of the Taoiseach visiting the American President at the White House was started by President Regan.

I attended several Irish-American events in Washington, D.C. after I became a senator. Brian Donnelly was one of the most helpful and impressive American congressmen of Irish heritage I met. His background was not that different from Margaret Heckler's. Born to Irish-American parents in Boston, he would distinguish himself as a representative in the Massachusetts state legislature, and later as a representative in the United States Congress, where he was widely respected for a series of healthcare reforms. I enjoyed a very warm relationship with him during my years in the Irish Seanad.

I first met him at a convention organised by the Knights of Columbanus. He struck me as a good man, and someone who was very proud of his Irish roots. He was very passionate about the bond between Ireland and the United States. He was very eager for more of his Irish-American constituents in Boston to visit Ireland, the 'home country' as they called it, and to learn more about the land of their ancestors. He was also a cute politician. He knew how to work the system, and he knew how to get what he wanted. This impressed me. I joked to him once that he would have won a seat for Fianna Fáil in Connemara if he wanted to, where his ancestors were from.

When I first met him, he explained his idea for a new type of visa, one that would advantage young Irish immigrants. He thought the current visa programme was hard for Irish applicants. He felt that his colleagues in the Senate and the House of Representatives favoured immigrants from other countries, and I agreed with him.

He explained to me that he was eager to create a visa system tailored to Irish immigrants. Originally, the basis for the new visas, the 'Donnelly visas' as they would become known, would be reuniting families; an Irish person could apply if an extended family member of theirs was resident in the United States. I thought it was a great idea. The theme of reuniting families also resonated with me. My family had been scattered across the globe on account of emigration. The photo reproduced here is very special to me for that reason. It was the first time all the members of the Kiely family, all my sisters and brothers, as well as my mother and father, were together in one place. Emigration is a good thing, but the inevitable separation of families that goes with it is hard.

When the visa programme was eventually launched, the visas would actually be allocated randomly, a 'visa lottery', but as it was focused on Irish applicants, many families were reunited as a result of it, and that means a great deal to me.

When Brian Donnelly asked me to help him with the programme, I imagined myself doing political things. I imagined helping would entail giving speeches, briefing ministers, liaising with ambassadors, that kind of thing. I never dreamed helping would involve doing the things I ended up doing. In retrospect, I think this is what Brian imagined too – no one could have predicted the adventure that was in store for us.

Getting the visa programme passed through the US Congress, the Senate and the House of Representatives, was actually the easy part. I thought it would take a frightful amount of lobbying, but no, American politicians were broadly sympathetic. The Donnelly visa programme was passed successfully.

The next step was getting Irish people to apply. As I have already mentioned, the visas were allocated randomly, they didn't factor in things such as profession, education, age and so forth. It was very much a lottery, names picked randomly out of a hat. Once your country of origin was deemed to be underrepresented in the US, you could apply.

That is why it was so important for Irish people to apply. If they weren't in the hat, they couldn't be picked out.

Once the programme had passed Congress, I really thought the hard part was over, and so did Brian. We were already talking about organising an event in Gaelic Park to welcome the new Irish immigrants. As both of us were seasoned politicians, it is remarkable how we overlooked a certain thing, something every politician should be afraid of, a strike!

Yes, there was a postal strike in Ireland the month the visas were due. It was a disaster.

Not one to give up easily, I went on Mike Murphy's radio show. I knew Mike from my time running the Ballybunion Gay Bachelor Festival. He loved making fools out of us country folk, but he was also a friend, and he didn't let me down.

I explained to his listeners that I was Dan Kiely, a Fianna Fáil politician from Kerry, who had helped Congressman Brian Donnelly organise the visa programme. I explained that the deadline for the applications was fast approaching, and, because of the postal strike, I had agreed to go to America to deliver the applications personally! I was going in two days time. If they wanted to apply for the visas, they could drop their applications into my office on Molesworth Street, and I would deliver them for them.

I was feeling quite satisfied with myself as I left the RTÉ studios, and drove home to my Dublin accommodation. I was expecting a few hundred at the very most to arrive at my office the following day.

When I arrived the following morning, I nearly crashed the car. I tended to drive to work via Stephen's Green, and that morning I saw a long queue. When I turned the corner onto Kildare Street I noticed the queue continued, and it was only when I took a left onto Molesworth Street, that I realised the people queueing were my visa applicants!

What I had expected to be over and done with in one morning, dragged on for two days. My office soon resembled a busy postal depot and if it was not for my two daughters, who were back home from America, I'm not sure I would have coped.

I remember having mixed feelings about the whole thing. A long queue of young men and women, waiting in line on one of Dublin's main thoroughfares to post applications for an American visa lottery, was very much symbolic of where the country was at that time, in 1987, mired in recession.

At the same time, I knew that emigrating to the United States was a great experience. I knew that many of the new emigrants would come back, as I had, and bring the skills and talents they had learned in their host country back with them, just as I had.

I was also proud of my daughters. It was tough going for a few days and they put in a real shift for me. I was also having marital difficulties at the time, and I had left my wife of many years. I was worried about the effect it was having on my kids, and bonding with them that week in Dublin, as we organised heaps of applications, was heartening.

I imagine I was some sight when I arrived at Casement Station Tralee, carrying many bags. A *Kerry's Eye* reporter and photographer, Pádraig Kennelly, had got word of my arrival, and they were there to meet me. While smiling, I remember being tired after the week. I thought that the worst of it was over – how wrong I was.

My next task was to arrange a flight from Ireland to the airport in Washington, D.C.. With everything going on, I had forgotten to book a flight! I contacted Aer Lingus. I explained why I needed a seat at such short notice. I was perfectly happy with a standard seat; my main priority was my precious cargo. Remarkably they said no, they couldn't accommodate me. Thousands of new visas would have meant thousands of extra passengers for Aer Lingus, but they still said no. Companies can be strange at times. I eventually managed to secure a flight through Aeroflot, the Russian airline. They very kindly agreed to transport me and the cargo to the United States. I had recently visited Russia in my capacity as a senator.

As before, I thought the worst was behind me, but that was a lack of hindsight on my part. This was the latter days of the Cold War, with Russia and the US still vying for world supremacy. Arriving into Washington, D.C. on an Aeroflot flight, with numerous sacs, all addressed to a government building in Virginia, was of course likely to arouse suspicion, and it did.

Customs stopped me and insisted on searching the bags. I explained that I was a politician in the Irish Senate and that I was delivering

The Final Count

Dan standing outside the visa processing centre in Virginia.

visa applications. I also explained that there was a postal strike in Ireland, but the customs official seemed unimpressed.

I mentioned previously how Brian Donnelly was a cute politician, and he was. I rang him and he had the whole mess sorted within minutes. I was out of the airport and into a chauffeur driven car within a blink of an eye, all courtesy of Congressman Donnelly.

Before checking into my hotel, I asked the driver to take me to the visa processing centre, which was situated in a small town in rural Virginia. (For readers unfamiliar with America, Washington, D.C., the capital of the United States, is buttressed between the states of Virginia and Maryland, but officially part of neither. It has its own quasi-state status; D.C., District of Columbia.)

The visa processing centre was a big, intimidating building with barred windows. I had a brief discussion with the receptionist inside the door, and I explained to her my situation. While Americans are like us in many ways, they don't have the relaxed Irish attitude to rules – everything has to be by the book there. The visa system was no different. It was in fact, as I discovered, ruthlessly inflexible. The visa applications had to arrive at seven the following day. If they arrived a minute before seven, they were considered null and void, and if they arrived a minute after seven, they were similarly declared null and void.

I could understand one minute after seven, there had to be a cutoff point. One minute before, however! I stared at the woman for some time. I found the bureaucracy shocking. In the bags I was carrying, full of visas, were people's hopes and dreams. To have the whole direction of your life hinge on a postal van in rural Virginia being one minute too early was too much. I couldn't get over the randomness of the whole thing. As if waging my own private war on the situation, I left the centre a determined man. I was determined that all the applications would arrive the following Saturday, at exactly seven pm.

When I got back to my hotel, I had a conversation with Brian Donnelly, and he filled me in on their unusual posting system. The postal system in D.C. operated according to an unusual sweeping system. There were post boxes scattered everywhere, and mail was collected at regular half-hour internals. I had to time it perfectly. I had to find a post office near the centre, and determine at what times the post was collected. The applications had to arrive at the centre at exactly seven o'clock, not one minute before or one minute after. Otherwise, all the applications would be null and void, and all our work would have been for nought.

After some searching, I eventually located a small rural post office near my hotel. Inside, a postmistress with spectacles greeted me. I explained I was from Ireland and the situation with the visa applications and the postal strike. She smiled and asked me how many stamps I would like. I had 15,000 applications with me, to be precise. I had counted them in my hotel room the night before. '15,000 please.'

She stopped smiling after that. This was a small rural post office, not much bigger than the post office in my home town of Tarbert. I was worried that she wouldn't have enough in stock.

Luckily, she did have enough. She laid a series of big cards with stamps on them on the counter for me. It all came out to $3,000. It was a lot of money then, but I came prepared. She also very kindly gave me a small stamp gun to make the process easier.

I also explained to her my dilemma with the visa processing officer. She explained that the post box was emptied every day, between half past three and half past six, as part of the sweeper system. I thought about it for a moment.

It was tight, but even if it came closer to half past six, it should make it. The visa processing centre was very close. I told her I would return Saturday, and make sure that the postman collected my applications in person. When I arrived back at the hotel, I realised that stamping and properly addressing 15,000 applications in one night was quite the task. Even armed with my stamp gizmo, it was tough. After a few hundred, I decided to seek assistance.

I rang Senator Donnelly's office, but all of his staff were dealing with the same problem; they were overwhelmed, trying to process an unprecedented amount of visa applications. The Irish embassy in Washington, D.C. was also mired in visa trouble, with thousands of applications flooding their system.

I eventually went back to the lady with the spectacles in the post office. She smiled at me again when I walked through the door. I think she knew I would be back. I asked her if she would be so kind as to lend me two postal workers, to assist in the stamping and addressing of the applications. I said I would pay them for their trouble.

She said she would be happy to, and the two postal workers proved to be very helpful. We got it done. The three of us got all 15,000 of them stamped and correctly addressed. I was back in the post office at three o'clock the following day, which was a Saturday, and visa D-day.

I remember being a little apprehensive; standing outside the post office in the blistering Virginia heat. I was worried that the postman wouldn't accept the applications, or refuse to take all of them in one sweep, which would of course prolong the agony. I was worried that all my work had been in vain. I was lucky! The postman was very friendly. He agreed to transport all the applications in one sweep.

For the sake of security, however, I trailed him in a taxi as he went on his round through the small Virginian town. He must have thought I was half crazy. When we arrived at the visa centre, he was whisked straight through, and my applications were transferred to the depot.

Dan pictured in his hotel room in Virginia, with some of the 15,000 visa applications.

I breathed a sigh of relief. The feeling of satisfaction was sweet. I felt even more relieved when I saw what was happening at the centre.

There was a long, noisy queue of people lined up in front of the centre's own post boxes, queuing to submit their applications in person. The people queuing looked frustrated, and the post boxes were already overflowing with applications. This wasn't the protocol at all of course. The protocol was that the applications had to be received at seven, through the state's sweeper system. I was worried these applications wouldn't be processed at all, and that the applicants had wasted their time; had their dreams shattered on account of pointless bureaucracy.

As we drove away in the taxi, I was forced to duck down to avoid a familiar face. Just as I had been ambushed by the *Kerry's Eye* reporter in Tralee, the cavalry was waiting for me in Virginia as well. Niall O'Dowd of *The Irish Voice*, which was a new newspaper then, aimed at Irish immigrants, spotted me and hailed down the taxi. Eventually, I agreed to talk to him and tell him what I was doing. It didn't change the tone of the article of course. I was referred to as a 'whippersnapper from Kerry'. To be fair to both O'Dowd and *The Irish Voice*, the press in those days called me worse things than a whippersnapper from Kerry.

It also transpired that Niall O'Dowd hadn't just come down to pester me, he was also delivering visa applications on behalf of Irish immigrants. Unlike me, however, he wasn't privy to the strict rules and was under the false impression that he could simply show up on the day and hand deliver sacs of applications. This wasn't how things were done in America; I had lived there long enough to know that. When the American government says they want something done a certain way, they want it done that way. Applications had to be delivered via the sweeper system.

I have no idea what happened to those hand delivered applications, whether they were even processed, never mind considered, and it worries me to this day. I know there was an Irish-American lawyer by the name of Walsh, practising in the Washington, D.C. area, who was assisting immigrants with the application procedure, and his applications were delivered the correct way, through the sweeper system. Similarly for those that managed to be delivered via An Post, the Irish postal service strikes notwithstanding.

Flying back on my Aeroflot flight the following day, I wasn't too concerned about the press. I was really only interested in what one group of people thought of me, and there was only one group of people on my mind. Of the 15,000 people who applied for Donnelly visas through me, almost all of them got visas. It clearly pays to do things by the book in America. I hope the United States was as good to them as it had been to me. I hope that someday they will have reason to be thankful to the whippersnapper from Kerry!

The Boss – Working with Charlie Haughey

Love him or loath him, Charlie Haughey dominated Irish politics in the '80s, casting a long shadow over it. As I was a Fianna Fáil senator during this time, I am often asked for my view on the man, the 'boss' as we Fianna Fáil representatives often called him. I have also been asked my opinion on the various controversies he became embroiled in: the arms crisis, the phone tapping scandal, and the various controversies around his personal finances. I was lucky enough to have a front row seat while many of these tumultuous events were taking place. I was at the table when the decisions were being made.

I have no desire to impose my views on readers, however. Others have recorded the facts on these matters, better than I can, perhaps. Let people read them and make up their own minds as to the rights and wrongs of what Haughey did or did not do. I would prefer to record my own personal experiences with the man and allow readers to draw their own conclusions.

One thing I will say about Charlie however – he was a great leader. For a man who was small in stature, he had real presence and charisma. When he walked into a room, people took note. He was the kind of person who automatically commanded respect and attention. Whether he was at a party meeting in Leinster House, ahead of a crucial vote, or a Cumann in Duagh, Charlie owned the room.

This is an old-fashioned way of looking at things of course. These days the emphasis is on respect and equality. That is fine, but I feel modern leaders could still learn a lot from Haughey.

Unsurprisingly perhaps, he had a foul temper. He could be nasty when he wanted to be. I got my first taste of this after I lost my Seánad election bid in February of 1982. I phoned him in order to make a request. In retrospect, the phone call was a mistake, and one I would later regret.

As readers may recall, I was first elected to Sinead Éireann in 1981, to much fanfare. In a stroke of political misfortune, the government lasted less than a year, and I was forced to contest two more Seanad elections the following year, failing to get elected on both counts. I felt hard done by because Noel Brassil, a constituency colleague from Ballyheigue, had been pressured to run through the same panel by the McEllistrims. Brassil's entry had the predictable effect of splitting the Munster, Kerry and rural Fianna Fáil vote, depriving both of us of a Seanad seat, and benefiting no one except Fine Gael and our other rivals.

I have discussed my battles with the McEllistrims in previous chapters, but to give readers some of the context of the phone call, I had better go back. The McEllistrim family are a contradiction in many respects. Tom McEllistrim Sr, the first of the three Tom McEllistrims to hold a Fianna Fáil seat in North Kerry, was an honourable figure. He served his country valiantly during the 1916 Rising, the War of Independence and the Civil War. Before the Rising, he was one of a group of volunteers who aided Roger Casement's attempt to import arms through Banna Strand.

Both he and other members of his family would carry on this honourable tradition of republican leadership in the years that followed. As elected representatives, however, they were fiercely competitive and at times, downright cynical. They were always desperate to stop any TD emerging in the Listowel and North Kerry area. They felt that a strong Fianna Fáil TD from Listowel, with a constituency

Rallying the troops. Pictured (l-r) is Dan Kiely, former Taoiseach Charlie Haughey, John O'Leary, former Minister for State in the Department of the Environment, and eight-time All-Ireland winner with Kerry, Páidi O Sé.

base in North Kerry, would rival their fiefdom in Castleisland and Tralee. Unsurprisingly, they seriously neglected the northern part of the constituency.

When Denis Foley became a TD in '82, he did, to his credit, make some attempt to provide representation to constituents in the north. He had a regular enough clinic in Ballybunion, and he occasionally had one or two in Listowel. I can't ever recall any McEllistrim having a clinic in Listowel, Ballybunion, Tarbert or anywhere in the north of the county at that time. Not if you paid him, would Tom McEllistrim (or 'Mac', to use the moniker by which he was known) have a clinic in Listowel. This neglect would eventually cost the party dearly in the polls, and the Fianna Fáil party is currently in a dire state in North Kerry, with the entire organisational structure (which I and others helped build up) having collapsed.

Having his back. Dan Kiely pictured with former Tánaiste and presidential nominee Brian Lenihan Sr.

It was for this reason that I approached Charlie Haughey. I wanted him to nominate me for a Senate seat. I was bitter about being shafted by Brassil and the McEllistrims, but I also felt the McEllistrims' antics were seriously hurting the party's standing in Listowel.

When I eventually got Haughey on the line, I put my case to him. At forty years of age, I was still relatively young. I was also relatively inexperienced on the national political stage – my national experience at that stage consisted of six months as a senator. The boss's reply that day would be a lesson in national politics.

'I tell you this for nothing Kiely, you fucking ring me again about this nonsense, and you will never run for anything in this party again. D'ya hear? I'm sick of ye culchies humming and hawing about this thing or that; get with the programme or fuck off.' He hung up before I had a chance to apologise.

Though he was hotheaded, Charlie could be personable and chatty; he was certainly 'one of the lads'. When I met him at the Ard Fheis the following year in '83 – at that stage, he was Leader of the Opposition – he was warm, and asked after my family. He didn't mention the phone call or my request for the Senate nomination. He suggested we go pheasant hunting when he was next in Inishvickillane, his island retreat off the Kerry coast.

I also remember him taking me aside and trying to convince me to run in the next election. This was a welcome surprise in one respect, as I felt I was out in the cold as a result of the phone call. Running again wasn't something I was overly enthusiastic about at the time, however. Predictably, he didn't take no for an answer. He would keep applying pressure until the next general election was called in '87. (The Fine Gael Labour coalition lasted the full five year term, meaning there wasn't another general election until February '87.) That was another thing about Charlie; he nearly always got what he wanted, and he got his way with me as well.

I wrote about my '87 general election campaign in the previous chapter, and how Foley and the McEllistrims tried to scupper my campaign before it had even started by delaying the nomination procedure. Haughey was a cute politician of course, and he knew my chances of getting elected, in a constituency with two sitting Fianna Fáil TDs, were slim. He felt that my surplus votes would help either Foley or McEllistrim over the line however, as had been the case on two previous occasions, February and November '82.

In March of '87, the year Charlie was elected Taoiseach, I contested the Senate election and was successful in my campaign to be elected. Being nominated to the Senate was a good boost for me personally, but it was also good for Listowel and the North Kerry area. The area now had a local Fianna Fáil representative with a national platform from which to build for the next election.

Despite this however, the 1987 election was a disappointing one for Fianna Fáil and our leader, Charlie Haughey. After five years of a Fine Gael and Labour coalition government, the expectation was for a turn towards Fianna Fáil. As I have written in previous chapters, I had my battles with that particular Fine Gael government. I witnessed first-hand their neglect of rural Ireland. The fact they were pushing for everything to be centralised in Dublin, including the creation of a national port authority, was a stark omen of things to come. I was surprised by the election result, having fully expected Fianna Fáil to be returned with an overall majority.

People predictably began to question Charlie's leadership of the party, and whether he could ever lead Fianna Fáil to an overall majority, which is what we had promised people on the doorsteps, and what we had delivered countless times in the past, under Éamon de Valera, Sean Leamass, and Jack Lynch.

Haughey did manage to become Taoiseach, but only after making a very unusual arrangement with the main opposition party, Fine Gael. Fine Gael, then under the leadership of Alan Dukes, agreed to abstain on motions of no-confidence and budgets, which allowed Haughey and Fianna Fáil to rule as a 'minority government'. It was similar to the recent arrangement between Fianna Fáil and Fine Gael after the 2016 general election, only with the roles reversed; in '87, it was Fine Gael supporting a Fianna Fáil government from the opposition benches.

It was unprecedented then, and it was, in many respects, against everything we had campaigned for. We had campaigned for a strong, stable Fianna Fáil government, and we ended up 'going into bed' with Fine Gael, to quote a popular media catchphrase.

I stayed loyal to Haughey during this time. After I had been elected to the Senate, Charlie appointed me official government representative for the undocumented Irish. This was important work and I took the role very seriously. One of my first duties as a newly elected senator, however, was more modest - it involved deer!

For readers who are unfamiliar, young readers perhaps, Charlie's personal residence was a 250-acre estate in North County Dublin, called Kinsealy. For someone like myself, who grew up in a small house attached to a Garda barracks, the estate was breathtaking. Haughey lived in Abbeville House, a large eighteenth century mansion situated on the grounds of Kinsealy. It had a big, sprawling ballroom, Aubosson carpets and antique furniture. As you would expect from a champion of culture and the arts, works from modern Irish artists like Robert Ballagh and Louis le Brocquy adorned the walls.

The estate also had a population of wild red deer, and that's where he needed my expertise. Charlie told me their numbers were getting out of control and he wanted them culled. Out of all the members of the party, I wasn't surprised he turned to me. He knew I had run a successful fox fur business in the 1970s , and when he visited Inishvickillane we would go pheasant hunting together.

The reason I bring the cull up is not to discuss the red deer population, but rather a remark Haughey made afterwards. Shooting and skinning deer is a messy business of course, as many of you will have guessed – even the city folk among you. A week after we completed the cull, I just so happened to pass the Taoiseach in Leinster House. I remember he was in conversation with Albert Reynolds and Ray MacSharry – at the time, two die-hard Haughey loyalists. The Taoiseach caught my eye and called out, 'Hi Kiely, get those fucking guns out of my hall, will you? They are making a bloody mess.' He then went back to his conversation with Reynolds and MacSharry, as if the remark was the most normal thing in the world to say! He was just that kind of person I'm afraid. He said whatever he wanted to say.

Unsurprisingly, the 'Tallaght strategy' arrangement with Fine Gael didn't last. I think it eventually fell over funding for an HIV-AIDS initiative. Fianna Fáil lost the motion and the government collapsed as a result, with the election scheduled for June '89. Take it from me, however – Charlie's decision to call the election had nothing to do with funding for AIDS, and more to do with the opinion polls. All the polls suggested we were on course for a big win and the overall majority we craved.

The North Kerry constituency lived up to its reputation for surprises. Tom McEllistrim, who had dramatically lost his seat in '87, won it back, at Denis Foley's expense, beating him to the third seat by 200 votes. While pressured to run (the party was again counting on the three-candidate strategy) I decided not to, with Ned O'Sullivan running in my place. I concentrated on getting reelected to the Senate, which I succeeded in doing. I ran through the Labour Panel, securing the nomination thanks largely to the support of the ICPSA (the Irish Conference of Professional Service Association), Ireland's 'white collar' representative body, which included groups such as the Association of Garda Sergeants.

Back in the Senate, I would find myself dragged into another national controversy. I would have preferred to stay out of things of this kind of course, but that is the price you pay for being involved in politics.

Seán Doherty was perhaps one of the most controversial political figures in the 1980s. Doherty served as Minister for Justice in Charlie Haughey's second term as Taoiseach, between March and December of '82. You couldn't find a person more qualified for that role, him being a former Special Branch detective and a qualified barrister. After Fianna Fáil left office in '82 however, an *Irish Times* investigation revealed that Doherty had authorised the tapping of three journalists' phones, Geraldine Kennedy, Bruce Arnold and Vincent Brown.

For many commentators, Doherty embodies the darker side of Irish politics in that era. I have no desire to get involved in that debate. Whatever the rights and wrongs of what he did, I got on quite well with Seán Doherty, to such an extent that when he lost his seat in the '89 GR, he asked for my assistance with his Senate campaign. I remember him approaching me in the summer of '89 to ask me if he could use my Seanad office – by this time, senators were afforded the privilege of an office and secretary. When I first entered Leinster House as a senator, senators were very much the poor relations of the Oireachtas, forced to beg a seat off a TD and beg the use of a TD's secretary. This had thankfully changed by '89.

I could see that Doherty was deflated after his Dáil defeat (something I knew about all too well) and was desperate for a Seanad seat.

Seán Doherty wasn't the only person disappointed in Leinster House at that time.

June '89 proved to be another disappointing election for Charlie Haughey and Fianna Fáil. We did manage to cobble together a government in the form of a coalition between us and the Progressive Democrats, a Fianna Fáil breakaway party founded in '85 by Des O'Malley, a longtime critic of Haughey, and his leadership of Fianna Fáil.

Unsurprisingly, the coalition arrangement was not popular with the Fianna Fáil faithful. We had promised a strong one party government and again failed to deliver on that mandate. Haughey's leadership of the party was again under question. It was with this background that Seán Doherty rang my office one night and asked to speak to myself and Tom Fitzgerald, a senator from Lispole in West Kerry.

Seán made it clear to Tom and I that if the Taoiseach didn't nominate him as Cathaoirleach of the Seanad, he would inform the public that Haughey had authorised the tapping of phones. As far as the public was aware, Charlie, who had been the Taoiseach at the time, knew nothing about the phone tapping; it had been authorised by Doherty as Minister for Justice, without the Taoiseach's knowledge.

If Doherty went through with his threat, it would have had serious repercussions. Charlie Haughey would almost certainly have resigned as Taoiseach, and the government would most likely have collapsed.

To be truthful, I wasn't overly surprised by what Doherty told us. Many members of the party, myself included, always had our suspicions that Charlie had authorised the tapping. Doherty's revelations merely confirmed something I had always suspected.

Nor did Seán's ransom surprise me – that he wanted to be Cathaoirleach. Being Cathaoirleach was a considerable step up from being a regular senator. The Cathaoirleach is Seanad Éireann's presiding officer. The best way to explain, is to say the Cathaoirleach is the Seanad's equivalent of the Dáil's Ceann Comhairle. The Cathaoirleach presides over the business of the house, including debates and questions, making calls on points of order and other procedural business. I doubt it was these administrative responsibilities that attracted Seán, it was rather the role's prestige and power.

The Cathaoirleach's salary is considerably more than a regular senator's. They get a Garda driver and are usually invited to official state banquets and events. If a foreign dignitary visits, for example, the Cathaoirleach will be on the invitation list. The Cathaoirleach also sits on the prestigious Council of State, a body which advises the president on the constitutionality of bills. It was the perfect ointment for a politician's wounded ego.

Tom and I did what Doherty asked us to do. We visited Haughey in Kinsealy and told him what Doherty had requested. After, I remember him leaving the room for about twenty minutes and returning in a quiet, sombre mood. He then told us to tell Doherty that his request would be granted. Neither Tom nor I left immediately, and when Haughey noticed this, he shouted, 'Have ye anything else for me lads? Get back to fucking work will ye.' Signs on, Doherty was nominated as Cathaoirleach of the Seanad some days later.

I would also play a part in the other major scandal that rocked that particular government. A presidential election was scheduled for the following year in 1990. For international readers unfamiliar with the subtleties of Irish politics, the office of the President of Ireland is largely a ceremonial role, similar to that occupied by the monarch in Britain. A bit like the Cathaoirleach of the Seanad, however, it is often coveted by ambitious politicians coming to the end of their careers, as it comes with all the trappings of state power.

For the 1990 presidential election, we nominated Brian Lenihan. Brian was an old stalwart of the party and had occupied a series of senior positions, including the portfolios of justice, transport and power, and education. At the time of his nomination, he was both Minister for Defence and Tánaiste. Brian had nominated Bertie Ahern, the Minister for Finance, to be his director of elections. As I was friendly with both Brian and Bertie, I wasn't surprised when they asked me to assist with the campaign.

Brian's campaign was to climax in Kerry with a big rally in Killarney a few days before the election. I was tasked with organising events and rallies in the north of the county. It was something I was happy to do. Lenihan was likeable, enjoyed an amicable personality and had years of experience in a high office. I thought he would make a great president.

Brian's two competitors for the presidency were Mary Robinson, a socially liberal senator, who, while running officially as an independent, was endorsed by Dick Spring's Labour Party, and Austin Curry, Fine Gael's nominee.

When campaigning kicked off in autumn of that year, confidence was high in our camp. On October 12, about a month before voters went to the polls, an MRBI poll for The *Irish Times* had Brian with forty-nine percent, Robinson with thirty-two percent, and Fine Gael's Austin Curry with nineteen percent We knew that if those numbers were repeated on voting day, Brian would win comfortably.

Then, all hell broke loose. That October, Lenihan became embroiled in a controversy over something that had happened back in '81. Before I explain how Brian was dragged into it, I had better refresh your minds on what exactly happened in '81, and why it suddenly became relevant to the election in 1990. In January of '81, the Taoiseach of the time, Garret Fitzgerald, had asked the President, Paddy Hillary, to dissolve the Dáil and call an election. Fitzgerald's government had lost the support of the socialist TD, Jim Kemmy, over a proposed VAT on children's shoes.

An allegation would emerge in the media some years later, that a group of Fianna Fáil TDs had contacted President Hillary (Paddy Hillary was a former Fianna Fáil TD and Minister for Industry and Commerce) and tried to pressure him into not dissolving the Dáil, as Fitzgerald had requested. Their motive was (apparently) to give Haughey time to form an alternative government. If it had happened, it wasn't successful, as the Dáil was dissolved and an election was held in February of that year.

This suddenly became relevant for the 1990 presidential election, however, as Brian Lenihan was allegedly one of those TDs. *The Irish Times* ran a critical piece on Brian implicating him in the incident. Their source was a series of interviews Brian gave to a UCD graduate student, Jim Duffy, during which Brian had told Duffy that he did ring the president in order to pressure him into not dissolving the Dáil.

While the *Times* and other newspapers were commenting on the situation, it didn't appear (to me at least) to be having an adverse effect on Brian's campaign, and if it was, it wasn't showing in the polls. The *Times'* own polling data had Brian, as of October 12, at forty-nine percent. Then Brian appeared on the RTÉ programme *Questions and Answers* and got himself into an awful lot of trouble.

Brian categorically denied having ever phoned the president in '81. Duffy then released the tapes of the interview to the public, and this of course caused considerable embarrassment, as Brian appeared to have completely contradicted himself. Early in '81, he had told Duffy that he did call the president, then in *Questions and Answers*, he had said he didn't. Brian was eventually forced to appear on a special RTÉ televised broadcast, to tell the public that what he had told Duffy was, after considering it for some time, false; he had not called President Hillary that year.

It was then that Brian's poll numbers began to suffer, and support for him began to shrink. A poll of Kerry constituents in late October, commissioned by Dr Gearóid O'Donnchadha, took us all by surprise. Fifty-two percent of respondents said they would give Mary Robinson their first preference, with Brian trailing in second, at forty-four percent. Even more worryingly, Robinson was set to receive almost sixty-six percent of Austin Curry's transfers; unsurprising of course, as Labour and Fine Gael had done a voting pact.

As bad as all this was for Brian, his troubles didn't end there. As I mentioned earlier, Fianna Fáil was in coalition with the PDs at this time. The whole Jim Duffy tapes debacle had put an already fragile coalition under additional strain. After Brian's appearance on RTÉ, the opposition, Fine Gael and Labour, tabled a motion of no-confidence in the government. The PDs threatened to support the motion, which would collapse the government unless Haughey either sacked Lenihan or ordered an inquiry.

Haughey initially tried to pressure Lenihan to resign. When he refused, he sacked him. Not only did this do further damage to Brian's campaign, but it caused a rift within the party. Some sided with Lenihan and believed Charlie should have called O'Malley and the PDs' bluff, while some sided with Charlie and thought the Taoiseach was right to prioritise the stability of the country over Lenihan's campaign.

Despite all of these shenanigans, Brian Lenihan put up a real fight. As Kerry played a crucial part in his campaign itinerary, me and my fellow Fianna Fáil reps from Kerry were determined to play our part, and we did just that. I organised a large rally for Brian at the Listowel Arms Hotel on Saturday, 27th of October, just a week before the election. Mary O'Rourke, who is Brian's sister and the Minister for Education at the time, gave an impassioned speech, as did Gerry Collins, the Minister for Foreign Affairs. I was pleasantly surprised by the turnout. The hotel was packed to the rafters with over a thousand people, and I wasn't surprised to hear the tide was beginning to turn again in Brian's favour. The final MBRI poll before the election had Brian trailing Robinson by five percentage points, but the gap was narrowing; momentum was visibly shifting in Brian's direction.

The photo on page 228, with me to Brian's right, is from that rally in Killarney, just days before the country went to the polls. Brian was very well received that day; people on the streets really warmed to him. I felt if we had another week, he would have made up the ground. Lenihan was that kind of man, he was a 'never say die' kind of guy and the tide was certainly turning.

My most enduring memory of that day, however, involves a different politician entirely. I will never forget meeting Jackie Healy Rae in Killarney, just before Brian was about to go on stage. Bertie has asked me to manage Brian's campaign in the north of the county and Jackie in the south. Being in Killarney that day, I had wandered into Healy Ray country, and Jackie didn't let me forget it; 'Give me that, Kiely,' he said to me, pointing to the megaphone I had clasped in my hand.

As I mentioned, there were tensions within the party at that time, with the faithful breaking into two camps: for Charlie's decision to sack Brian, and against. Jackie was very much against the sacking of Brian, believing the Taoiseach had capitulated to the upstart PD party. A few days before the rally, he had told Conor Keane, *Kerryman* journalist, that Charlie 'was only out for himself'.

We didn't fight over it, however. I handed Jackie the megaphone and told him to do Brian proud, and he did. After Jackie's impassioned introduction, Brian had a fantastic rally in Killarney, and it turned out to be a great climax to what was an extraordinary campaign – with one more week, I think our man would have won.

Many commentators believe the sacking of Brian weakened Haughey, damaged his standing within the party, and contributed to his eventual downfall, which would come two years later. Seán Doherty would finally go public with the phone tapping story, and inform the public that the Taoiseach had authorised it. Consequently, Charlie resigned as the leader of Fianna Fáil and Taoiseach on the 30th of January 1992.

He was replaced by his old ally, Albert Reynolds. This created another strange situation for me. The man I had first met through the ballroom business was now Taoiseach and leader of Fianna Fáil. Reynolds had been managing showbands in venues across Limerick

Dan pictured with US Congressman Brian Donnelly, after a meeting with Gerry Conlon and Paul Hill, two members of the 'Guildford Four', Irish men wrongly convicted of the Guildford pub bombings. Also pictured are Dan's daughters, Noelle (fourth from right) and Joan (first on the right).

and Dublin, while I was doing the same in Ballybunion and Dublin; we had often 'locked horns', and competed for bands and venues.

As people often say, there is no rest for the wicked, and that is certainly true of Irish politics.

Albert & Bertie

So, it finally happened. The boss was gone! In June of '92, Charles J Haughey resigned as leader of Fianna Fáil. I remember the tension was palpable in the room that afternoon, when Charlie, more downbeat than usual, announced he was to resign. In his resignation speech to the Dáil, he famously quoted Shakespeare's Othello, but there was nothing Shakespearian about his speech to us (the parliamentary party). He simply informed us he was resigning for the good of the country as the PDs couldn't guarantee their support for the government if he remained.

This was very different in tone to the previous heaves against him, some of which I witnessed. During his tenure, Charlie had faced numerous motions of no-confidence and challenges to his leadership from backbenchers. I remember one where there had been a question mark over Michael Kennedy's loyalties. People were wondering whether he was going to vote for Charlie or if he would side with the rebels. Charlie was seated at the main table when I arrived, projecting authority and self-confidence, as he usually did. Having cast his vote, Michael Kennedy walked across the room and took a seat by Haughey. While nobody in the room uttered a single word, the symbolism wasn't lost on anyone. By sitting next to Haughey, Kennedy was indicating how he had voted, where his loyalties lay.

After Charlie's resignation, the word on everyone's lips was, 'Who would replace him?' Bertie Ahern, Albert Reynolds, Mary O'Rourke and Michael Woods, a former minister for agriculture, were all touted as potential replacements.

I was happy to take a step back and not actively campaign for anyone, as I didn't want to be dragged into an acrimonious leadership contest. Somewhat accidentally, however, I was dragged into a spat of sorts. After leaving the parliamentary party meeting after Charlie's resignation, I was stopped by reporters. They asked me if the Taoiseach resigned, and I said he had, assuming it was public knowledge, and if it wasn't, it was bound to be in a matter of seconds. The prime minister of the country had resigned after all, it isn't exactly something you can keep secret.

The next thing I knew my voice was being broadcast across RTÉ radio, and the newspapers were running with 'Dan Kiely announces the Taoiseach's resignation', or something to that effect. When I returned to my office my secretary told me Dermot Ahern, the Fianna

Dan Kiely on the campaign trail with former Taoiseach Bertie Ahern.

Fáil 'chief whip', had been looking for me all day. When I rang him back, I got a ferocious going over. He told me the announcement of the Taoiseach's resignation was the prerogative of the party's communications department, and my statement to reporters had not been 'authorised'. I was tempted to say to him that perhaps the party's 'communications department' has better things to be doing than badger me about 'unauthorised statements'. I was right in one respect, my intervention was soon forgotten about, and everyone turned their attention to who would be the next leader of Fianna Fáil.

As it happened, Bertie Ahern and Albert Reynolds would strike the first of their many deals. Bertie agreed to support Albert's leadership bid on the condition that he would remain Minister for Finance. In hindsight, this was a wise move by Bertie, as Albert would only last two years, after which Bertie was nominated unopposed.

Reynolds was elected leader of Fianna Fáil on the 6th of February that year, and was voted in as Taoiseach on the 11th.

Having Albert as a leader was a little strange for me. I first met Albert Reynolds in a very different context to national politics: the world of ballrooms and showbands. Albert and his brother, Jim Reynolds, went into the ballroom and showband business in the early sixties, just when I was starting out. As I wrote about in previous sections, I started off with the Red Mill on Jerome Avenue in the Bronx, before graduating to run a series of ballrooms in Ireland, including the East End, Hibernian and the Atlantic in Ballybunion, and my ballroom on Camden Street in Dublin. Albert and Jim Reynolds' first ballroom was in their hometown of Roosky, Co Leitrim, appropriately called Cloudland. They would go on to manage numerous other venues across the country, including Lakeland in Mullingar, Dreamland in Athy, and Jetland in Limerick. In the height of the showband craze, in the sixties and seventies, when my ballrooms in Ballybunion were flying, I was competing with people like the Reynolds brothers. Sometimes, however, we could collaborate to our mutual advantage.

My East End ballroom was modelled on a design I got from Jim Reynolds, and I'm grateful to him for that, as it was my first large entertainment venture in Ireland. Limerick is only an hour's drive from Ballybunion, with many Limerick city people holidaying there during the summer, and this was something I used to my advantage. When the Reynolds had a band at the Jetland, be it Joe Dolan, Dicky Rock, Butch Moore, or whoever, I would also try and get them to play in Ballybunion, and more often than not it worked; the closeness in distance worked in my favour. If they played the Jetland on a Friday night, they may as well take a gig in Ballybunion on Saturday. I know it worked vice versa as well. If we managed to secure a top performer for the East End or the Hibernian, the Reynolds would poach them for the Jetland.

When we met later as politicians, I remember having one or two chats with Albert about our showband days. As I mentioned in previous sections, when I arrived in New York in the early sixties, I felt that the entertainment scene was behind the latest fashions and tastes. Even the Central Manhattan Ballroom, run by the formidable Bill Fuller, still had traditional orchestras, playing folk classics like the 'Siege of Ennis'. I had seen the beginning of the showband craze in Ireland, and I knew they would take off stateside as well. The old, stuffy orchestras would eventually be replaced by colourful suits and more upbeat music, and I was right. I think Albert and Jim Reynolds saw a similar niche in Ireland and we all deserve a lot of credit. Our ballrooms introduced a new style of entertainment to tens of thousands of people. We also brought several international stars to Ireland, like the legendary Roy Orbison. The father of rock and roll music played in my ballroom in Ballybunion.

I did have one or two run-ins with Albert Reynolds over the years, which is probably what you would expect from two old stalwarts of the showband scene. My first run-in with him was over a lifetime project of mine, the industrialisation of the Shannon Estuary. As I mentioned in previous sections, I was eager to see the Estuary developed for industry. In 1987 for example, unemployment in Kerry was seven percent, double the national unemployment rate, with tens of thousands of young people emigrating yearly. Failing to develop such a strategically valuable site was a terrible shame.

In '88, the IDA, the Irish Development Authority, put the landbanks on the estuary up for sale, with an asking price of £500,000. As Minister for Industry and Commerce, this came under Albert's authority, and he had approved the sale. I disagreed with him. I thought it was very unlikely that a private enterprise would be able to generate the kind of funds necessary to develop the property. I also thought the amount of money the state was asking for it was scandalously low. The state had purchased the Shannon property in 1980 for a cost of six million pounds, which, as I calculated at the time, factoring in cumulative interest, amounted to a total cost of forty million pounds. The proposal didn't make financial sense.

I convened a meeting of all the relevant stakeholders, including the IDA, inviting Reynolds, but he didn't show. Albert could be stubborn when he wanted to be. The private sale didn't go through and, sadly, to this day, I feel the estuary's potential has never been fully realised.

This wasn't to be my only run-in with my old rival. As I wrote previously, I felt the Listowel and North Kerry region was suffering from chronic neglect. We needed a strong, dynamic local TD, who would fight North Kerry's corner. I was a senator, of course, but I would have achieved more as a TD. I would have wielded more influence and gotten more done. With this in mind, I approached Albert just before the November election of '92, with an eye to running in North Kerry. I had been pushed by the party, against my will, to contest the '87 election, but I was always open to running. I told him exactly what I had told his predecessor, Charlie Haughey, that Fianna Fáil was losing support in the north of the constituency, and that constituents felt abandoned on account of the lack of investment.

Predictably, he dismissed my concerns. He assured me Tommy Mac had been working hard for Listowel constituents, and was steadily growing his support base. This wasn't surprising. Albert Reynolds and Tom McEllistrim went back a long way. They were both part of the infamous 'gang of five', a group of five Fianna Fáil TDs who supported Haughey's bid to replace Lynch as leader after Lynch lost a series of by-elections. The other three were Seán Doherty, Killilea Jr and Jackie Fahey. Reynolds saw McEllistrim as an old comrade and he wasn't going to betray him for me. Unfortunately for Fianna Fáil, McEllistrim had not been as successful in expanding his base in Listowel as Albert believed. Tom McEllistrim lost his seat in that election, haemorrhaging 2,137 first preference votes.

Reynold's tenure as Taoiseach and leader of Fianna Fáil was short-lived. He resigned in November of '94, after our coalition partner at the time, Dick Spring's Labour, withdrew from the government. The government eventually collapsed over the tardiness in extraditing Brendan Smyth, a paedophile priest, who was facing child sex abuse charges in the north. (Smyth was subsequently convicted.) In truth, tensions between the parties had been simmering for some time. To some people's surprise, although not mine, Albert proved even more inept at managing 'liberal' coalition partners than Charlie had been; tensions over the X Case and the Beef Tribunal brought down our coalition with the PDs.

After less than two years, the party found itself back to square one! We were leaderless again. The one election Albert led us into had been a disappointing one, with the party's vote share dropping by five percentage points.

After Albert resigned, Bertie Ahern emerged as the clear favourite to replace him. He was overwhelmingly popular with the party, including myself. According to an *Irish Press* piece from November '94, all but ten Fianna Fáil TDs had already declared their preference for Bertie. As often happens in politics, things are never straightforward. I was close to Bertie at this point, and I would play a part in his leadership campaign.

Albert's preferred successor was Máire Geoghegan Quinn, the then Minister for Justice. This was unsurprising. When Reynolds won the Fianna Fáil leadership in '92, he culled the cabinet of Haughey loyalists; sacking Mary O'Rourke, Ray Burke, Gerry Collins and many more, and promoting David Andrews, Seamus Brennan and Charlie McGreevy. For someone like myself, who has engaged in one or two blood sports over the years, there are few things more gruesome than an Albert Reynolds' cabinet reshuffle.

Máire had been loyal to Reynolds during her time as Minister for Justice, and he had needed her, having been involved in several controversies. One such controversy involved the wealthy Arab investors, the Marsis, who had invested hundreds of thousands of pounds into Reynolds' pet food company, C&D. In return for their investment, Reynolds helped them avail of what was known as the Business Migration Scheme. This was something the Irish government had introduced way back in 1956. It granted citizenship, or naturalisation, to investors who could prove their business activities were creating wealth and employment in the country. As Minister for Justice, Máire had refused to order an investigation into the matter, much to the chagrin of the opposition at the time.

She wasn't just popular with Albert, however. The Dublin press also liked the idea of a Máire Geoghegan Quinn Taoiseach. Stephen Rae, a journalist with the *Sunday Independent*, described her as a 'tough talking and articulate minister, she has never hidden her desire to be the first female Taoiseach'. While she didn't declare her intention to run until late October, there was an expectation in the Bertie camp that she would run.

As often happens in politics – and in life – a deal was struck. I happened to be in the room when it happened. Bertie promised to support Máire's European ambitions in return for her withdrawing from the race. He was tipped to win regardless of whether she ran or not, but was eager for his nomination to be unopposed. During the previous decades, during the Lynch, Haughey and Reynolds' tenures, Fianna Fáil had been torn apart by internal divisions, with different factions vying for supremacy. Bertie was eager for his election to be unanimous, which would present a united front to the public. He also knew that if he was elected unopposed, he would be the first Fianna Fáil leader to do so since Seán Lemass, the man widely considered to be Ireland's greatest Taoiseach.

He got his way in the end. Máire dropped out of the race and supported his bid. She would eventually get her European portfolio, being nominated to the European Court of Auditors in 2000, and becoming Ireland's Commissioner to Europe in 2010.

I remember being at the meeting where the 'deal was done' so to speak. It was my first opportunity to see Bertie's negotiating style in action. He had a very unique and particular approach to diplomacy. I certainly had never seen it before, and none of my colleagues had. He had thought through all of the issues exhaustively, seen them from every possible angle, and was able to put forward his position in the clearest possible way. He was a very persuasive and forceful negotiator. The fact that he went on to become one of the principal architects of the Good Friday Agreement wasn't surprising. Today, he is recognised internationally for his negotiation and diplomatic skills.

Bertie could be ruthless when he wanted to be too. Leaders probably need to be; they wouldn't be able to achieve anything otherwise. While he had served as Minister for Finance in Albert's government, and built on his accomplishments in Northern Ireland, there was no love lost between the two. After Albert resigned, he didn't disappear into the background, as some would have wanted. He remained a backbench TD, and would actually remain in the Dáil until 2002, as a TD for Leitrim Westmeath.

I remember the tensions between Bertie and Albert flaring up at the time of the '97 presidential election. It was an election Fianna Fáil and Bertie were very eager to win, as Brian Lenihan had lost the previous presidential election due to unfortunate and calamitous circumstances. It was also an election we were hotly tipped to win. Fianna Fáil's fortunes had improved since Bertie became leader, and we were flying high in the polls. '97 was therefore a very eventful year in Irish politics, with both a general election and a presidential election.

I didn't contest the '97 election in North Kerry. The party changed tactics, opting for two candidates as opposed to the traditional three. We fell short, unfortunately, with Denis Foley being elected at Tom McEllistrim's expense. The most notable aspect of that election was the rise of the former Provisional IRA militant Martin Ferris, who shocked everyone by accruing almost 6,000 first preference votes, higher than both Foley and McEllistrim. (I went head-to-head with the former gun-runner in 2002, when I ran again, something I will write about soon.)

Nationally, Fianna Fáil did much better, increasing their seat total by ten. The result was another coalition between Fianna Fáil and the PDs, the PDs then led by Mary Harney, O'Malley having resigned. No sooner was Fianna Fáil back in power than Albert was badgering the party about a presidential bid. It was pretty obvious to everyone, myself included, that Albert was not Bertie's preference. Over the course of '97, Mary McAleese, a Trinity College law professor who hailed from Belfast, emerged as the favoured candidate.

This left Bertie, the new Taoiseach, in a conundrum. He had allegedly given Reynolds personal assurances that he would back his bid for the presidency, even though McAleese was his preference. These shenanigans about the presidency were a distraction of course, especially considering how many important things were going on at the time, including the peace process. As it happens, I did play a small part in the drama, so it's worth putting it in writing.

It soon became apparent to all of us that Bertie was doing a double act. Publicly, he was supporting Reynolds' bid, but privately, he was supporting McAleese. He gave an interview to the *Sunday Independent* newspaper, soon after becoming Taoiseach, where he talked up Albert's credentials, and assured the public there was going to be no other Fianna Fáil candidate put forward. Soon, however, both McAleese and Michael Kennedy threw their hats in. Come voting day, Albert easily won the first round of ballots, eliminating Michael Kennedy. For the second round, Kennedy's supporters defected to McAleese, handing the Belfast woman the nomination. Whether the whole thing was intricately planned by Ahern, I'm not sure.

I can now, for the record, put one rumour to bed. There was some speculation in the press about which candidate Bertie voted for. Did he vote for Albert, as he said he would, or did he cast his ballot for McAleese? On some accounts, Bertie endorsed McAleese over the cabinet table some hours before voting, but he didn't vote for her. I can confirm that he voted for Albert. I witnessed it. He showed me his ballot slip before he put it into the box. He wanted it publicly witnessed, publicly known that he was a man of his word. It was yet another piece of Leinster House theatre, not the first one, and definitely not the last one I would witness during my time there.

I also remember catching a glimpse of Albert after McAleese's victory was announced. He looked weary and defeated.

Not that I can talk of course! Albert wasn't the only one weighing up a political return at that time; so was Dan Kiely! Looking back, in hindsight, I should have probably exited the stage then. I had achieved a lot in politics; my work on behalf of immigrants into the United States, and bringing President Regan to Ireland were some of the highlights.

The political bug is a funny thing, however. Once bitten, it is hard to shake off. Bertie Ahern wanted me to run as well, and he could be convincing. I guess if he could convince Ian Paisley to sit down and talk to the IRA, he could convince Dan Kiely to run in North Kerry. Like I said, a master of diplomacy and negotiation.

One Last Hoorah!

So, I relented! I agreed to one last hoorah. Bertie's power of persuasion got the better of me! I put my name forward for the 2002 General Election. Initially, the signs were good.

I had an incredible team of canvassers and supporters behind me, and we knocked on doors up and down the constituency. The economy was flying at that stage, with all regions, North Kerry included, buoyed by the Celtic Tiger boom. Bertie Ahern opened my new constituency clinic on Charles St in Listowel to much fanfare, and people seemed generally happy with the direction the country was going in.

The opinion polls were mixed – as they often are. An IMB national poll predicted that I would take the third and final seat, with Martin Ferris, the Sinn Féin candidate losing out. A poll from *The Kerryman* newspaper suggested the opposite, however; that Fianna Fáil would struggle in the constituency, with Ferris pipping me for the final seat. *The Kerryman* poll shocked the party bigwigs, but I wasn't surprised that Ferris was projected to poll well. The former gun-runner had been building on his impressive performance in '97, where he raked up 6,000 first preference votes, and, worryingly for Fianna Fáil, took nearly a quarter of McEllistrim's transfers, after McEllistrim III was eliminated in the third count.

Despite these ominous signs, I was enjoying being back in the thick of things – it was my first Dáil election since 1987. I remember debating Dick Spring, Martin Ferris and Jimmy Dennihan in Tralee's

Time for comic relief. Dan relaxing after some busy campaigning. Also pictured is former Taoiseach Brian Cowan, and Dan's mother Hannah Kiely.

Siamsa Tíre, with the debate anchored by journalist Pat Kenny. It became apparent in that debate that one of Sinn Féin's strategies was to target disaffected Fianna Fáil voters. While the economy was booming, with record growth rates and tax surpluses, some of our traditional republican voters were vulnerable to Sinn Féin.

Ferris also brought up the skirmish I was involved in, the one where a disparaging remark about my father was passed. As I explained before, I am not proud of that incident. I lost my cool, but I wasn't going to take lectures on law and order from a man who had been a central figure in the Provisional IRA. I'm proud of my performance in that debate.

Going into the election, confidence was high in my camp. The press was up to its old antics of course, with Donal Hickey from the *Irish Examiner* characterising my campaign as 'colourful' and 'flamboyant'.

Unfortunately, my political luck had run out. I polled a disappointing 4,000 first preference votes. The bleak *Kerryman* poll came to pass. Ferris and Dennihan were elected, while Tom McEllistrim III, the son of my old rival, scraped through for the third final seat, with the help of my transfers.

Not one to give up, I ran to retain my Seanad seat that same year. The Seanad election was held that July, just two months after my gruelling Dáil campaign. Disappointingly, I failed to get elected, which brought the curtain down on my nineteen year tenure in the Seanad. I wasn't too disheartened, as I felt I had achieved so much during my time in the country's upper house. My work and activism on behalf of Irish emigrants to the United States being the highlight, particularly the vital role I played in both the Donnelly and the Morrison visa programmes, and in President Reagan's successful visit.

I was a little sad, clearing out my office in Leinster House that summer, but if there is anything I had learnt during my career as a politician, it is that disappointment is part and parcel of public life. Don't put yourself forward for an election if you can't bear the sting of losing.

Nor was it to be my last political defeat, unfortunately. In the next ten years, I would experience two local election losses, in 2004 and again in 2009. This was disappointing, as I felt I had a lot to give at the local level; advocating for my constituents, and battling for the kind of issues I had championed throughout my political life: industrial development, unemployment and rural interests.

I lost my seat in Kerry County Council in 2009. When the local elections came around again, in 2014, I was eager to throw my hat into the ring. It was an interesting time to be involved in local government, as the then Fine Gael/Labour government had introduced a series of structural changes, many of them bad. Phil Hogan, then Minister for the Environment and Local Government, had passed a bill disbanding all the urban councils, concentrating all power in the county councils, which, in the case of Kerry, was Kerry County Council, based in Tralee. For someone like myself, who had advocated all my life for local government, for the idea that the decisions that affected local communities should be made by the community's own local representatives, it was a bad decision. As a result of the Act, all decisions that affected North Kerry, towns like Tarbert and Listowel, would be made in county buildings in Tralee. The urban councils that had served the state so well were dissolved with one stroke of a ministerial pen.

Still hungry, still eager to make a difference, I approached Fianna Fáil with the intention of contesting the 2014 local elections. The initial signs were good. Unsurprisingly, I received massive support from the party faithful in Listowel, with the majority of the Listowel cumanns endorsing me. At the candidate selection convention, I received the second highest number of nominations; 183 to John Brassil's 230. Much to my shock and surprise however, it transpired that Fianna Fáil was operating a two candidate policy for the election; one candidate was to represent the 'urban' part of the constituency, the town of Listowel, and the other the 'rural', the surrounding hinterland. As I was based in Ballybunion, party HQ had categorised me as 'rural', and therefore, despite the fact I had received more nominations than Jimmy Moloney, the Listowel-based councillor, he was categorised as urban and received the nomination ahead of me.

I was shocked. Firstly, I received more nominations than Jimmy Moloney at the convention. That was the bottom line for me. Was Fianna Fáil a democratic party, or was it being directed by the bigwigs from the top? I was also surprised by the fact the party was content to run two candidates in what was a seven seater election. As the local town councils had been subsumed into the county council, the number of councillors allocated to each area had increased, meaning Listowel was entitled to seven councillors. The party was going through a difficult time, still struggling in the aftermath of the financial crash. So

A prize fit for a senator. Included in this photo are Dan Kiely and former US Senate Majority Leader Senator George Mitchell.

the idea that Fianna Fáil would be happy with two seats in a seven seater was shocking. When I got elected first, Fianna Fáil won four of the six seats in the North Kerry constituency. It struck me as very defeatist, and it sent a terrible message to both our supporters and our political enemies; it effectively said Fianna Fáil was happy with second best. And maybe they are! The present leader of Fianna Fáil, Micheál Martin, would often give you the impression that he's happy playing second fiddle to Fine Gael.

Despite my protests, the party was not for turning. In the end, I made the hard decision to leave Fianna Fáil and run as an independent.

It was a sad day in so many respects. I had given so much to the party. My father had joined Fianna Fáil when Éamon de Valera established the party in 1926, and his sons, myself included, had continued that tradition of political involvement and activism. Many of my brothers, sisters and extended family have been involved in the Fianna Fáil organisation over the decades, canvassing up and down the country for candidates, and managing local cumanns and other grassroots organisations. Acknowledging my family's contribution to the party, Brian Cowen, the then Taoiseach, visited our family home in Tarbert in 2008, and the picture of him with my mother, reproduced in this book, is very important to me. I think families like ours represent everything Fianna Fáil is as a party and what the 'movement' was supposed to represent; republican values, hard work, community spirit and giving something back.

After the financial crisis, and Fianna Fáil's subsequent difficulties, there was a change in leadership, and their values were, in many respects, different from the values of old. The new leadership, led by the current leader, Micheál Martin, took the view that the personnel needed to be changed; the old guard needed to be replaced with the new. The party was in electoral difficulty of course, and I can appreciate why attracting new blood was important, but families that had given so much to the party suddenly found themselves out in the cold. If the strategy had led to a dramatic increase in support, then you would agree, but it hasn't. As I write, Fianna Fáil is languishing in the polls.

Martin's performance as Taoiseach was also very mixed, to say the least. As I am writing this, he has been Taoiseach for over a year, and I still think he is being overshadowed by Fine Gael's Leo Varadkar.

As for the future of the party, I fear Fianna Fáil has some tough years ahead. Jim O'Callaghan is often touted as a potential successor to Martin. He was part of the legal 'dream team' who represented the state during my Supreme Court case, something I will tell you about in the next section. Being from Dublin gives candidates an electoral advantage these days, of course, considering how populous and dominant the capital has become. This is an unfortunate development for the country, as many rural areas are in danger of being left behind, but it is the reality, and party leadership may favour a candidate from there, especially with Fianna Fáil struggling in Dublin. Michael McGrath, the Cork-based TD, and current Minister for Public Expenditure, is also popular among the faithful and may be preferable to O'Callaghan in the long run.

One name that isn't mentioned enough, in my opinion, is Norma Foley. She is the daughter of my old rival, the Tralee TD Denis Foley, and is currently the Minister for Education, a tough brief in what are exceptional times. I actually predicted her ascent after the last election. I remember telling her husband at the counting centre that she would be a minister in the next government, and I'm happy to state here, on record, that I wouldn't be in the least bit surprised if she is a future leader of the party. She is personable, hardworking, and formidable.

Having a woman as Taoiseach would mark a change, of course, though, some changes are positive, some not so. While active in politics in the seventies and eighties, I did acknowledge the need for change, and I embraced it when I felt it was the right thing to do. I voted for the liberalisation of contraceptives for example, in the 1980s. I had my reservations, particularly around the availability of contraceptives for sixteen year olds, but society was changing, and I felt that change needed to be reflected in our laws. I didn't, however, support calls to relax our abortion laws, and I voted no in the recent referendum. I have always been proudly pro-life, and if that makes me old-fashioned in some way, then so be it. Like I say, change is unpredictable; some changes are positive and other changes are negative.

So, in 2014 I did something I had never done before as a politician, I contested an election as an independent. It was a challenge, but I was up for it. Many former Fianna Fáil stalwarts, Jackie Healy

Rae included, had left the party in similar circumstances to mine and achieved so much as independents.

The local election did indeed prove dramatic, but not for the reasons you would think. I arrived at the John Mitchels GAA grounds on the evening of the election only to discover that I had lost out on a seat by two votes. The result surprised everyone. As Owen O'Shea and Gordon Revington write in their book *A Century of Politics in the Kingdom*, 'Kiely performed much better than many predicted. Despite being outside the fold, many Fianna Fáil members canvassed with him and he ran a strong campaign.'

All I could concentrate on was the fact I had lost out by two votes! I had been involved in many close elections in my day, but never one that close. I couldn't believe it. It was painful to take! Little did I know, that losing by two votes wasn't the only thing surprising or strange about that election! That night was the start of a very big adventure. My last big battle in politics!

Pictured at the 'American Ireland Fund Gala' (l-r) are Congressman Bruce Morrison, Dan Kiely, and Paddy D'Arcy, former General Manager of Kerry County Council.

One Last Battle

My last battle in politics would begin at the John Mitchels GAA Club in Tralee. Come to think of it, it was an apt location. Long before I got involved in politics, I had fought my battles on the football field, first with the New York Juniors, and later when I was the manager of the Kerry Minors. I would like to think my footballing background stood to me during the difficult times to come, but, take it from me, nothing prepares you for suing the Irish state. They proved to be the fiercest opponent I ever took on. Despite all my years in politics and business, I can safely say I learnt something new from the whole ordeal.

When I arrived at the Mitchels grounds that evening, the initial count had been completed. I had lost out by two votes. I had had my share of bad luck in politics, but two votes! I was two votes behind Fine Gael's Mike Kennelly, and five behind Fianna Fáil's Jimmy Moloney. Remarkably, losing out by two votes wasn't the biggest shock of the night, worse was to come.

I was told that the returning officer, Michael McMahon, had permitted the other candidates to oversee his inspection of the 'dubious ballots', meaning ballots that could potentially be spoilt, ie, not permissible as votes. My immediate reaction was, why hadn't I been called? Surely, I, as a candidate, was entitled to oversee the inspection? To make a long story short, I discovered the custom was for returning officers to announce they were making the inspection at the count centre. They would either tell candidates or their representatives in person or announce it over an intercom or something to that effect.

I was told that this was the way it had always been done, and as I had run all my previous elections as an Fianna Fáil candidate, a Fianna Fáil solicitor would have overseen the process for me. They were right in one respect. It was my first election as an independent, and running on your own is, in many ways, more challenging; you don't have the support of a party machine behind you. In another sense, I felt what was being said was misleading. I agree that party representatives, such as solicitors and directors of elections, should oversee the adjudication of dubious ballots, but whether they are particularly good at it and whether they were fair to all candidates is another matter. I knew of one Fine Gael solicitor, for example, who would often oversee the vote counting on behalf of Fine Gael candidates, but it was clear to everyone he was biased towards one particular candidate; he wanted his man to win at the expense of the other Fine Gael politicians. I'm sure there were similar shenanigans in Fianna Fáil. If my experience

Dan decided to contest the 2014 Local Election in order to continue his work as a local community representative. In this image, he is pictured with Listowel Parish Priest, Fr. Declan O'Connor, other community members and representatives, and current members of the Army Reserve, at the old FCA Hall in Listowel.

in politics proves anything, it is that rivalries within Fianna Fáil and Fine Gael are as bitter, if not more so, than those between the two parties themselves.

As it happened, an even bigger shock was yet to come. After speaking to Michael McMahon, I spoke to some of my supporters and friends. Some of them had been in the John Mitchels grounds all day, and they filled me in on what had been happening. Apparently, Michael McMahon had accepted ballots that began with numbers like 3, 4 and 5 as legitimate votes. In other words, a number 3 next to a candidate on a ballot had been taken to indicate a first preference, as opposed to being nulled and 'spoilt'. Why this matters, and why this came as such a shock to me, requires some explaining.

I have already explained the intricacies of our proportional representation voting system, if any reader wants to refresh their minds. In the PR system, voters select candidates in order of preference, beginning with a number one, which indicates their first preference, down the list, to second-preference, third preference and so forth. As I explained previously, second, third, etc matter if the voter's first preference candidate has been eliminated or they have reached the electoral 'quota', in the event of which their surplus is then distributed among the remaining candidates. We don't need to concern ourselves with the intricacies of the system here. What matters in this case, was what was actually written on the ballots.

The Irish state (or at least I thought) is quite strict about what you can and cannot write on your ballot slip. We were always told to advise voters to simply write the number 1 next to their first preference, the number 2 next to their second and so on. This is what the electoral commission had always advised. If you wrote 1 in word format, ie, the letter 'one', you will get away with it, but, other than that, they are quite strict. If you scribble something unflattering about one of the candidates, for example, which happens often enough, your vote is considered spoilt. If you write out

'Mayo for Sam' in letters next to the candidates' names, as one voter in a Dublin local election did recently, then, no prizes, your vote is spoilt.

I had always believed returning officers were hard-nosed when it came to dubious ballots, that's why I was so surprised. My first thought was, this just flies in the face of common sense, how can 3 indicate 1? If a voter had placed the number 3 next to a particular candidate, how can the returning officer consider that a first preference vote? It just didn't make sense to me. I instinctively thought it was wrong. I managed to grab Michael McMahon again before the night was over, and I put my concerns to him. Eventually, either through him or another official, I got an explanation, or at least something close.

It apparently had to do with the fact that the European election was being staged on the same day. For some time, the convention was that the state would host European elections on the same day as local elections. So voters had two ballot slips on those days, one for the European elections and one for the local elections. Because of this, voters had a habit of jumbling up both ballots or, in other words, taking both ballots as if they were one. Some voters, therefore, marked their preferences on the European ballot first, before continuing the sequence on the local ballot as if they were the same. So, a voter might place 1, 2 etc on their European ballot, and 3, 4 etc on their local ballot, continuing the sequence as if they were the same ballot. The state's argument was that although (in the above example), the voter had written 3,4 etc on the local ballot, because, in the voter's head, both ballots were the same, 3 indicated a first preference.

I appreciated the fact that voters were confused, that was fair enough, but accepting these ballots as legitimate struck me as plain wrong. I felt it was very unfair. The state had always been so strict when it came to spoilt votes. For example, consider a recent RTÉ report on spoilt votes in a Dublin constituency, after Fianna Fáil senator

Catherine Ardagh exposed certain practices. If a voter stuck an X in a candidate's box, and left all the other boxes empty, this was considered spoilt. 'Why?' you would wonder. Surely the voter's preference here is clear? Similarly, if a voter placed a 'Yes' next to their preferred, first preference candidate's name, the ballot was rejected as spoilt.

My question was how could they be so finicky about spoilt ballots generally, but allow the dubious practice of considering 3s and 4s to indicate number 1s. Surely, I argued that night, a voter could have forgotten to indicate his or her first and second preference, and number 3 really did mean number 3. How could Michael McMahon and the Irish State take that chance?

My complaints that night were futile. I remember going to bed with a bad feeling in my stomach. I felt that the whole thing was wrong. As often happens in life, I went to bed deflated, but I woke up with fire in my belly. I sat in my car and drove to the town of Killorglin. Killorglin is famous for the annual puck fair, where locals trek around the surrounding mountains in search of a wild goat. It wasn't a goat I was travelling to Killorglin for that day however, but the next best thing, a solicitor.

I had asked solicitor Paul O'Donoghue to meet me, and he agreed. He was a former Fianna Fáil local councillor, and the brother of the former Minister for Justice, John O'Donoghue. He had politics in his blood, and I felt he would appreciate the predicament I was in. 'Two votes Dan, that's hard luck,' was the first thing he said to me. He then asked whether McMahon had ordered a recount, and I explained he had. Even after the recount, I was two votes short. He looked at me as if I was a beaten man.

When I explained the issue with the 173 dubious ballots, however, his expression changed. The fact they were accepting number 3s as first preferences was as much news to him as it was to me. As he said later to Owen O'Shea and Gordon Revington, 'I had been scrutinising doubtful papers since the age of eighteen, and I had never heard of

3s, 4s or 5s being admitted as first preferences in a count. I felt there was something perverse about that.'[2] Perverse was the word.

Luckily, he felt we had a case. The first step was to bring our case to the Circuit Court in Tralee, as there was a provision under the Local Elections Act of 1974 to contest a local election result. He also explained to me that we needed additional legal firepower, so he brought a barrister on board, a lady by the name of Elizabeth Murphy. We would contest the results on a number of points, including the fact McMahon should have allowed the 173 doubtful ballots to be examined at the second count. This sounded reasonable to me; if there was a second count, surely every candidate deserved a second chance to view the dubious ballots. Most importantly, McMahon was wrong to allow ballots that began with numbers like 3 and 4 to be included in the final count. I felt this was our strongest argument. I felt that considering 3 to indicate a first preference sounded very dubious, and I thought it undermined the whole process. When I got home that night, I had a good chat with my partner Nuala. She fully supported my efforts to have the result overturned. I had several tough months ahead, and I wouldn't have gotten through them without the support of Nuala and my family; I owe them all a great debt of gratitude.

Judge Carroll Moran heard our case in July of that year. I thought both O'Donoghue and Murphy performed quite well throughout. We discovered that a number of county returning officers, including Kerry's Michael McMahon, met to discuss how government guidelines were to be implemented. O'Donoghue argued, rightly in my view, that this constituted an unwarranted extension of their powers: That if they were meeting informally to discuss the implementation of guidelines, surely they were interpreting the guidelines, and the guidelines must have been fuzzy and vague to warrant such a meeting. O'Donoghue also mentioned that many people deeply

---

[2] *A Century of Politics in the Kingdom*, page 146

familiar with the electoral process, himself and myself included, had never heard of the practice of considering 3s and 4s to indicate first preferences. Both O'Donogue and I had been around the block, I had contested countless local and national elections, and neither of us had ever heard of it. None of the journalists and political commentators I had spoken to had heard of it either. The impression I got was that the electoral guidelines were being devised in secret, and discussed and debated among a select few; the public had never been given an opportunity to debate and discuss them. I felt that the whole thing was wrong.

Unfortunately, Judge Carroll Moran didn't agree. He found that there was no basis for the dubious ballots to be re-examined in the event of a recount. He said the decision of the returning officer was final in this matter (it was a 'quasi-judicial' decision). Re-examining them in light of a recount would also, according to Moran, create numerous practical difficulties for returning officers and officials. More disappointingly, he also found against us when it came to 3s 4s etc. being considered 1s. He found that McMahon had followed the guidelines issued to returning officers prior to the election and that the election regulations provided for such practices. He also defended the practice on merit, saying it showed good common sense on the part of officers. This last point of his angered me a little. It was as if their attitude was, follow common sense when it suits us, to hell with common sense when it doesn't. As I mentioned previously, ballots have been rejected for far smaller irregularities and anomalies.

Judge Moran's ruling was disheartening, to say the least. I don't like unfairness, and I felt I had been robbed. Losing elections is never nice, but to lose one by two votes, and under such dubious circumstances, takes some beating. I was encouraged by the discussions I had with both Murphy and O'Donoghue in the aftermath of the ruling, however. Both disagreed with the judge's ruling, and both felt there were grounds for an appeal. They advised me to go home and think it over.

At home that night, my feelings were mixed. The unfairness of the situation was eating away at me, but I also appreciated how big a financial risk it was. I would need €10,000 upfront in order to lodge my appeal, and that was just the start. After that, the legal expenses would spiral. The only course left open to me was the Supreme Court. My lawyers advised me that the Supreme Court functions differently from the lower courts, and they can disagree with the judgements of the lower courts on very technical, complicated points of law. Not only did they think we had a shot, they were quietly confident we would win.

I decided to go for it. I remember visiting O'Donoghue and Murphy in O'Donoghue's office in Killorglin on the day I decided to proceed. While O'Donoghue and Elizabeth Murphy agreed to take the case on a no win, no fee basis, the administration cost, including the filing of all the necessary paperwork, was €10,000, something I had to pay upfront. In the event of us winning, I was promised that this €10,000 would be reimbursed.

My case was formally lodged with the Supreme Court on the 2nd of August 2014. I remember being with my partner Nuala on the night it was officially confirmed we were going to court. We were nervous, but I was also quietly confident we would win on the dubious ballots. Having fought numerous elections, I felt that my instincts on political matters were good, that there was just something wrong about the practice. I was less sure when it came to being awarded a recount, and I was nervous about the financial implications.

I remember Paul getting a little worried when the state lined up their 'dream team' of lawyers. I took a different view here, and saw it as a sign that they were concerned; that we had a good case after all. When I entered the Supreme Court that summer, for the first time, I remember thinking to myself we had come a long way from my initial conversation with Michael McMahon, that night in the Mitchels GAA grounds when my legitimate concerns had been dismissed. That day, I was in the highest court in the land.

Paul O'Donoghue was right about the lawyers on the opposing bench. It was obvious to me from the moment I stepped into the court that the state had spared no expense. Clearly, someone in high places didn't want Dan Kiely to get a recount. The state's legal team was headed by barrister Noel Whelan, also a political columnist for *The Irish Times* and former candidate for Fianna Fáil in the '97 general election. Whelan has since passed away. I thought he conducted himself ably enough, outshining his more experienced colleagues. The other lawyers included Jim O'Callaghan, now a Fianna Fáil TD for Dublin Bay South, and Frank Sutton and Frank Callinan, two of the most illustrious senior counsels in the country. I remember joking to a friend of mine that the Irish state would give OJ Simpson a run for his money when it came to assembling a legal 'dream team'. Luckily for me, I had the best of the bunch. I was represented by Michael McDowell, former Attorney General and Minister for Justice, who put in a great shift for us.

The biggest anxiety for me and my family, however, wasn't whether we would get a recount or not. I have no shame in admitting that I was worried about the financial consequences of losing. I had invested all my remaining savings into the case. I had also borrowed from loyal friends and supporters, relying on their generosity, as I had on occasions in the past. If I lost, I would be broke; it was as simple as that.

After a series of hard knocks, however, my Kiely luck was back. Much to my shock, and the shock of everybody in the court, all five judges ruled in our favour on both the dubious ballots and on the recount. We didn't just win, we won emphatically. I was expecting a close call, with the various judges inching in our favour or against based on subtle points of law, but all five agreed emphatically that the returning officer was wrong on the ballots. They agreed with us that the practice defied logic and common sense. Justice O'Donnell argued, correctly in my view, that numbers only make sense as part of 'sequence including one', so, in other words,

Dan emerging victorious from the Irish Supreme Court, after all five Supreme Court Justices ruled in his favour on the dubious ballots, with four of the five ruling in his favour on the recount.

3 only makes sense if it follows 1 and 2. They also agreed that the practice breached provisions laid out in the Local Elections Act of 1974, which stipulated what needed to appear on the ballot to constitute a first preference. Justice William McKechnie argued that the Memorandum of Guidance, issued by the department for returning officers, was, in his language, 'sub-legal', meaning it constituted merely an interpretation of the existing act, which it was actually in breach of, in his judgement. One of the five judges, Justice Peter Charlton, did 'dissent' on the matter of whether there should be a recount, but the other four, including the Chief Justice, Frank Clarke, agreed that there should.

I was elated. I had come close to bankruptcy and humiliation, but I survived. The picture reproduced here is of me outside the Four Courts on the day of the ruling, and I think it tells its own story. Unfortunately, the recount didn't change the results in my favour.

Kennelly gained three votes at Jimmy Moloney's expense, but this unfortunately was not enough to change things in my favour. My two rivals were still ahead of me, Kennelly now by five votes and Moloney by two. Winning on the recount would have been the sweetest of sweet victories, but it doesn't change my view on our case. I am proud I stood up for myself and beat the state in our highest court. I feel our case should be an inspiration to all citizens. If you feel you have been wronged, fight it, don't just take it lying down. While it came late in my political career, I think it is safe to say I left the best for last; the sweetest victory just as the sun was setting on my decades long career as a public representative.

𝔜ou are cordially invited

to attend the Grand Opening of the

Hibernian Ballroom,

Ballybunion,

on Wednesday August 2nd, 1967

Music by Dermot O'Brien & his Clubmen.

An invitation to the opening of the Hibernian Ballroom, Dan's first business venture in Ballybunion, described by the *Kerryman* newspaper as an 'innovation' and a product of the owner's 'fertile mind'. 4,000 people attended the 'grand opening'.

Dan Kiely pictured with his brothers Tim and Pete Kiely, all in the uniform of the Irish Army Reserve, the FCA.

Dan Kiely in action at the Ballybunion Gay Bachelor Festival.

Who needs 'Beatlemania', when you have Ballybunion mania? Eager fans await an announcement at the Bachelor Festival.

People gather for a local community meeting held in Dan Kiely's Hibernian Hotel. Present include Dan Kiely, Jimmy Harris, former Head Postmaster, and Brendan Daly TD, former Minister for Defence and Minister for Fisheries and Forestry.

Eligible bachelors at the Gay Bachelor Festival line up for the photographer.

Senator and proud son of a Garda Dan Kiely marching with rank-and-file members of the Garda Representative Association. Dan credits the GRA and other members of the ICPSA for his successful election to the Seanad through the Administration Panel.

Dan Kiely pictured with his sister Cathy Skae (née Kiely), who Dan credits with doing so much to help him and other family members when they first immigrated to the United States.

Dan pictured in his hotel room in Virginia, with some of the 15,000 visa applications received under the Donnelly visa scheme. Dan personally delivered 15,000 applications to the visa processing centre in Virginia, a story recounted in the chapter 'More Ups and Downs'.

Some cross-party collaboration, as Dan Kiely, then Chairperson of the General Council of County Councils, shakes hands with former Tánaiste and Labour TD for Kerry North, Dick Spring.

Legendary Hollywood actor and director Paul Newman was a guest of honour at the Ireland American Gala Dinner. Pictured here with Dan Kiely.

Best of friends, best of enemies. Pictured (l-r) is Dan Kiely, former Taoiseach Charlie Haughey, Tom McEllistrim, former Minister for State in the Department of Defence, and Tommy Foley, Tom McEllistrim's campaign manager.

A united front of Irish and American representatives at the Ireland American Gala Dinner. Pictured (l-r) are former Congressman Joseph P. Kennedy II, Dan Kiely, and Congressman Richard Neal.

Dan pictured with former US Senate Majority Leader, Senator George Mitchell, whose work was instrumental in persuading the various parties to sign the historic Good Friday Agreement.

Pictured at the Ireland American Gala Dinner, are (l-r) Dan Kiely, John Hume MP, former leader of the SDLP and renowned diplomat who did so much to advance the peace process in Northern Ireland, and Paddy D'Arcy, former General Manager of Kerry County Council.

Dan Kiely pictured with US Congressman Brian Donnelly, who did so much to advance the cause of Irish immigrants in the United States. This picture was taken at Tarbert Ferry terminal, where Congressman Donnelly helped organise a raffle to raise funds for a community hall in Tarbert.

Hollywood legend Paul Newman 'shooting the breeze' with the great and the good of Kerry political life at the Ireland American Gala Dinner. Pictured (l-r); Dan Kiely, Paul Newman, Paddy D'Arcy, former General Manager of Kerry County Council, and Denis Foley, former Fianna Fail TD for Kerry North and father of Minister for Education Norma Foley.

Dan represented Kerry in every way he could, including presenting this lampshade, designed by Kerry resident artist Louis Mulcahy, to Irish billionaire businessman Tony O'Reilly.

Dan pictured with the 42nd President of the United States, Bill Clinton, who did so much to bring peace to the north of Ireland. He enjoyed an excellent working relationship with former Taoiseach Bertie Ahern and former British Prime Minister Tony Blair.

Senator Dan Kiely pictured on a diplomatic mission to Russia.

An Taoiseach Bertie Ahern visits Dan's constituency office in Charles St., Listowel ahead of the 2002 General Election, and receives a rapturous welcome. Dan's late mother Mrs Hannah Kiely is also visible in the photo.

An Taoiseach Brian Cowen wouldn't allow the rain to dampen spirits, as he embraces Hannah Kiely surrounded by her family and the Fianna Fáil rank and file.

An Taoiseach Brian Cowen visits a very proud Hannah Kiely at her home in Tarbert, with her sons, daughters, grandchildren and great-grandchildren present to witness.

Trip on a golden carriage. Dan Kiely pictured with former Taoiseach Enda Kenny, during a diplomatic mission to Russia.

Dan Kiely's father, Dan Sr., pictured at the Seán O'Ceallagh Na hÉireann society breakfast, held in the in the Concourse Plaza Hotel, on the anniversary of the 1916 Rising where Dan Kiely Sr. was a guest of honour. Also pictured is Jack McCarthy, originally from Kiskeam, who managed 'local' labour union branches in New York for what is now LIUNA (Labourers' International Union of North America).

Proud father Dan Kiely pictured with his four children, son Donal and daughters Joan, Noelle and Eileen.

Dan Kiely and his parliamentary colleagues enjoying a view of the Taj Mahal, in Agra, Uttar Pradesh, during an Irish diplomatic mission to India.

Dan Kiely enjoying the sights during a diplomatic mission to Russia.

Dan emerging victorious from the Irish Supreme Court, after taking a case contesting the State's decision not to call a recount of the Kerry Local Election despite his concerns regarding dubious ballots. All five Supreme Court Justices ruled in his favour on the dubious ballots, with four of the five ruling in his favour on the recount.

A family reunion fit for a quintessential emigrant family, with all fourteen surviving members of the Kiely family, along with their mother Hannah and father Dan Sr., present in one location for the first time, for this reunion in their hometown of Tarbert, Co Kerry.

Epilogue

I recently became aware of a famous quote from the English politician Enoch Powell: 'All political careers end in failure'. For someone like me, who has had his fair share of political setbacks, it was certainly sweet to end my career on a high note. What made our triumph in the Supreme Court so satisfying, was there had been so many naysayers discouraging me from taking the case. Just as they had been on many previous occasions, the naysayers were wrong; we won, and my case was a risk worth taking.

If I was to pass on any advice to young people interested in getting involved in politics or business, it would be to take the plunge. If you believe in yourself, and you believe in the cause you are fighting for you, then go for it. I don't regret anything from my years in local and national politics. I provided strong local representation for the people of North Kerry and Kerry overall, and I championed some very deserving causes. I still feel, to this day, that local councils should be more empowered to make decisions that affect local people. I only discovered recently that Ireland is the most centralised country in the EU, meaning the central government in Dublin has a massively disproportional share of power when it comes to health, housing and other vital areas that affect people's lives. The abolition of town councils by the Fine Gael/Labour coalition government was the culmination of a long process towards centralisation, and it was one I opposed all my political life.

I still feel, to this day, that we are underutilising the Shannon Estuary. There is so much more the government could be doing for the North Kerry and West Limerick regions.

The work I did on behalf of Irish immigrants in the United States, and the work I did to build on Ireland and America's unique relationship, are perhaps the political achievements I am most proud of. It moves me to think of the people and families whose lives were changed as a result of a successful visa application. Many of the people I secured visas for went on to rear families in the US and build and lead businesses that are still running and thriving. It means I changed many people's lives for the better, and you can't pay a politician any greater compliment than that. If that doesn't constitute political success, I don't know what does.

For advice to young people interested in politics, I would quote my fellow Kerryman, Lord Kitchener (he was born in Ballylongford, Co Kerry), 'Your Country Needs You'. Don't listen to negative voices. If the negative voices had their way, nobody would do anything. It's easy to find excuses not to do something; excuses are a dime a dozen. If you feel a task is too difficult, or if you ever feel exhausted or overwhelmed, read the earlier chapters from this book. I'm sure my accounts of those hard days in the bog, and dragging water from the well in Tarbert, will give you pause for thought, a reminder of how hard your ancestors had it, how they still got by and reared their families, and how many of them thrived despite everything. I often tell my grandchildren how they should use my own father and mother, their great-grandparents, as role models, as they were exemplars of hard work and commitment.

I still think of them often. My father in his waterproof clothes, coming home shivering from the cold after a day on the beat. My mother kitting into the late hours, making bedclothes from old sugar sacs. They worked every day God sent them, and each member of my family owes them so much.

I haven't retired from politics, far from it. These days, I am active in organising and managing campaigns and canvasses in North Kerry for my friend Michael Healy Rae. Michael's father Jackie, also a good friend of mine, exiled himself from Fianna Fáil on account of the party machine's narrow-mindedness and incompetence. His battles with the party machine parallel mine. While the Healy Rae family may no longer wear the party colours, they embody the very best of the republican tradition; specifically work ethic, strong community representation and a commitment to development, progress and helping those that need it. They, along with some other like-minded representatives, from across the party and political spectrum, keep the flame of that tradition burning in the Dáil.

Despite my disenchantment with party politics, I feel very positive about the country. I think Ireland is doing very well on the whole, and I am not in the least bit embarrassed to state my view that it is the best country in the world to live in. On most international metrics, whether that be life expectancy, clear air, job opportunities, and so on, the country does very well and frequently ranks best.

My loving partner Nuala and I still live in Ballybunion, North Kerry, where I ran a string of successful nightclubs and hotels, and I am very happy to live in the beautiful seaside village. Ireland has come on leaps and bounds since I was a young fella. Ireland can afford to give its young people today opportunities my generation could only dream of. The testament to this is my four children, Donal, Joan, Eileen and Noelle; Donal, who is retired now, had a very important position in the Tarbert ESB plant, Joan is chairperson of New York GAA, and Noelle and Eileen are running their own successful businesses.

They all have something of myself and their late mother in them if you ask me. They are also a credit to the success the country has had in creating new opportunities for its young people. Of course, the country has problems, and there are many things it could be doing better, but my advice to young politicians, campaigners and journalists is to *be positive.* If you don't have a positive mentality and give credit where credit is due, you won't achieve anything. Politics is full of naysayers at present, perpetually negative people who are always complaining about everything, and putting the country down. You can't disagree with them either. They will shout you down, which is why I stay away from some social media platforms. In my day, many of them would shoot if you didn't agree with them. These days, they simply abuse you on social media, so I suppose that's progress.

One thing I hope this book achieves is to make people aware that there is more to Dan Kiely than politics. Politics is a relentless beast, it swallows you up. Many younger people, I suspect know me principally as a former senator, local representative and former general election candidate. Many of my proudest achievements, however, have nothing to do with politics. We call the house Nuala and I live in today the 'East End', in tribute to that nightclub and entertainment complex I built there in the early sixties. When I reflect on the bands and performers I managed, I am filled with pride. Bringing international acts to audiences in rural locations, like Ballybunion, was a privilege and something I would do all over again. I still think of the person who is perhaps my most famous act, rock & roll and blues legend Roy Orbison. After losing both his wife and two young sons in unrelated tragedies and enduring such profound misfortune, he was able to not only continue to write and create music, but also perform at sold-out venues for millions of fans. His life story has stayed with me as an example of human endurance. If I could go back in time and say something to that young man with a dream of building something in Ballybunion, I would say go for it. You will experience some setback and knocks, but you will also achieve so much. As an older man now, I have no regrets. If I were to quote something at him, I might even borrow a line from Roy Orbison, 'You got it'.

About the Authors

Dan Kiely

Born in 1942, businessman and politician Dan Kiely's remarkable and often colourful life included becoming the youngest manager of a nightclub in New York state, a stint as Kerry Minor football manager, importer of fox furs and one of Fianna Fáil's longest-serving senators. Dan managed some of the world's liveliest ballrooms, hosting some of the biggest names in the Irish and international showband scene, including Joe Dolan, Dicky Rock, Butch Moore, 'Big Tom' McBride and the 'father of rock 'n' roll' Roy Orbison.

During his time as a Fianna Fáil senator, he was a close confidant of former Taoiseach Charlie Haughey. In the words of Michael Healy Rae TD, 'Charlie Haughey had many secrets, and Dan Kiely knew every one of them.'

In 2014, Dan lost a local election by two votes and contested the result in Ireland's Supreme Court. The result was a victory for Kiely and a change in Irish law. It was a fitting end to an often dramatic and combative political career. A final act of courage from this son of a War of Independence volunteer.

Jeremy Murphy

Jeremy Murphy is an Irish publisher, agent and former journalist. He established 'JM Agency, Publishing and Marketing Consultancy' in 2018, and it has, to date, helped numerous authors, publishers and businesses bring their publications to life. These include Eddie Hobbs, Theresa Lowe, Robert Pierse, Irish companies Lettertec Ireland Ltd and Orpen Press, and international publishers Aleph Book Company (India) and Editora Estrela Cultural (Brazil).

Broadcaster Joe Duffy described *One Last Bend* by Vincent Henry, edited, designed and produced by the JM Agency team, as a 'beautiful production'. Photographer and author Orla McConnon Bakeberg has described Jeremy and the team as 'the most supportive, sensitively creative and collaborative of publishers'. Bestselling author and former Economics Editor at *The Irish Times* Marc Coleman has described the transcription, editing and design services Jeremy has provided to his consultancy company Octavian Economics as 'exceptional' and 'professional'.

Jeremy holds a BA and MA from Trinity College Dublin and University College Dublin, respectively, as well as postgraduate qualifications in business and marketing from Technological University Dublin and the Digital Marketing Institute of Ireland. He lives in his native Listowel with his wife, Dr Carol O'Hanlon, a former winner of Ireland's 'Young Scientist' competition, an achievement Jeremy will always be in awe of.

Jeremy would like to thank the fantastic team at JM Agency for helping him bring *The Final Count* to life. These include senior copy-editor Susan Lewando, whose editing of early drafts and knowledge of the book's genre proved invaluable; editor and proofreader Niamh McAuliffe, whose thorough proofread and editorial insights helped get the manuscript over the line; and Joanne Cafferky, for her fast and exceptional editing, that allowed the team meet the deadline. The team also includes designer Parvathi Venkitaraman, whom Jeremy would like to thank for her exceptional and professional design work, for turning what was a raw Word draft into a professionally designed book. He would also like to thank photographer and artist Daria Piaseczna for all her advice on how to create the perfect portrait image for memoirs, and particularly for the two images of Dan Kiely that grace the book's cover.

Jeremy would particularly like to thank former Senator Dan Kiely for the opportunity to work with him on his memoir. Helping Dan Kiely document his extraordinary life, create a record for both the readers of the present and the future, was an honour.

www.ingramcontent.com/pod-product-compliance
Lightning Source LLC
Chambersburg PA
CBHW041604220426
43661CB00014B/1179